BACKCAST

BACKCAST

*Fatherhood, Fly-fishing, and a River
Journey Through the Heart of Alaska*

Lou Ureneck

St. Martin's Press
New York

www.stmartins.com

Excerpt from the traditional narrative, "One Must Arrive with a Story to Tell," reprinted by permission of the Alaska Native Language Center and by the Lower Kuskokwim School District.

Excerpt from "Nostos" by Louise Gluck, copyright © 1996; reprinted by permission of HarperCollins Publishers.

Excerpt from "Two Tramps in Mud Time" from *The Poetry of Robert Frost,* edition by Edward Connery Lathem, copyright © 1969 by Henry Holt and Company. Copyright 1936 by Robert Frost; copyright © 1964 by Lesley Frost Ballantine. Reprinted by permission of Henry Holt and Company, LLC.

Book design by Michelle McMillian
Sockeye Salmon illustration by David Cain

Library of Congress Cataloging-in-Publication Data

Ureneck, Lou.
    Backcast : fatherhood, fly-fishing, and a river journey through the heart of alaska / Lou Ureneck.—1st ed.
        p. cm.
    ISBN-13: 978-0-312-37151-7
    ISBN-10: 0-312-37151-9
    1. Ureneck, Lou—Family.   2. Fathers and sons—Case studies.   3. Divorced fathers—Biography.   4. Divorced fathers—Family relationships—Case studies.   5. Fly fishing—Alaska.   6. Alaska—Description and travel.   I. Title.

HQ755.85.U74 2007
306.89'2092–dc22   2007019467

10   9   8   7   6   5   4   3

For my mother

CONTENTS

LEONTES: *My brother,*
            Are you so fond of your young prince as we
            Do seem to be of ours?
POLIXENES: *If at home, sir,*
            He's all my exercise, my mirth, my matter;
            Now my sworn friend, and then mine enemy;
            My parasite, my soldier, statesman, all;
            He makes a July's day short as December;
            And with his varying childness cures in me
            Thoughts that would thick my blood.

— WILLIAM SHAKESPEARE, *The Winter's Tale*

His father exclaimed, "Arenqiapaa! Oh my goodness!
When, I wonder, would anyone
Not have a story to tell
After returning
To the village?
One must always arrive with a story to tell
After having gone to the wilderness;
That's how it is!"

— TRADITIONAL NARRATIVE, TUNUNAK, ALASKA

BACKCAST

I. ON THE RIVER

Inside the small circle of our tent, I listened to the rain that had blown in from the Bering Sea and the whisper of my son's breathing as he slept beside me. We were camped on a gravel bar that shouldered the Kanektok River on the western face of Alaska. The storm that was lashing our tent had begun as a typhoon northeast of Japan, rolled across the North Pacific, and shimmied up the chain of Aleutian Islands to the great Kuskokwim River delta, where it was sputtering in a rattle of wind and rain. Our two-man tent billowed and snapped as if it were a luffing sail. We were more than a hundred miles from the nearest link to the outside world, and that was a dirt landing strip at Quinhagak, a Yupik Eskimo village. We were without a phone or radio, without a guide, and without the slightest bit of firsthand knowledge of the country we were in.

This is where my memory of our trip usually begins, on the morning of the third day when the rain came down in sheets. Maybe that's because there was another storm blowing, the one between Adam and me. Memory is like that: It has its own intelligence. It holds on to what matters, and it sees connections between events in our lives that we sometimes miss when we are living them. My memory has put these two storms together, both of them hammering me with my failures as a father. Already the tent was beginning to leak, an early premonition of how ill prepared I was for a trip into the Alaskan bush. The bigger failure was my divorce. I had taken apart a twenty-year marriage. Adam was angry about the breakup of our family and the loss of me as a perfect father and upright man. I had learned there was no explaining a divorce to your child, and the more I had tried, the worse I had made things between us. I had stopped trying.

On that morning of the third day, I wasn't sure I could place our position on the crude map that I had drawn back home in Philadelphia and kept folded in the pocket of the flannel shirt I had been sleeping in. I guessed that we had covered about thirty miles of river. I was cold and hungry. I wanted a cup of coffee, but lighting our small camp stove to boil water would be difficult in this weather, so I slipped deeper into my sleeping bag and told myself I didn't need it. I guessed the time at eight o'clock. The night before, we had fished past midnight in the purple twilight. We had caught pink hump-backed salmon and glorious red-and-green char until our shoulders ached, and I knew Adam would sleep for another hour or more if I didn't rouse him. He had slept like a stone since he was an infant, and he was no different now as six feet, three inches, of sinewy boy-man. I let him sleep. I enjoyed the temporary peace between us. Memory also grants its concessions.

I was fairly sure that we were safe from the brown bears that were stalking the river. The bears were enormous, tall as church doors, wrapped in great blankets of heavy brown fur, the color of cocoa. In late August, with the salmon runs at their peak, the bears had moved in from the surrounding country—mountains and tundra—and swarmed the river and its tributaries, feasting on fish flesh. It made no difference to the bears whether it was alive or dead. They raked flopping sockeyes and silvers out of the swirling water, and they ate the black carcasses of the big kings that had come up the river in June, spawned, and died. This was gorging season. We had been careful the night before to keep a clean camp. Our food, freeze-dried packets of noodles and Thai chicken, instant coffee, and a dwindling number of PowerBars, was stored in dry bags and stowed in our raft, which we had beached several hundred feet downstream, well away from where we slept. We already had experienced two close calls, one with a headstrong yearling, and I wasn't eager for another. I felt for the shotgun that I kept between our sleeping bags. It was there, cold to my touch, with its breech safely open and slugs in both chambers. I tried to get a little more sleep, but I wasn't having any luck.

Adam and I took our trip to Alaska the summer he graduated from high school. I was forty-nine, and Adam was eighteen. I was deep into middle age; he was on the verge of becoming a man. I had been divorced for a year by then, though my former wife and I had been apart for three years, in different cities separated by hundreds of miles. A chasm of anger, disappointment, and sadness had opened between us. We communicated through lawyers. During most of that time, Adam and I had lived together as father and son and sometimes as warring parties. I was his custodial parent.

I had hoped that the trip to Alaska would settle some of the trouble between Adam and me. It would be good, I thought, for us to go fishing together one last time. In the woods and on the river, maybe we would regain something of our old selves before he went off to college and on to the rest of his life. Looking back, I have to admit the trip was a little desperate. I had been willing to take the risk. My life was in a ditch: I was broke from lawyers, therapists, and alimony payments and fearful that my son's anger was hardening into lifelong permanence. I wanted to pull him back into my life. I feared losing him. Alaska was my answer. What I had failed to appreciate, of course, was Adam's view of the expedition. For him, the trip meant spending ten days with his discredited father in a small raft and an even smaller tent. It was not where Adam had wanted to be, not now, not with me, and not in the rain. The trip would take us through 110 miles of rugged Alaska, some of it dangerous and all of it, to us anyway, uncharted. I had no inkling of what lay ahead: fickle early-fall weather, the mystery of the river, and unseen obstacles that already were silently forming themselves in opposition to my plans.

2

We came into southwestern Alaska on a Sunday, the third Sunday in August 2000. We had flown from Philadelphia, our home, to Anchorage and from Anchorage to Dillingham. Adam had spent the flight from Anchorage to Dillingham silently studying the snowy peaks of the Alaska Range from the plane window and napping. He was talking to me as little as possible.

Dillingham is a cannery town tucked into the huge seaward prominence of Alaska between the Yukon River and the long upswept beard of the Alaska Peninsula. Our stay in

Dillingham was to last only three hours. From Dillingham, I had arranged for us to fly to the headwaters of the Kanektok River, where we would begin our trip, about one hundred miles farther north and west into the bush. That would put us about eight degrees of latitude south of the Arctic Circle, deep into the Alaska wilderness. I had planned for us to raft from Kagati Lake westward to the Bering Sea.

We landed at noon at Dillingham's small airport, where we were scheduled to meet our outfitter, Denise Grant. She and I had exchanged e-mails through the summer as I was planning the trip from my apartment in Philadelphia, where I worked as a newspaper editor. I had picked Denise because she and her husband offered the cheapest flights into the bush. I had put the trip together on a shoestring, cutting corners wherever I could on gear, food, and travel. After Adam and I came down the steps of the small plane, he separated himself from me immediately and left the waiting-and-baggage building to look for Denise. He was underscoring his silence with distance.

Denise arrived, and we hopped into her van and pulled out of the airport.

"So you got here okay?"

She spoke in the tinny accent I remembered from our phone call. Australian, I guessed. Denise, in her thirties, was blond and compact. She wore a tank top and jeans. She turned hard on the wheel and punched the accelerator, tearing us out of the gravel lot. We climbed onto the tar road. Dillingham looks like it was thrown up in a week from the corrugated scrap metal and waste-wood left behind by a retreating army. It is a kind of Caribbean redoubt of the North: a muddy and coniferous Trinidad in the 1950s. We rode to Denise's house on the town's outskirts, a wooded subdivision of dirt roads, scattered cabins, and sled dogs chained to doghouses. They looked up, their wolf eyes trailing us as we went by. With the exception of our sleeping bags and fishing equipment, I was renting all the camping and rafting gear for the trip from her: tent, raft, oars, patch kit, cooking utensils, bottled-gas stove, fuel canisters, cooler, roll-up table, plastic tarp. It was spread out on the cement floor of her garage like a yard sale. Some of it looked awfully beat up. Well, I thought, this is what you get when you pick an outfitter by price.

"Are you boys ready to catch some fish?" Denise asked. I could picture her slinging beers in a waterfront bar.

She and Adam had established a quiet rapport as they walked and sorted through the used equipment. It was as if they were culling a garden of the bad tomatoes, keeping some and tossing out the rotten ones. Denise picked up one end of the heavy rubber raft, which was folded flat in quarters, and Adam had picked up the other, and the two of them rocked it twice and then on her count of three heaved it into the back of the van. We drove down to the town's little supermarket. I went inside with Adam, who walked five steps ahead of me, keeping the distance he had established at the airport, while Denise went to gas up the van.

The store had a couple of cash registers, a white-enameled meat counter, a table with some shriveled oranges and brown bananas, and aisles of dusty cans of beans, beets, and cooked meats. To save money on lunch, I bought bread, cold cuts, mustard, and cheese to make our own sandwiches for the day. Adam disapproved. He went to the cooler and picked out a pricey roast-beef sandwich in a cellophane wrapper and a can of root beer. He grabbed a big bag of vinegar-flavored potato chips.

"Take that, Dad," he seemed to be saying.

I let it ride. He knew I was watching my money closely, but I didn't want to wreck the trip with an argument over a sandwich before we had even gotten started. He was entirely capable of saying, "I want to go home." He held the option like a hidden card, and he knew I wasn't willing to call his bluff. A chubby Yupik Eskimo girl, maybe fifteen, in a sleeveless housedress, rubber flip-flops, and thick black-frame glasses that magnified her eyes took my money at the checkout register. The lunch and bug spray came to twenty-eight dollars. Adam wandered out of the store as I surrendered the money to the girl's brown and pink palm.

In the van and seated up front, I separated the slices of fatty bologna, peeled the American cheese from its plastic wrappers, and assembled my sandwich on the squishy white bread in my lap. Adam, in the backseat behind Denise, tore open his bag of chips.

"How can you eat that stuff?" he asked.

"What?" I said. "It's bologna. What's wrong with that?"

He munched his chips with a look that said my question was so lame that it didn't deserve an answer. When he finished his sandwich, he asked me to make him one with just cheese. I set mine on the dashboard and made one for him without bologna. I gave him his sandwich, and then I rolled up a piece of cheese in a slice of round bologna and ate it without bread.

"I don't know how you can eat that stuff," he said.

"It's delicious," I lied. "Alaskan finger food."

I asked him for a swallow of his root beer. He held the can away from me, as if I were going to reach back and grab it from him.

"Come on, just a swig," I said.

I turned to the backseat and put out my hand. He squinted

at me skeptically and then passed the can to me over the seat but warned, "No backwash. I don't want to find any bologna chunks in my soda."

I took a long drink and rolled another slice of bologna.

We jostled down the road that passed the town dump on the way to the pond where we were supposed to meet Denise's husband, Rick, in his floatplane. We came to the pond, but the plane was not at the dock. The pond was empty, lined by scruffy trees, a green-black serrated edge of conifer. Denise's face dropped at the sight of no plane. She parked the van, and Adam walked over to the dock with a duffel bag and lay down with it as a pillow. His attitude seemed to be: "If I'm here in Alaska, I might as well get some sleep." I wondered: Was this the same boy who used to pepper me with questions about everything around him in the outdoors? There had been a time in our lives, not that long ago, when his fascination with the world and trust in me had kept us in a steady stream of conversation.

"Dad, what do you think is the biggest fish in this lake?"

"Dad, how long can a duck hold its breath underwater?"

"Dad, what is stronger, a bear or lion?"

"Dad, do birds sleep at night?"

"Yes, Adam, I think they must sleep at night. Otherwise, they'd get awfully tired from flying."

"Well, if they sleep at night, how come they don't fall out of the trees?"

I yearned for one more unanswerable question.

Soon I heard a buzz in the sky. The plane grew larger and took on wings and floats and then dropped on the pond. Rick pushed open the door and stepped out. He was trim and outdoor-natty in blue jeans, pressed plaid-flannel shirt, leather boots, visor cap, and aviator glasses. He looked like he had just flown in from a movie about a wilderness trip to Alaska.

"Ready to go?"

After we loaded, the plane lifted ponderously from the pond, like a big old dog getting up from the rug, and barely cleared the tips of the black-spruce trees. We turned away from the broad waters of the coast that spread to the horizon like a sheet of wrinkled tinfoil. Below us, I saw deep-green marshlands with silver-sequined ponds and bright bands of finger lakes to the north. In a few minutes, as we were still climbing, we reached the Ahklun Mountains and followed a course between their jagged snowy peaks and steep black flanks.

Fat slushy drops splattered on the windshield. In late August, Alaska weather pivots from summer to fall, and it can turn ugly fast; I knew that, but I was surprised to see that we already were in the snow. I dismissed it as a consequence of the altitude. We would be fishing at least a thousand feet lower, and we were unlikely to encounter any sustained snowfall. At least I hoped so. We weren't prepared for snow. I had packed us for a summer trip.

The Ahklun Mountains march in a two-hundred-mile line northeast from Togiak Bay and divide the Bristol Bay lowlands from the great Yukon-Kuskokwim deltas to the north. The mountains are cut lengthwise by a long river valley. The Goodnews River flows south and west to Kuskokwim Bay and the Bering Sea. It was a river floated by expensive guiding operations, which charged upward of a thousand dollars a day. Had things gone differently for me in the last few years, we probably would be fishing the Goodnews on this trip. Its fishermen slept on comfortable cots in big canvas wall tents, ate gourmet meals prepared by their guides, and drank single-malt scotch at the end of a day.

Our river, the Kanektok, drained the north and west sides of the range. We passed over alpine glaciers that seeped pencil lines of black mountain scree into milky-blue lakes that looked like abandoned paint pots. Rick banked the plane right and left, pulled up and pushed down, and we moved in and out of rain and snow. Often we were in the clouds, and then we would suddenly break into slanted columns of subarctic sunshine that seemed to pick up and wiggle every shiny stone on the vast landscape for maximum sparkle. After about forty-five minutes of pounding through the lumpy air, my seat fell out from under me, the way a New York elevator drops from under your feet on the way down from the hundredth floor.

The sky disappeared and the slopes of the mountains filled the plane's little windows. I felt the rapid *tap-tap-tap* of the plane's pontoons meeting the wavelets of the lake. It was the sensation of running one's fingernail over a washboard. I looked over Adam's shoulder, through the windshield, to the gray-blue surface of the water. This was Kagati Lake, principal source of the Kanektok River. We glided to the shoreline behind the slowing watery *slop-slop-slop* of the propeller. Rick opened his door, stepped onto the left-side pontoon, rocking the plane, which was now a boat, and tied us off to a clump of blueberry bushes on the shoreline. Adam and I unfolded ourselves and stepped from the plane.

Kagati Lake fills the bottom of a giant bathtub-shaped basin of tundra and woody scrub, and, on either side of the tub, massifs comprising several peaks thrust steeply skyward.

The highest, Mount Oratia, to the north, rises forty-seven hundred feet. It was snow covered. The lake itself is shaped like a set of lungs, two deep-blue lobes separated by a long sternum of purple and green tundra and low silver-green bushes. The sternum ascends quickly on its easterly, or upstream, end into a mountain, Ata-ai-ach, and then descends to rise up again into a higher and unnamed mountain. On either side of Ata-ai-ach, the lake's lobes are fed by streams that are in turn fed by smaller streams and ponds. At the western, downstream end, the lobes connect to form a wide pond with bays. It was into one of these bays that Rick had dropped the plane and where the three of us stood and watched hundreds of salmon—bright red sockeyes—porpoising in the slate-colored lake. Some of these fish had already released their skeins of orange eggs, and others were still traveling to the upper streams, beyond Ata-ai-ach, where they would propagate their species and die.

Rick called us out of our gaze, and we began to toss our gear ashore. With Rick at the plane's door, Adam on the end of the left float, and me on the shore, we made a bucket brigade, with each bag and case passing through three sets of hands. The mosquitoes were fierce and exploded out of the tundra with every step I took on the spongy ground. They formed balls around our heads, gray buzzing halos. The mosquitoes were in my ear canals and up my nose, and I was breathing them into my mouth. I choked on one that stuck to the back of my throat. I tried to cough it up. I called a halt to the unloading and pulled a bottle of repellent from one of the backpacks.

I covered my arms, face, neck, and ankles and rubbed a palmful of the greasy liquid in my hair and ears. It burned. The stuff could melt the varnish off a fishing rod. I lobbed the bottle to Adam, who covered his face, neck, and ears and the backs of his hands. He offered the bottle to Rick, who scoffed that we even acknowledged the bugs. I thought of the old line about Alaska mosquitoes: big enough to stand flat-footed and have sex with a goat. We went back to work.

As he was pulling out the last bag, Rick stopped and pointed toward the head of the bay. I looked up. A young bear had come out of the puckerbrush and was ambling toward the lake and us. He seemed carefree and oblivious until the moment he caught our scent, or the scent of the mosquito repellent. He stopped short and peered toward us, snoot first, like a boy who had lost his glasses. He was about five feet tall, maybe two hundred pounds. He wanted the fish in the lake, but we stood between him and the water. I couldn't tell if he could see us or just smell us, but our presence, however perceived, was causing him no small amount of distress. He turned in place and started toward us again. He closed the distance quickly on all fours, to about two hundred feet. A bear can cover two hundred feet in less than five or six seconds. Even a yearling bear can be dangerous, maybe especially dangerous. He's a kid with no judgment. I reached for my backpack and pulled out a can of bear spray Denise had given me back in the Dillingham garage. It was a pressurized solution of high-powered pepper juice that can shoot thirty feet and sometimes repel a curious bear. Of course, it can also make the bear madder than hell. I felt a little ridiculous holding the can in the air. It felt like a charge of oversize deodorant.

"Forget that stuff," Rick said. "I've got something serious for him."

He reached into the plane and pulled a leather holster from under the seat.

"Let's see if he gets any closer," Rick said.

For Rick, that many words in a row constituted an oration. The bear claimed a single step, and Rick slipped out a long-barreled handgun with a bore as big around as a butcher's fat finger. The bear stood high on two legs and looked fierce, stretching his neck upward, but he didn't advance. Rick raised the gun. I waited for a blast.

Damn, I thought. We are going to begin the trip with the killing of a bear.

It didn't seem like a good omen. Bears, owls, ravens, otters—killing some animals seemed like an invitation to disaster. Call it bad medicine. I had a friend, an archery hunter, who had shot a black bear with an arrow back in Maine. He told me how the bear, manlike, had gripped the arrow sticking from its chest and tried to pull it out. Crying and moaning, the bear went into a death scene worthy of opera. It lay down and clawed the ground and moaned. It rolled from side to side on its back and then staggered off into the woods. My friend gave up hunting bears. They were too high in the order of things. There was enough about this trip that was worrisome. I didn't want to add an insult to the spirits that hovered over the lake and river. Here was a dilemma: I didn't want to see the bear dead, but neither did I like the alternative of letting him get any closer. Bears killed people in Alaska. I had grown up on outdoor magazines with gruesome photographs of men mauled and eaten by bears. Rick held the gun steady. He clearly was a lot less troubled by the prospect of offending the spirits. One move forward and Rick was prepared to deliver the lead slug of the .357 Magnum cartridge somewhere to the left side of the bear's chest. We waited, and then the bear backed away on all fours. He took a broad arc around us and entered the lake three hundred yards from the plane. Almost immediately, he hoisted a big sockeye against the gray sky.

"Well, Dad," Adam said to me. "Welcome to Alaska."

I took his words as a gesture of kindness.

3

Among the words that Rick had rationed to us as we un-loaded our gear from the plane at Kagati was the advice that we should try to reach the point where Klak Creek flowed into the river by nightfall or early the next day. It was a good long run on the first day, he said, and it would put us closer to the best fishing. He described it as a better-than-middling-sized tributary that entered the main river from the left. My map, which I had drawn from the Internet, did not show the creek. It was a rough sketch of the lake, the course of the river, and some of the prominent mountains. I pressed him for more information.

"Don't fish the upper river," he said. "Just float the first ten miles or so."

I asked him how we would know Klak Creek when we came to it.

"You can't miss it," he said.

Why can't I miss it? I wondered.

I didn't like the way this was shaping up. I had gotten this kind of advice before from people who lived and worked in the country they were directing me through, and it was always useless. Once, on a hunting trip with my brother and nephew in northern Maine, I had spent the better part of a day trying to find my way out of a swamp because of directions like the ones we were getting from Rick. The guide had driven us in his pickup truck into the woods early in the morning and de-posited us at points along an old logging road. The plan was for each of us to slowly hunt our way toward a secondary road about two miles through the woods. My turn to get out of the truck came, and I hopped out of the truck bed. The guide leaned out the window and told me to walk down the ridge to a line of black growth and then along a stream.

"Just follow the stream out to the road," he said. "You can't miss it."

It sounded simple standing there next to the truck. I followed the line of the ridge for a good long way and then descended into the low ground where I thought I would find the stream. I slogged through mossy pools of black water, hoping to catch sight of the stream through the dense growth of trees. I found nothing but more swamp. On that day in November, in among the fir, hemlock, and cedars, darkness began to gather under the boughs around two in the afternoon. There is nothing as gloomy as a cedar swamp in late November. The light is gray and murky; the trees and moss muffle sound. There is no horizon, and even the sky can be hard to see through the branches. It is hard to know where you are. I was sure that I had walked more than the guide's two miles. It seemed closer to three or four.

I considered the possibility that I was lost, that I had managed to turn in the wrong direction somewhere along the way. In places, I could only see four or five feet in front of me. I pushed through the balsam thickets and at one point caught the backlash of a branch in my right eye. The pain turned my stomach. I had to sit down on a wet stump for several minutes, my eye tearing and blurry, before resuming my search for the stream. Blocked by soft mucky ground that sucked and swallowed my boots, I had to backtrack to higher ground. Twice I fell. The zigging and zagging and the backtracking left me without any sense of the course I had traveled. Had I been walking in circles? I checked the compass pinned to my coat. I doubted what it was telling me. Had the compass been damaged? I tapped it, changed my position, and watched the floating ball swing its north-marking arrow around to a direction that seemed all wrong. It pointed me on a line of travel that my intuition argued would plunge me back into the woods and away from the road. I scolded myself for not bringing a second compass to check the first. I kept walking, and still I couldn't find the stream.

My heart began to race. The trees spun around me. I prepared myself to spend a night in the woods. It would be okay, I kept telling myself. I could build a fire, cover the ground with spruce boughs, and put my back against a tree. My hunting partners would come looking for me with flashlights. They would fire rifle shots into the air, and I would mark my location by firing back. It would be embarrassing, but they would find me. As I kept moving, huddled inside my wool coat, it began to snow. The murk deepened. There were no birds in the trees. There was no life anywhere. Why had I ever decided to go hunting? It was a stupid way to spend my time. I could be home cleaning my basement or doing paperwork at the office. Why had I gone into these woods? I liked everything about the woods except this, being lost. It had happened to me more than once, and always there was that feeling of panic that had to be pressed down into the chest: Don't run; stay calm; breathe. Remember to breathe.

A game warden friend in Maine had told me stories of his days on lost-hunter duty in the Big Woods, above Greenville in the Telos country near the Canadian border. He and other wardens would find the lost man, after a night in the woods, almost naked, his clothes torn off from running through the thickets and tangles of blowdowns. He would be cut and bruised from banging into trees, stabbed by the sharp ends of broken limbs, crazed with fear. Often the man would have to be restrained, even sedated.

There's something about not knowing where you are, not being able to put your eyes on something familiar, a star, a mountain, a street sign, that throws the mind into despair. Of course, I had come to know in the last few years that a man can also become lost when he cuts himself loose from what's familiar and important in his life.

Sanity requires at least one fixed point on the landscape. In that Maine swamp, I had none. I had my compass, but a compass is merely an idea when you are feeling lost, a leap of faith into the abstraction of magnetism. I brought myself to a halt. I had been going too fast again. I collected myself and my thoughts. I stopped and counted to one hundred. I ordered myself to follow the direction of the compass. I resumed walking, slowly, and finally I broke out of the woods to a road. Thank God! I wanted to get down on my knees and kiss the pebbled tar that was slowly turning white under the gathering flakes.

"You can't miss it," Rick said.

This was Alaska, and the entire state of Maine could fit into the pocket of wilderness we were rafting through. Many streams entered the Kanektok along its length, some were bound to be "middling sized," and I guessed that at least half would enter from the left as we passed downstream. Was there an overhanging tree, a pile of boulders, I had asked him, or the remains of an old skiff that would identify the stream as Klak Creek?

"You can't miss it," he said.

There were no roads to step out onto here, no hope of hearing the roar of a distant pulp truck grinding through its gears on the way to the pulp mill in Madawaska, no tar road that could take me back to the lopsided cabin and a roaring woodstove.

Rick climbed into his plane, taxied to the middle of the lake, and lifted off, disappearing behind the mountains. Well, I thought, we are going to float down a big river, and rivers flow to the sea. At the end of this river, where it meets the sea, there is a town and a landing strip. I know that much for sure. How far wrong can we go? We just won't leave the stem of the river. It will take us to our destination. I spent a few lonely minutes considering our situation and then suggested to Adam that we assemble the raft.

When we had landed on Kagati Lake, the clouds had parted briefly and the wind had died or at least slowed for a while. The sun had come out, too. It had made the lake bluer and had given the landscape a cheerful look. I am one of those people whose mood tracks the weather. While we had been unloading, the clouds had closed back together, mixing and shifting in a sky that was a cauldron of blacks and grays. My spirits dropped with the loss of the sunshine. A steady rain began to fall. I remembered the lines that I had committed to memory years ago from the poem by Robert Frost about the "two tramps in mudtime."

The sun was warm but the wind was chill.
You know how it is with an April day
When the sun is out and the wind is still,
You're one month on in the middle of May.
But if you so much as dare to speak,
A cloud comes over the sunlit arch,

A wind comes off a frozen peak,
And you're two months back in the middle of March.

Frost helped: He was familiar. He was a point on my landscape. Adam and I put on our waders and rain jackets to stay dry and hold our bodies' warmth. The rain that came down was cold and penetrating, and it felt like pebbles when it struck my face. It didn't fall to the ground so much as it shot downward in an angled line, straight as a kite string. Some of this rain was gathering in the folds of my yellow rain jacket, and I saw that it was hail, hard-frozen rain, as fine as corn meal. I lifted the hood over my head, tightened the drawstring, and put my back to the wind like a Vermont cow in a November snowstorm. Kagati was being whipped into a gray chop. The pretty lake had turned into an angry sea. I wasn't eager to set off into it. I wondered what the hell I had gotten us into.

The raft came in several parts: There was the big rubber bladder that was the raft itself and a steel-tube frame that needed fitting together. The frame went inside the raft to create a rowing and sitting platform. It gave the bladder some rigidity. As we attempted to put it together, it quickly became apparent that Adam and I were working simultaneously but not together. I was holding a piece that Adam was looking for, and he had set aside a piece that I needed to complete my portion of the assembly. The pieces were not interchangeable: There were pieces for the right and for the left sides, and the pieces had tops and bottoms. As we were discovering its complexity, the mosquitoes began to swarm again. This occurred whenever the wind died down.

"I'll do the frame," Adam announced.

"Okay," I said. "I'll pump the raft."

I had a foot pump, thanks to Denise, to do the job. Separately, Adam and I went about our tasks and accomplished them in silence. We pushed our craft into the lake, going into the waist-deep water with it, and loaded our gear: tent, sleeping bags, food, clothes, gun, stove, chairs, table, cooler, six fly rods. I lashed the gear in place with a long piece of nylon line and kept two fishing rods and the gun, a 12-gauge shotgun I had brought for protection against the bears, free and quickly accessible.

Adam was still guarding his thoughts and mostly staying quiet, but for a while, at least for the present moment, I let go of my close observation of his moods. I was enjoying my own sensations of work and the cold, clean air. It was good to open my lungs and my eyes to this big unspoiled place. The air felt fresh on my face, and even the frozen rain was a tonic and invigorating.

I lifted my head and stuck out my tongue to catch the ice crystals as they came down from the low sky of gray cotton. It felt good, too, to use muscles and simple skills that I had so long neglected and to be standing crotch-deep in an alpine lake making the raft ready for the river. I had been deskbound in Philadelphia, and I had taken on the soft and pasty look of a man beaten down by a divorce. It was a small pleasure, this act of putting a bowline loop in the end of a coil of line and threading it through the eyelet of the raft and then passing the whip end through the bowline loop to make a cinch that I could tighten to hold our gear. I was good at knots, and this knot, the king of knots that held but never tightened on itself, would hold our gear in place in case of a bumpy ride or, God forbid, a capsize.

I pulled down hard on the line and made the lashing fast with two half hitches. I put a slip loop in the second half hitch so I could pull it loose in a hurry. The slip loop was a little bit of showing off, a fillip of my knot-tying expertise. It was a trick I had learned from my stepfather a long time ago. He had been a merchant seaman, and he taught me many knots. I didn't have much to remember him by except seven or eight good knots.

The river flowed mostly east to west, with two half loops that took it first north, then south, before running straight to the west. From the air, it would have looked like a piece of blue thread that had been tightened and allowed to snap back into the shape of a stretched-out and tipped-over S with lots of squiggles, small turns, and bends. I had estimated that the trip would take us ten days. When we started out, with no sure sense of what lay ahead, it seemed a good long time. We could run some sections of the river, loaf and fish others. Making 11 miles a day with the current would be easy. I didn't want to hurry the trip. This was precious time with my son, and there weren't doors out here that he could close and put between us. I even thought that we might have to slow ourselves down to keep from traveling the distance too fast and arriving early at Quinhagak.

Adam took the oars and rowed us across the lake. The waves splashed water in the raft and I pulled a cup from our cooler to bail it out. With some muscle, fighting the wind, Adam brought the raft to the lake's outlet, where the river sluiced against a canyon wall of orange gravel. We were off, and we were moving fast in the swift, cold water. At its beginning, the Kanektok is already a river. It doesn't start as a trickle and gather small streams to make a river. It begins as a river, spilling over a lip of stones at the end of the big lake and exiting with force.

"Whooooooooaaaaaa!" I shouted as we slipped down the chute.

The raft swung completely around in the current. Adam was grinning and working the oars to point the bow downstream. Soon he got it right, and we were sliding along silently and in wonder at the mountains that rose from the river's edges. This river was unlike other rivers I had fished. On the Madison in Montana or the Kennebec in Maine, I had always begun a river trip in the usual way of a lifelong fisherman: I took the measure of the river and assessed its character and activity. What could I learn by watching the water and the life just above and below the glassy plane of the river's surface? I would look for mayflies drying their wings or caddis flies that hovered like moths just over the surface or the swirls that said the fish were taking nymphs that were escaping the muck and rock of the bottom and rising toward the light. This river was different. It had a foreboding aspect, in its surge and sweep out of the lake, and I felt that in some sense it was taking its measure of me. Who was I, and why had I come here? Was I prepared for what would follow? It was like a mustang when the rodeo gate is thrown open. We were on its back. Adam gripped the oars, and I held tight to the lashings on the frame. The raft flexed where the water rose up over rocks, and it spun when the current ricocheted off the banks. No dams hobbled this river. Its only restraint was the eroding seismic folds of the upheaving frozen land itself. It was kept in its channel by the resistance of ancient geology. It swept down through the mountains with fierce determination, driven by snowmelt and incessant cold rain, following its hollowed-out course, a watery locomotive. Along the way, it moved tons of gravel, picking up and depositing islands and bars. It uprooted trees, carved steep cliffs, and cut new channels in the permafrost tundra.

It was different from the other rivers Adam and I had fished in another way. It held tens of thousands of salmon, some of which were now finning in the clear water under our raft as we left the lake. This seemed nothing short of a miracle: Head to tail and cheek to caudal fin, in a long line, the fish looked like a ragged red ribbon waving in the breeze, except that the breeze was crystalline water that was as distorting to our eyes as oily sunlight. I wondered if the red ribbon extended all the way to the Pacific.

"Holy shit, Adam," I said. "Look at the fish."

The great quantity of water rushed downward, pushing off banks, riding high in the curved sweep of the outer bank walls, flexing, scraping, swirling. The river currents required constant steering with the oars, touching and pulling the water, first on the right and then on the left. Only one of us could fish at a time. The raft needed one man's complete attention. Without one of us at the oars, the raft would spin, or bounce off the banks, or get tangled in the shoreline brush. After we left the lake and made a short distance down the river, I volunteered to take raft duty from Adam to let him be the first to fish. We exchanged places. It wasn't so easy walking in the raft. It was soft underfoot, like stepping across the skin of a relaxed trampoline, and I kept my hands on the frame as I made my way to the rowing seat. Adam went to the bow. Before I got the hang of the oars, the nose of the raft pointed first this way and then that way as we moved downstream. We must have looked to the fish hawk wheeling high above us like some crazed and swollen water bug. Once I got us straight and under control, Adam leaned into the pillow of the bow so he could stand and cast the fly line. He threw the line out on the water several times and then turned to me.

"How do you catch these fish?" he asked.

This was a good sign: He apparently wanted to catch a fish badly enough to ask me a question. I knew something about fishing for Atlantic salmon from our trips to eastern Canada, but the Atlantic is a different fish entirely from these Pacific salmon. The Atlantic spawns and returns to the sea and then returns another time to the river to spawn again. The Pacific salmonids, the king, silver, chum, pink, and sockeye, all of which entered the Kanektok, make one ascent. They spawn and then they die. In the river and on the shore, we saw the black carcasses of the king salmon that had run up the river in June and July. Some were half-rotted and caught between rocks, and some were on the gravel strands, eyeless, stinking, and half-eaten by bears. Except for the reading I had done over the summer, I knew nothing about fishing for the Pacific salmon of Alaska. Everything I had read suggested that catching fish in Alaska was ridiculously easy, and trying to learn how to do it made as much sense as trying to learn how to hit the floor when you fell off a bar stool. Nearly all of the literature was about cooking the fish, not catching them.

"They're not feeding in the river when they come to spawn," I said. "They're going to strike out of aggression or annoyance. Put the fly right in front of them. I think that's the trick."

Adam worked the water carefully from the raft, making some short casts first and then lengthening them to cover more water. Nothing struck. He changed flies, and still he raised no fish. He was laying the line out beautifully. We could see sockeyes in the river, and I had read that the Upper River also held grayling and arctic char. The grayling is a graceful fish with a tall, sweeping dorsal fin. Its exotic look is tropical. The char is a colorful brute. It gobbles the eggs of the spawn-ing salmon. The big Kanektok rainbow trout, the prize that brings fishermen this far out into the bush, would come later, toward the middle of the river in the area the guides call the Braids. The rainbows were powerful fighters and voracious feeders, swallowing small mammals that fell into the river. I had even packed some flies made from spun deer hair that looked like plump mice.

As we slipped along, we passed innumerable spots in the river that looked like they held fish—deep pools, overhanging banks, pockets, back eddies, and pillows where the water piled up behind rocks. It was beautiful water, by any fisherman's measure. Back in the East, any of these spots would have held several fish. In fact, on some of the overfished streams of the Adirondacks or New England, many of these pools, aesthetically perfect, would have merited plaques with Proper Names and wood-plank tables for eating a gourmet lunch with a bottle of good wine. On the Tobyhana in Pennsylvania or the Beaverkill in New York, these runs would have been the property of prestigious old fishing clubs with wealthy industrialist pedigrees. They would have inspired a corpus of their own fishing literature, bearing the imprints of fancy small publishing houses. Our eyes were bugging out at the sight of so much good water. It was Eden, and it was all ours.

But we could not catch a fish. Several hours had passed, and we hadn't experienced so much as a single strike. We were no longer seeing the sockeyes, either. The red ribbon had been cut, and the river seemed dead. We saw not one lonely fish. I was getting worried. Maybe all of the fish were at the lake and the head of the river. Sockeyes were known at times to be lake spawners. Were all the fish behind us? Had we come all the way to Alaska to fish a river that was a big, beautiful dud? Had I been suckered by promotional literature? Had we traveled three thousand miles to be skunked?

I had seen these rivers before, inviting but sterile to fishermen. There were some rivers like that in western Maine that tumbled out of the White Mountains—clear as the air on a

January morning, picture-perfect, and yet completely unable to give up a fish. The Swift River in Oxford County was one of them: A man could flail it all day and never turn so much as a minnow or a dace. It was a good place to have your picture taken looking sporting in hip boots, but utterly and maddeningly fishless. I put the best face on the situation, telling Adam that it was the Middle River that was known for its amazing fishing. We had another day or two before we would get there, and we could just enjoy the scenery until we reached it. We could rest up for the action ahead. He gave me the bologna-sandwich look.

I had coaxed him into the trip by telling him the Kanektok was probably the greatest fishing river on earth. I was sorry now for my hyperbole. Since we had left Philadelphia, I knew that Adam had been searching for the flaw in my planning, and it was beginning to look to both of us like my screwup was not forgetting the split shot, failing to pack an extra pocketknife, or leaving the instant coffee at home. I had achieved a first and, some might say, a pure impossibility: I had brought us to an Alaskan river where we would not be able to catch a fish. I kept my concern to myself. Had I staked this trip, and all that it meant, on the wrong river? Maybe I had. It was possible that we had arrived between pulses of the salmon runs and that the fishing had been phenomenal last week and would be phenomenal in another week or two, but that now it was nothing and we would endure ten fishless days. I had heard it from guides so many times before: "You should have been here last week."

I said to Adam, "The Middle River's what we want."

Maybe he would buy it. His face offered no clue.

For several hours, we floated and watched the landscape. We made cast after cast and got not a single strike to our flies.

It was beginning to look for sure like one more thing that I had botched. After a long silent stretch, we switched places in the raft. Adam was sick of fishing—or rather, sick of casting. He took the oars, and I picked up a rod. I stripped line from the reel and let it lie on the floor of the raft as I worked the flex of the rod, back and forth. It was fun to be casting, even if I wasn't catching fish. I enjoyed the mechanics of the cast. The graphite spine of the rod was alive in my hands and responding to the way I worked it back and forth. It felt good, like standing in the batter's box and false-swinging a baseball bat. I took the rod through its familiar quarter arc, keeping my wrist stiff, and worked its resistance from my elbow and shoulder. I was in my sphere of pleasure, meditatively casting and not rushing the line in its journey through the air, when Adam spoke up.

"Dad," he said, "you're bringing the rod back too far on your backcast."

I adjusted my backcast. It had been a little sloppy, for sure, and occasionally the line had caught the water behind me. I probably had played out more line than I could comfortably handle. I shortened the line by reeling some in, moved the rod through a tighter arc, and showed better control.

A little farther downstream Adam spoke again.

"Dad, you almost hit me with the fly."

I was fishing with a weighted fly, which tends to drop on the forward cast. It had zipped by our ears a couple of times. A weighted fly that smacks the ear or side of the head is painful and not uncommon when fishing in the wind, so I snipped it off and replaced it with an unweighted pattern. It didn't fish as well, but it was safer. I went back to casting. The fly swam just below the surface, above where the fish were likely to be in lie.

"You're not covering the water," Adam said.

I tried harder.

After a half mile more of river: "Dad, you're missing the best runs. You're wasting all the best water."

I could see that his criticism wasn't going to stop until I stopped fishing, and even then Adam would probably find a new failing of mine. He hadn't liked my rowing, either. It was too this or too that. I decided to overlook it: I was used to this by now. I knew it was my presence, and not my fishing, that was annoying him. Some of this has to be his age, I thought. At least I wanted some of it, a small piece of it, to be his age. Did it all have to be my fault? I knew that the parents of teenagers are pitiful and hopeless in the eyes of their children. I took some solace in the thought. In the last year, at various times, Adam had advised me that I had bad breath, thinning hair, body odor, a protruding gut, and that I slouched and made too much noise when I ate. Of the two parents, fathers are especially disgusting to children: They have patches of hair on their shoulders, and hair grows out of their ears and nose, they eat onions and sardines, and their toenails grow brown and cracked. One morning, I had made the mistake of coming out of the bathroom after a shower in my underwear.

"Dad, that's gross!"

Nothing was as vile to Adam as the sight of his father in his underwear. I had trained myself to chew slowly and quietly. I even swallowed with care. Adam had watched me across the kitchen table, listening.

"Nobody eats as loud as you do, Dad. I don't even know how you do it."

I kept a supply of breath mints. I sucked in my stomach around him. And I never, ever, went around in my underwear. As the parent of a teenager, I had learned to keep my capacity for being disgusting to a minimum. But there wasn't much I could do about my presence now. We were stuck with each other in the raft.

"Dad, you're splashing the line on the water."

I took a deep breath. I figured it was time for us to take a break and have some hot tea on the shore. It was 7:00 P.M., so I might as well make dinner, too. The sun made a brief showing, and we beached the raft on a narrow gravel bar of white pea-sized stones that was sprouting willow bushes. I set up the stove and put some water to boil for hot tea and another pot for freeze-dried chili.

We were at a bend in the river that created a long, deep pool against a high bank opposite where we had beached the raft. The bank showed bands of colors, red and orange. It looked like some huge modernist painting, one horizontal bar of color blending into the next. Adam took his rod and started at the head of the pool, working it methodically downstream as if it were a Cartesian plane. This was the way he had been taught by the French-speaking guide I had hired when we had fished the Margaree River in Canada four years ago. We had made that trip at the end of the summer before Adam had entered high school. It was our last trip before I separated from my wife. As I watched him working the pool, I recalled how the guide, Robert Chaisson, had stood with Adam in the river, shoulder to shoulder, and showed him the importance of covering all the water. The fish could be lying anywhere, and the beat we had been fishing was too valuable to ignore any piece of it. Adam began with short downstream casts and lengthened them in increments, a yard at a time, sending the curve of the line in sweeps over every bit of water as it slid by in a flat plane from the head to the tail of the pool. There was not a piece of river bottom to which he didn't expose the trailing fly, a No. 2 Black Leech. He had not forgotten the lesson that Robert had taught him on the Margaree. That had been a good trip. Life then had been simpler for Adam and me.

As I pulled the box of tea bags from one of the packs, Adam, who had worked his way down to the pool's exit riffle, let out a shout.

"Dad!"

He had a fish on. The rod bent almost to the point of snapping. The fish appeared hooked well, and Adam was trying to turn its head and move it out of the fast part of the current. Adam knew how to fight and land a fish, and he was playing this one with skill, though it still had the better of him. It rushed out into the heavier current and stripped line off the reel. The key to playing a big fish is to tire it so it can be beached or netted without breaking the line, which tapers to an almost-invisible hundredth of an inch, light enough to fool it into striking in the first place. Fishermen use the rod's bounce and the reel's two-way spool, which lets line out as well as takes it in, to absorb the fish's struggle and prevent the line from snapping. The more it struggles, the more it fatigues, and the force applied through the rod and spool is never more than the tensile strength of the line. Eventually, the fish lacks the strength to continue the fight, and it can be brought to hand or shore. Playing a fish is a form of jujitsu. It is a contest that rests on a single cruel irony. One of the combatants has knowledge that the other lacks: the futility of struggle. An old, smart fish understands the game. It changes the rules and evens the game. It will not fight back. It holds in the current, confounds the fisherman, and stalemates the battle.

For the skilled fly fisherman, the art of fighting fish is this: to balance the loss of the fish from a broken line against the death of the fish from exhaustion. A fighting fish expends enormous amounts of energy and oxygen as it strains against the resistance of the line, rod, and reel, taking it to the edge of death and sometimes over the edge so that it floats lifeless to the boots of the fisherman. Its fate is in the hands of the man holding the rod. I had taught Adam that it was better to lose a fish than to kill it.

Adam had taken naturally to the lesson. I had been bringing him along fishing with me since he was five or six. If he wasn't searching for frogs, he would sit patiently on a rock, Gandhi-style on his heels, holding a landing net and waiting for me to hook a fish. When I brought one to my waders, he would splash over to me in his sneakers and shorts and slip the net under the defeated fish. He always insisted on its release, alive and unharmed.

"Let it go! Let it go!"

From the beginning, when I first put a rod in his hands, at age seven in a brook near our home in Maine, he had fished with intensity but without aggression. It was a rare combination in a good fisherman. I had known lots of good fishermen. Many felt the need to land and kill every fish they hooked, and some weren't happy until they took every fish out of a stream. It was their aggression that gave them focus. They were fish killers. Adam's focus came from another place. I don't know that I had ever seen him happier than the day, when he was about six years old, that he discovered a nest of baby mice in the barn. He called me out to see them, full of wonder at their hairless pink bodies, each small enough to curl up on a penny. He watched them for an hour before I insisted that we cover them back up with duff and leave them alone for their mother. He had that same look each time he caught a fish.

Another day, he ran into the house as I was reading the newspaper, eager to show me what he had caught in the clover in the front yard. He thrust out his hand. I looked closely over my newspaper. Pinched between his thumb and middle finger was a fat bumblebee, furiously pumping and straining its stinger.

"Adam," I had said slowly, "don't let it go. Let's walk to the door. Just hold it carefully. When I tell you to, and not a second before, throw it out as hard and fast as you can. Then stand back because I'm going to slam the door."

It was easy to turn him into a fisherman. I just put him near water.

Adam had been what parents call an easy child. He had not fussed much as a baby, and as he grew up, his early easiness developed into a gentle nature. He took the world as it came to him, and he sought ways to accommodate himself to it without antagonism or conflict. Even now, a lot of what he was angry about, I guessed, was the fact that I had made life difficult for him by causing him to be angry. He was angry at me for putting him in the position of having to be angry. He didn't want to be angry. He saw me as the cause of his distress, and of course he was right. He had loved living his life inside our family. When he was small, he made gingerbread houses with his mother at Christmas and he liked to set the table at Thanksgiving. Each setting had a paper turkey or Pilgrim with a name on it: Mom, Dad, Elizabeth, Yia Yia, Uncle Paul. In the sixth grade and eager to please his older sister, Adam had let her relieve her boredom one night by dyeing his hair green in the bathroom sink.

Of course, he also had a maddening side: He was constitutionally incapable of hanging up his clothes or putting anything away or taking a shower that lasted less than forty-five minutes and required no fewer than three large bath towels, and he had a stubborn streak. His stubbornness was now fixed on me as the person who had torn apart our family.

I watched him fight the fish. He was knee-deep in the river, and his line was tearing across the pool. He was tall, loose in his long limbs, and muscled in his arms and shoulders. He had his mother's high cheekbones and light complexion. He held the rod saber high as I had shown him when we had fished in Maine. It gave him leverage over the fish in the strong current. Yes, watching him, I had to acknowledge the extent to which I had come to value my life through my children. They were good kids, Adam and his older sister, Elizabeth, and they gave me—or I selfishly took from them—a handhold on a better sense of myself. Their presence had helped me put some of the damage of my childhood behind me. I had created a life—important job, house in the country, family—that was a bulwark against the disorder and disappointment of my past. My children were at the center of it. The piano lessons, vacations to Disney World, summer camp, pony club, private school—the very fact that they depended on me and that I was capable of providing them with a safe middle-class upbringing—had given my life substance, even heft. I had preached the gospel of aspiration and achievement. Isn't that what had saved me and pulled me up? When my daughter was in elementary school, I paid her to memorize Shakespeare, a dollar for a passage or a poem. I loved her high-pitch recitations of the opening of *Henry V* over blueberry pancakes and hash:

> *"O for a Muse of fire, that would ascend*
> *The brightest heaven of invention,*
> *A kingdom for a stage, princes to act*
> *And monarchs to behold the swelling scene!"*

Elizabeth had just graduated from New York University and now was throwing herself into the hard work of becoming an actress in New York City. Adam was on his way to Bowdoin College as a classics major, back to Maine, not far from where we had lived and not far from his mother. At night, back in Philadelphia, I would ask him to read aloud to me from *The Iliad* and relish the sound of him forming the Greek syllables.

"Menin i-ede thea, Peleiadeo Achilleos . . ."

As he waded deeper into the river, I saw in my son a person who would go farther and be more than his father. I didn't want him to have my life: There had been too much hurt in the beginning of mine. Things had gone wrong. I wanted something better for him, and I wanted to break the curse that I felt had been set down on me. Yet I had put all of this at risk. In the last few years, I had met many men who no longer had any contact with their children because of a divorce. These men didn't see their children at holidays and missed their graduations. They seemed bereft as they told of learning secondhand about their children's careers and weddings. I couldn't bear the thought of losing my son. I wouldn't let it happen, even it meant taking the risk of a self-guided and underfinanced trip in Alaska.

After a prolonged battle with the fish, too long really, Adam brought its heavy flattish body to the beach. It was a sockeye salmon. It had a big green head, fierce hooked jaw, and blood-red body. It looked like a demon cut from the top of an Indian totem pole. It was downright scary lying there on the beach, gasping for air and pumping its gills. Adam had foul-hooked it, in the tail. The fish hadn't sought the fly; it simply had been snagged as the fly passed over it. The odd hookup accounted for the long fight. It was a wonder that he had landed the fish at all. It hadn't been caught in the right way, for sure, but still it was a fish. And not just any fish, it was an Alaskan salmon, an honest-to-goodness Alaskan salmon, and it was our first fish of the trip.

Hallelujah!

For a few minutes, we were on top of the world. I took a picture of Adam: my son and his fish in Alaska. He knelt with the fish and held it forward with both hands toward the lens of the camera to make it appear even bigger. He was smiling. I was smiling. This was what I had been hoping for: a father-and-son moment. Maybe this trip was going to work out after all. We were back in the old groove, celebrating over a big fish. For a moment, our troubles fell away. I snapped several more pictures, and then Adam cradled the fish in the water until it swam out of his hands and disappeared in the deep channel. We drank our tea sitting on the edge of the raft and ate our chili, satisfied with our fishing prowess and overall excellence as men of the wilderness, and then we set back onto the river.

In many places, the river moved between high banks, and often the banks were spotted with hundreds of small holes bored into the gravel. They were homes to river swallows. The birds popped out of the holes and swooped over the river picking up mosquitoes. The swallows flew spirals and loops and arabesques. They reminded me of the barn swallows I had come to know so well one summer in Maine twenty-five years earlier. That was the summer, in 1975, when I was twenty-four, that I had spent hatching my plan to build a house. I had only been married a year then, and my wife, Patti, and I were renting an apartment in a run-down neighborhood of Portland, which, in those days, was a run-down city with a run-down waterfront. Patti was not yet pregnant with Elizabeth. I was working at the city's daily newspaper. The pay was $164 a week. We had no savings. Our only asset was the Volkswagen bus Patti had brought into the marriage. We lived from paycheck to paycheck. Buying a house was beyond our means—dinner at Denny's and a night at the movies were beyond our means back then.

We looked at several houses with a real-estate agent, but always the financial calculation was a dead end. We needed money for a down payment and enough income each month to cover the mortgage payments. I put pencil to paper and determined that it would take us four years to gather the down payment. So, I decided on a different course: I would build my own house. I persuaded the credit union to give me a note for seventy-five hundred dollars and bought fifteen acres on a back road northwest of the city.

The lot I had bought was heavily wooded, with tall, fat pine trees and a brook that cut across the low corner of the property. It was a gorgeous sight with the sun filtering down through the leaves of the swamp maples and the brook wending its way through the ferns. The land had once belonged to the Flagg Lumber Company and had been managed for saw logs. I looked at the green-black trees rising to the blue sky and saw boards and beams and heavy timbers bundled beneath the bark. There was a sawmill just two miles down the state highway that could turn those trees into big-dimension lumber. Somehow, from the thought of all that cheap lumber stacked in my yard, which was still a woodlot, my mind leaped to the idea of building a post-and-beam house, one of those old-style New England homes that are framed with heavy timbers. This would be a big job, I knew, but the idea of it appealed to me. A post-and-beam house was snug and fitted together like a handcrafted chest of drawers, and it was strong and permanent. It was what I wanted in a house.

The prototypes for a post-and-beam home, eighteenth- and nineteenth-century farmhouses, were scattered throughout the surrounding countryside of southern Maine. Some were simple boxes with gabled roofs, capes with a center chimney; others were L-shaped structures, with tacked-on extensions that connected them to barns. With their siding of white clapboards, four inches to the weather, and twelve-over-twelve mullioned windows, and a lilac bush in the dooryard, they struck me as pure poetry, as finished and perfect as a sonnet. They were rooted in the places in which they had been built, and their lines and proportions seemed to me as natural and pleasing as the ponds, trees, and meadows with which they shared the landscape. They sailed through the seasons on granite foundations. I wanted to live in one. There were a couple of big problems with my plan: The skills it took to build them were mostly lost, and while I had worked my way through college on a summer construction crew, I surely didn't have the knowledge to raise up my own house. Nor did I know where I could get the drawings that would guide me through the construction. I wasn't even that handy with tools.

I had read Scott and Helen Nearing's book *The Good Life* and briefly considered a stone house of the type they had built in the 1930s for their idyll of simple living up the coast but rejected it in favor of the texture of wood and standing wealth of my woodlot. I carried the problem with me as I went back and forth from our second-floor apartment to the newspaper office, working from late afternoon until after midnight, editing stories of dairy-price battles in the legislature, the cost of No. 2 fuel oil, drownings, country fairs, grange meetings, and houses set afire by faulty kerosene heaters. All the time my mind was working on the question: How could I build this house?

Finally, the answer came to me. I could create my own set of drawings for a house by studying the old barns in the nearby countryside whose ribs and rafters had never been covered over with plaster walls. They were standing three-dimensional blueprints that had been exposed to generations of dairy cows, oxen, and draft horses. These barns were there waiting to teach me what I needed to know. The same techniques that had been used to build the old farmhouses had been used to build the barns out back. Downsized to the proportions of the structure I wanted to build, the barns would serve as models for my timber-framed house.

So, for two months, I prospected old barns, and especially the old barns owned by my neighbors, the Shakers at Sabbathday Lake in New Gloucester, the town where my pine trees were gaining girth in the July sun and where one day a house would look down a long slope to a brook. No one had built barns like the Shakers. It was one of life's fine coincidences that the only piece of land I could afford to buy was a short distance from a remnant Shaker colony. The Shakers were a celibate religious sect of the nineteenth century that had run down to a few old men and women. They had channeled their sexual and spiritual energy into making beautiful and practical objects: chairs, tables, houses, barns. Their handiwork was austere and eloquent and lasting. "'Tis the gift to be simple, 'tis the gift to be free," the town's elementary school children sang in their homage to the Shakers at holiday concerts. So I took my flashlight and sketch pad and went into their barns and the barns of others in the area to study the ancient art of making a home whose bones would be big pine timbers.

This was considered daft behavior by my neighbors, and

especially by Bob Hersey, who owned the land next door, on which he grew cucumbers for a pickle company in Lewiston. Fortunately, Mainers, like a lot of New Englanders off the beaten track, tolerate eccentricity in pursuit of an ideal. Bob Hersey, or Mr. Hersey as I called him, since I was twenty-four and he was closer to seventy, was himself an exceptional character in the town and displayed his own personal oddities, including an astonishing lack of enterprise. His little house at the edge of the pasture up the road lacked a floor in one room, and the walls inside the two bedrooms were plugged and stuffed with newspapers to keep the wind from howling through in winter. In any event, I was accepted among the farmers, woodcutters, and tradespeople in town as one of my generation's "back-to-the-landers," college-educated young people who had the misguided notion that life in the country, or on a farm, was a fulfilling spiritual alternative to the nation's materialism, that somehow burning wood or owning a composting toilet showed depth of character. I would admit to being an idealist, but I had never held a strong enough claim on the middle class to have had a basis for rejecting materialism. Frugality, for me, was not an indulgence; it was a necessity. I needed every dollar I could scrape together to build my house. My mission on that unpaved country road was to make a life, an orderly life, in a safe and snug house, but I let the "granola" stereotype ride since it seemed to amuse my neighbors.

Invited into their barns, I examined how the posts and beams, the vertical and horizontal members of the structures, had been fitted together. Lying on my back, I stared at the handiwork of house wrights who had been dead for a century. I found their design, workmanship, and rough aesthetics as engaging as any Etruscan mural or medieval arch. I measured

the distances between eaves and ridgepoles and the spans between rafters. I examined the connecting mortises and tenons
and calculated the carrying loads of oak and pine beams that
were twelve inches square. My house was taking shape in my
mind, even as I resolved its vectors and snow loads on pieces
of graph paper I had shoved inside the sketch pad. The swallows had been my companions in this work, often exploding
in flocks from dark corners of the barns and bursting out of
broken windows into the drowsy August sunlight. I wondered
if they had to blink as I did when they came out of the darkness of their capacious birdhouses. The Maine swallows were
bigger than their Alaskan cousins, but they had the same long
gray-black tail feathers and the same darting and turning
flight in pursuit of mosquitoes.

4

Sometimes, as our raft moved along, we heard loose dirt
rolling down the steep banks and into the river. By looking
carefully, I could see little balls of gray fur scurrying from hiding place to hiding place. They were arctic voles. We also
could see, above and behind them, the long black mink that
were hunting them. I put down my rod and rooted for the
voles.

In hours, Adam and I moved out of the mountains and into
the country that was a stationary sea of rolling hills, treeless
but whiskered with dark green bushes. The hills were in fact
the deposits of glaciers that had retreated thousands of years
ago, at a time when much of the earth's water was locked up
in ice and the oceans were hundreds of feet lower than they
are now. At that time, twenty-thousand years ago, a land
bridge had joined Alaska and Siberia. It had been trod by

mammoth and man, and the Kanektok had been five times longer, reaching well out into what was a more distant Bering Sea. In those days, the trip would have taken us fifty days and we would have been constantly on the lookout for saber-toothed tigers.

We slid along on the river, its glassy surface distressed here and there by an eddy or swirl boiling up from an invisible boulder or the steep ascent of the river bottom. In the open country on either side of the river, the tundra was dark and brooding in some places, bright and cheerful in others as the heavy clouds admitted pillars of sunlight to the earth. There were, in fact, a vast number of different weather stories playing out over the landscape, all visible from where we sat on the raft. In some places, rain was falling; in other places, mist softened the outlines of the hills. I could see other places where the air sparkled with sunshine. I was witnessing all of this, at times, as snowflakes swirled in gray light around the raft.

The effect of this was a dramatically lit landscape, the way it might have been seen by a Renaissance painter exploring the effect of light and shadow on the Italian peninsula. The expanses of light and dark, often with the light bursting from behind the dark, seemed to deepen the depth of the spaces, making a mile or two miles or the full distance to the horizon seem more spacious, the way the vault of a cathedral is made to feel more voluminous by the light pouring in through colored windows. Hills or trees bathed in the Arctic light seemed both far away and, by virtue of being precisely etched, as if they were at an arm's length. It was a landscape viewed through a stereoscope. Yet the most astonishing aspect of the play of light and land was the appearance of rainbows in the sky. The distant sunlight, refracted through the closer rain or snow, was making the sight of them common. Already we had seen four, though two were short-lived because the light and water moved so rapidly over the vast green and pink prairie of lichen. The entire landscape seemed to be breaking into shards of light and color like a crystal held up to the sun and turned first this way and then that.

As we floated downriver, we found bear tracks and scat at nearly every gravel strand. From time to time, when the tracks were far enough removed from the brush where a bear might be hidden, we stopped to examine them. The flapjacks of scat, full of berries, shimmered with fish scales. Some of the tracks were as big as dinner plates. These were enormous brown bears, much bigger than the yearling we had encountered at Kagati.

The deep tracks suggested animals as heavy as small cars. They would be wrapped in great blankets of lush brown fur. Occasionally, in pockets of dead air among the bushes, we could smell their wet-rug dankness. It hung in the air even after they had departed, the way diesel hangs in the air after the bus has pulled away from the bus station. I was fairly sure we were safe. Brown bears did not have reputations for unprovoked attacks, though it was always dangerous to surprise one or crowd its space. Besides, I had our gun lashed to the stern, where I could easily pull it out if I spotted danger. The gun was unloaded for our own safety, but I kept a handful of Magnum slugs in my front trouser pocket.

The standard procedure in bear country is to make yourself heard to warn an animal of your approach. "Make noise, sing, talk loudly, or tie a bell to your pack," advised a Fish and Wildlife bulletin that had come with our fishing licenses. That's what I did when we went ashore to investigate the tracks and scat. I sang. Whatever first came to mind, that's what I belted out. I went through the songs from grade school: "Oh, Susanna," "Clementine," and "Frère Jacques."

"Frère Jacques,
Frère Jacques,
Dormez-vous?
Dormez-vous?
Sonnez les matines,
Sonnez les matines,
Din, din, don!
Din, din, don!"

I hadn't sung them in forty years. Since I could remember only a verse or two of each, mangling even that little bit, I moved on to the songs of a later period, church hymns such as "Onward, Christian Soldiers" and "Mine Eyes Have Seen the Glory." Those, too, were soon exhausted, and I went on to the pop music of my teenage years: "Yesterday, all my troubles seemed so far away."

The performance among the bear tracks was an ontology of my musical development, such as it was. What the bears in the area made of this bawling I cannot say. When I depleted my memory of songs, I went to poetry. I recited Yeats's "Lake Isle of Innisfree" and the opening verses of Whitman's "O Captain! My Captain!" We got back in the raft, and the bears were spared my delivery of Lear's speech on the heath. As for Adam, who had inherited his mother's gift for music and could actually carry a melody, he was content to call out, "Hey, bear. Hey, bear. I'm coming through, bear." My singing had given him one more thing to roll his eyes about. He was already in the raft, at the oars, waiting impatiently, when I came back to it.

"Let's get moving," he said.

We went back to not catching fish. We spent a desultory afternoon and evening floating down the river and looking at the great hills set back from the river. They came in and out of the clouds. Often we felt that we ourselves were in the clouds, enveloped in their mist and rain, and occasionally it was hard to tell which was moving, the clouds or a single big hill that had been revealed momentarily in the purple-gray light. It was we who seemed stationary as the hills drifted upstream, to the east, back to Kagati Lake. An odd feeling of disorientation resulted, and I wanted to hold tight to the gunwales of the raft. At times, it felt as if the entire landscape were afloat and moving with different currents and streams. Were we on the river or floating on the cold mist? Were those spectral caribou moving in the other direction?

It had been a long day on the river since we had left the lake. Eventually, we decided it was time to start looking for a place to spend the night, even if we hadn't reached Klak Creek. In August, the Alaskan day is lit until after midnight. The sky was like the globe of a hurricane lamp with the flame turned low. It was already close to 11:00 P.M., so we had a couple of hours before darkness. The river continued to flow between steep banks, and when we found a place where we could clamber up the bank we brought the raft to shore and set about making camp. Adam pitched the tent, and I went to work on a late dinner. We were hungry again, very hungry. The temperature had dropped: into the low forties. We put on extra clothes.

We worked and ate quickly and got into our sleeping bags.

By now, it was dark, with only a faint glow on the western rim of the tundra. The moon, a transparent wafer, appeared intermittently between the scudding clouds and rain showers. I hung a candle from a grommet sewn into the low ceiling of the tent. It gave us light and a little heat. The small tent was made of a light yellow fabric. When I went out to pee, I could see that the candle had turned the tent into a Chinese lantern. The wind came up, and the candle rocked. It made a Punch-and-Judy show on the walls. Back inside, I felt for the double-barreled shotgun that I had put between our sleeping bags.

Adam wrote in his journal, and I paged through a field guide to Alaska wildflowers. I had already collected a half-dozen specimens along the river and pressed them between the book's pages. This was a habit of long standing with me: I had flowers in other books from other places, mayflowers from Penobscot County, buttercups from Cape Breton Island, beach peas from the Jersey shore, and in some cases the pages of my field guides pressed the dried exoskeletons and delicate wings of blue, white, and green mayflies. After returning his journal to the rucksack at the foot of his sleeping bag, Adam lay on his back and folded his hands behind his head. He was quiet for a while.

"Did you ever read *Invisible Man* by Ralph Ellison?" he asked.

It was one of the books he had read in his senior English class back in Philadelphia. I wondered if there was some relationship between the book and what he had just entered into his journal.

I said that I had.

"Did you like it?"

"I thought it was great," I said. "The fight scene is unforgettable."

"Is it your favorite book?"

"No," I said. "But it's probably in the top twenty-five."

I picked a high number because I knew Adam was impressed with the numbers of books I had read. The walls of our apartment back in Philadelphia were crowded with bookcases, and from time to time he would pick out a book at random, usually a fat one, and ask me if I had read it.

"What's your favorite book?"

"Favorite? I don't think I could pick a favorite," I said.

After a moment, I added, "I can tell you the best fishing story ever written. 'Big Two-Hearted River' by Ernest Hemingway."

Adam turned on to his side and looked over at me, interested for the first time since we left home.

"What's it about?" He rested his head on his elbow.

I told him the story of Nick Adams and his trip into Michigan's Upper Peninsula after returning from the war. "That was World War One," I explained. In the story, I told Adam, Nick hops a freight train that takes him deep into the woods, where he makes a camp and fishes for trout.

"Nick has suffered a trauma, the reader is made to feel, and he finds healing in the carefully observed sensations of the woods and the river."

"Is he a fly fisherman?" Adam asked.

"No. But he's a good fisherman, anyway," I said. "He catches grasshoppers and uses them for bait."

"What happens in the story?" Adam asked.

"Not much," I said. "At least not much that you can see. Mostly you feel it. It's a story where all of the meaning is unspoken."

"Doesn't sound like much of a story," Adam said.

He rolled over and went to sleep. I spent a little time thinking about Nick and then went to sleep, too.

5

On the second day, as Adam and I came swirling around a bend we encountered a sow brown bear standing knee-deep in the river. She was with her cub. This is the most dangerous way to meet a bear. A startled she-bear with a cub is the guaranteed exception to the rule that bears tend to leave you alone if you leave them alone.

She was fishing, looking down into the water and swatting salmon out of the current. Her pig-sized cub was on the bank, watching her. For the cub, it was both lunch and a life lesson in salmon fishing. For Adam and me, it was a serious no-shit situation, very possibly deadly for us or the bear, and even as we realized it, the current was bringing us nearer to her. She was unaware of our silent approach on the surface of the water. The river was narrow, only about four raft-widths across, and the current was moving swiftly, with a slim channel down its center. The edges of the river, right and left, were shallow and rocky, so if we held our course, we would be forced to pass within feet, within claw-reaching distance, of the big female. There was no way to run the raft past her. She would surely attack. At a minimum, the slash of her claws would deflate the raft, turning it into a waterlogged rubber pancake. We would be splashing in the water with a thousand-pound bear as our gear floated downriver.

I decided quickly to beach the raft and pulled hard on the oars to reach the meager shoreline. Adam reeled in his fly and stowed his rod on the bottom of the raft. I tried to row the raft upstream even as I headed to the nearer edge of the stream. I feared that an attempt at landing on the opposite shore, away from the bear, would carry us farther downstream and a few lethal yards closer to her. The raft scraped onto the sand and rocks, only about forty yards upstream from where she stood. In bear terms, this is absurdly deep in the danger zone. A brown bear can cover that distance in three seconds or less. In spite of their size, bears are fast, quicker even than Olympic sprinters. So there we were, in clear view, not much more than one hundred paces upstream, and on the same side of the river as the big sow. I heard my heart pounding in my ears.

I hoped that once we beached the raft she would spot us, see that we were not a threat, and amble off into the bush. Already, though, I was pulling the shotgun from the lashings on the stern. I took two lead slugs from my pants pocket and dropped them into the gun's two chambers. I closed the gun. It clicked. The bear looked up but not toward us. She didn't seem to know where the sound had come from. Then Adam stepped from the raft. At the crunching sound of his foot pressing down on the gravel, she looked toward us. My heart rose in my chest. I held my breath. Up until we beached the raft, Adam and I had been exchanging a string of variously low and modulated "holy shits," with him encouraging me to get the damned raft to shore as fast as possible. But we had gone silent on the shoreline. I didn't know whether our voices would warn her off or startle her into attack. The sound of the boot on the gravel fixed our position for her.

She put her porcine eyes on us. The air congealed. She lumbered from the water but maintained her eye contact. She was enormous, probably nine feet tall, and her paleolithic architecture showed through her heavy coat. When she walked, the giant triangular plates that were her ursine scapula shifted under the carpet of her pelt. She was long through the body and neck, with a massive head and prominent snout. It was a head big enough to fill a basement freezer. She stood up straight, pointed her nostrils into the air, and grunted. It was the amplified sound of a heavy chest of drawers being pushed across a wood floor. *Rrrrrrruuuuggg. Rrrrrrrrruug.* This I guessed is what a wild boar sounded like rooting for food. She rocked from side to side. She had seen us, and now she was trying to get a better sense of us through her most acute sense, smell. I hoped we didn't smell like fish or whatever the pheromone was that communicated fear. I could hear her breathing, a kind of windy whale sound traveling through long church-organ pipes. The sight of us obviously was a taunt to her, a challenge. Would she rush us? Would she attack? The instinctual belts and pulleys of her big simple brain apparently were at work, calculating distance, smell, shape, and movement. She was making up her mind.

I joined Adam by stepping out of the raft, ever so gently. All of my motion was away from her. I was careful not to make a move that was toward her or that appeared fast or aggressive. I gripped the shotgun in my left hand. I reached back into the raft and pulled out one of the long cans of aerosol bear repellent. I pushed the gun's safety into the firing position.

"Hey, bear." I spoke quietly at first. Then more loudly, affirming my identity as a human. "Hey, bear. Everything's okay, bear. No problem, bear. Just a couple of fishermen, bear." It was the voice I would have used had a mugger stuck a gun in my ribs back in Philadelphia: "No problem, man, take what you want. Here's my wallet. Just don't kill me or my son."

Ashore, Adam started to walk upstream on the thin strand of beach, away from her, and she got back down in the water to watch him. She was fixed on him, not on me. Was that because he was in plainer view? I wasn't sure what our next move should be. Now it was my parental mind that was making its own set of calculations.

My brain plotted the position of the bear, the cub, me next to the raft, and Adam behind me and walking upstream. It was a rectangle that could have easily fitted within the bounds of a tennis court. I felt myself move upward into a state of hyperalertness. Suddenly I was aware of everything around me, and all my senses sharpened. I could taste the metallic saliva in my mouth. I felt the size and shape of my tongue. I felt the wind on my face. It was moving from the bear to us. It lifted the tiny heart-shaped leaves of the alders and showed their lighter undersides. A small black bird, catapulted from upstream, shot between the bear and me and disappeared into the thicket. I heard the river gurgling, the wind moving through the bushes, and her breathing and grunting. Once before I had felt this level of superawareness: My car had been rear-ended by a tractor-trailer on the Maine Turnpike in a snowstorm. In the three or four seconds that it took for the car to flip over and land on its roof on the embankment, my mind filmed the scene in all its detail: two oncoming cars, the snow in the funnel of headlights, the *whoosh* of the truck's brakes from behind, and then a blast of its horn, the guardrails, the car turning over in the air, the deafening *boom* as the car came down on its roof, and the subdued crunch of the windshield.

The bear was rocking and grunting, and I noticed that the fur low on her body was darker, where it was wet. Her forearms seemed short for her long body, and twice she came down onto them but pushed herself back up into her erect and towering posture. We were without a place to retreat. The upstream beach narrowed and then disappeared, where the alders met the river. Adam walked away faster from the raft and then broke into a slow jog. The bear came down on all fours and moved toward him. She stopped and then moved again, a bit faster, splashing in the water.

"Adam," I shouted. "Stop."

My voice didn't turn her eyes from Adam. She seemed locked on him the way a missile locks on a plane. It was clear that the bear was reacting to his retreat. He just wanted to keep moving away from her, and I felt the same almost irresistible urge to run, but it was the moving away that was bringing her on.

"Adam, stop," I shouted again.

The opportunity to shoot before she went into a full gallop was disappearing. She was only twenty-five yards from me now, and I could smell her. It was the smell of a Labrador retriever that had been rolling in dead fish. Adam was still moving. If the bear were to reach him and attack, I knew that he knew to put himself into a ball and lie still on the ground. The victim of a bear attack could sometimes survive by playing dead and allowing the bear to bat him around. There would be flesh wounds, maybe worse, but death might be averted if the bear felt that its prey was no longer a threat. Adam knew this, too, but he also knew enough not to run away from a bear. He knew that running triggered a predatory response. Knowing and doing in these situations were two different things.

There was no question I would fire those slugs into the bear's chest if I had to, and it was looking as if I would have to. I was reluctant to shoot only because I was afraid that I wouldn't kill her. I certainly didn't need a wounded bear on my hands. What the hell would I do then, fall on her with my Swiss Army knife? Yet she was closing in, and I had to make a decision. I could fire a shot in the air to try to frighten her off, but if that failed I would be left with a single cartridge.

The shotgun was loaded with magnum-sized slugs. Packed with a heavy load of powder, the slug, a full ounce of lead about as big around as a spool of thread, would exit the muzzle with hundreds of foot-pounds of force. If it struck the bear, it would tear a big hole, break bones, and sever arteries. But that might not be enough to ensure her death. I was unsure that I could deliver a killing shot, even at this close range. A shotgun lacks the spiral scores, or "riflings," in the barrel that make a rifle's bullet accurate over distances. Shotguns have smooth bores, and they are made for firing loads of shot—multiple pellets—that cover a big circle. They are meant for shooting small flying things, like ducks. Slugs fired from a shotgun are powerful, enough to push an engine block, but wildly inaccurate.

I could fire at this bear and the slug might strike her chest, or it might miss by a foot or two, hitting her gut or paw or nothing at all. A shotgun is a point-blank weapon. If I wanted to be sure of placing a killing shot to her chest, I would have to wait until she was almost on me or passing me as she went for Adam. At a distance of five or ten yards, I could fire directly at her and hope that the lead slug would break through the cage of her heavy ribs and explode her heart. It would be like firing into the grille of an oncoming car. The engine might go dead, but the car would still be moving. I would have to stay cool and place a second shot before she landed on top of me, dead.

I prepared to shoot. I had no other choice. I would fire the right barrel first, then the left.

I shouted one more time.

"Stop!"

This time, Adam brought himself under control. He came to a halt. The bear stopped, too. She stood and watched us both, bringing me into the line of her vision by moving her head rather than shifting her eyes. She grunted, rocked some more, and then looked back toward her cub. The action was now stopped, but the scene might not be over. What would she do? I looked down the line of the barrels. The bead was on her chest. She was grunting but not moving. She looked downstream. Her cub had disappeared into the willows on the left bank. Mother bear looked back to Adam, then back for her missing cub. The big simple brain was making a new calculation.

I held off on firing. I waited for her decision. One step in our direction and I would gently press the trigger. My decision was made. I waited. She was angry, damned angry, and clearly she had intended to attack. Yet another impulse was tugging at her. It was her maternity. Her cub was nowhere in sight. She turned, splashed her way back to the fishing pool, and climbed the bank. Adam sprinted back to the raft, and we hopped in and pushed off. Adam took the oars and rowed ferociously downstream, hugging and brushing the opposite bank. We passed the place where she had been fishing, with no sight of her in the brush. I was still in a state of high alert. I drank in the sight of each leaf along the stream, the sparkle of the sun on the river's ripples, the clouds scudding overhead. I felt exhilarated, delivered, and sick in my stomach. My skin was tingling.

"Damn," Adam said, shaking his head and leaning back as he pulled hard on the oars. "That was close."

"Too damned close," I said. "Let's get the hell out of here."

The river maintained its narrow course. It seemed to have gotten narrower, and it was continuing to make blind left and right turns. There was the chance we would face a repeat of the situation we had just left behind, maybe with the same bear.

We went several hundred yards before either of us spoke again.

"We need to be extra-careful through here," Adam said.

"I'm thinking the same thing," I said.

"Do you have something, a pot or pan or something, I can bang as a warning?"

I dug into the cooler and took out a saucepan and a big spoon. I clapped them together as we floated along.

"Hey, bear," Adam sang out. "Coming through, bear."

I gave my Lear speech.

I was feeling a little giddy.

"Do you realize how goddamn close that was?" I laughed.

I thought of the bear joke my brother had sent me as an e-mail when I was planning the trip. I told it to Adam.

"It seems that the Alaska Department of Fish and Wildlife was working up a new warning to fishermen in bear country. It still told them to wear bells to avoid startling a bear and to carry pepper spray in the event of contact. But the new warning also said that fishermen should know the difference between the paw prints and scat of black bears and grizzlies. A grizzly's paws are larger, and its claws are longer. Black bear scat contains berries and rabbit fur. Grizzly scat has little bells in it and smells like pepper."

"Very funny, Dad. Ha-ha." He drew out each of the last two syllables. "Ha-ha."

Later in the day, we finally began to pick up fish, mostly arctic char. They were heavy big-bellied fish, glorious in their reds, pinks, and pale blues, with flanks that looked like a summer sky at sunset. They were monster versions of the brook trout we caught back in Maine. We saw that the char hung in the current behind the sockeyes and fed on the eggs as they released them into the river. It was a rich yoke diet that made for fat fish. Adam landed one that was well over eight pounds. I unhooked it for him and dropped it into the cooler for dinner. The river had widened again, and it was straighter and less prone to surprises. Even though we were still seeing plenty of scat, I was feeling good and not a little relieved. We were finally into fish, lots of fish, and we hadn't seen a bear in eight hours.

6

On the morning of the third day, when the rain that had been pounding us nearly all night finally eased, I pulled myself out of the tent and set to work on the ritual of our little propane stove: pump the cylinder, turn the knob with my thumb over the valve hole to maintain the tank pressure, open the spout, and light the gas. The burst of blue flame and the steady hiss of the gas were comforting. The stove gave us heat. Even if it was only a small circle of heat, as big around as a teacup, it was heat. Oh, glorious heat and pretty blue flames! It doesn't take long in the wilderness, when you are cold and wet, to connect heat with survival. The steps are short from heat to survival, and survival to hope, and hope to joy. Heat—it's the difference between feeling lost and feeling found, between a bleak and dark existential universe and a world watched over by a kind and understanding God. Soon we had hot coffee (praise the Lord!) and char, which I fried to a crisp in a skillet. (Amen!) Char is a deliciously oily fish, and I could feel my body absorbing its fattiness. I felt warm and strong. We ate standing up, probably a pound and a half of fish apiece. We were dressed in our chest waders and rain jackets as we shoveled in our breakfast and spit bones on the ground. I cleaned the dishes at the water's edge, and then we loaded the raft and set down the river. The water was high from the night's downpour. Our bellies were full, and we looked forward to the day.

I took the oars first, and Adam fished. My legs and back were stiff, but the rowing, which was more nearly steering and pulling away from the banks when the current pushed us too close to shore, soon loosened my muscles, and I felt good from the exertion. I positioned the raft so I faced downstream, which is an inefficient but pleasant way to row. I could see where we were going rather than where we had been. I was pushing rather than pulling the oars. I opened my raincoat and the underlayers of cotton and polypropylene to let out my body's steam. Adam stood in the bow, his knees against the rubber wall of the raft for steadiness, and cast toward objectives that might hold fish.

Adam is an athlete. I enjoyed watching him pick up the line from the water with a strong lift of the rod, and I felt his timing as he let the line lie down in the air behind him before bringing the rod forward, sharply, to put the fly far out on the water. As we swept along, we called out to each other as we saw likely places that would hold fish and we wondered aloud about Klak Creek. We still had not found it, and the pilot's directions to us had become a joke.

"You can't miss it," I said.

"Nope," Adam said. "Should make it by tonight, maybe tomorrow."

"Yeah, we just won't fish the first ten miles or so."

"Can't miss it!"

He seemed to be getting into the spirit of the trip. I was pleased.

In the early evening, when the thickening clouds and wind gusts told me that it was likely the rain would come down hard again, we decided to make camp and have dinner. We had put in a long day in mostly bad weather, but the fishing had been steady and we had even fished a pool where we caught grayling on dry flies. In the cosmology of fly-fishing, the dry fly is supreme. It floats on the surface and allows the fisherman to see the fish rise to the surface, kiss the glassy plane that is the ceiling of its world, and sip in the fly, which it assumes to be an insect. The grayling had been hitting our gray-and-white dries as if they were mosquitoes trapped on the surface.

Fishing this good made the weather tolerable. I planned the night's meal as Adam waded into the river for more fishing. He was still bragging about the size of the big char he had caught the previous day. After dinner we would float downriver a little farther and set up the tent well away from the place where we ate.

As I carried the cooking gear and cooler from the raft to the place where I would set up the stove and we could sit on some big rocks to eat, I realized that I didn't see the gun, so I went back to the raft to get it. I didn't want the gun to be out of sight or far from hand, even though there were no bears in sight. The gun wasn't in the raft. I checked carefully on the bottom and among the big plastic bags that were under the rowing seat. I grew worried but was unwilling to conclude that it was missing. I walked over to where Adam was fishing.

"Adam," I called out, "did you bring the gun with you?"

"No," he said, not turning to face me but watching his line. "Check the raft."

My heart sank. Had we lost the gun? I was forever losing car keys or leaving my wallet on restaurant tables, but this wasn't Philadelphia and it wasn't a credit card that I was missing. Bear tracks were all over the sandbar where I was standing. My mind ran back over the day. Maybe we had left it where we had camped the night before? No, I remembered putting it in its place on the stern of the raft. It was definitely there at the start of the day. Could it have fallen out of the raft into the river? That was possible. My practice had been to slip the gun under the rope that lashed our bags in the stern of the raft. The rope was tight enough to keep the gun in place but loose enough to let me pull it free if I needed it quickly. I checked the ropes. They did seem a little loose. Maybe the gun had worked its way to the edge of the raft and just slipped into the water. We might not have heard it hit the water. It could have slid in silently, barrel first, without a splash. This was easy to picture. I tried to slow my thoughts. Maybe we had left it at the place we had stopped for lunch? I was having trouble remembering what the place looked like. Was it a gravel bar, or had we climbed onto the tundra? What had I prepared? Maybe if I could recall making the meal, I could re-member what I had done with the gun. I couldn't pull up a picture of the place. The images of all our lunch stops were beginning to come to mind and blend in together. I couldn't keep them in order.

When I told Adam that the gun was definitely missing, he came ashore. I asked him if he remembered loading it from the place where we had stopped for lunch. He didn't.

"That was your job," he said.

I asked him if he remembered where we had eaten our lunch. He described it—a long rocky bar where a slow stream entered the river—and the scene came back to me. I remembered a big willow tree that tilted over the slow stream. I remembered the place where I had set up the stove, and the gun was probably right there where I had left it leaning against a rock.

"Good going, Dad," Adam said.

I felt the blood rise in my neck and face. How much of this did I deserve? We were supposed to be in this together, weren't we? My reserves of guilt apparently were running low. I checked my response. Adam turned and went back to the river to fish some more.

There was going to be no way to retrieve the gun. It was gone. The bar was probably four miles upriver, and the current would make rowing upstream impossible. Bushwhacking upstream through the willows was out of the question. The willows were jungle thick in places, and streams and swamps would have to be crossed. Besides, walking without a gun would be too dangerous. We were bound to startle a bear along the way. I was sick at the realization of its loss. The gun, a 12-gauge Ithaca side-by-side shotgun, had been a gift from my brother more than twenty years ago. It was a prize piece. I knew he would be disgusted with me for having lost it. Even worse, though, was the prospect of six more days and nights on the river without a firearm.

There was nothing to do but continue on—and redouble our efforts to avoid bears. I decided that we would lengthen the distances between the places where we cooked and tented. We also would take the added precaution of washing down the raft at the end of each day to make sure it didn't smell of fish slime. Another rule: We would store all of our food in the cooler, which closed tight, and we wouldn't keep any fish overnight. We simply couldn't risk meeting a bear without the gun.

I set about making dinner. I noticed as I dug into the cooler that we were drawing down our food supply much more quickly than I had anticipated when I planned the trip. We were consuming roughly twice as much as I thought we would at each meal, and we were eating four meals a day. Maybe because of the work or the cold, damp weather, which also caused us to burn calories, we were easily eating a pound of pasta at each meal. I was mixing the pasta with olive oil, which I had packed in a plastic bottle, and grated Parmesan cheese. The oil was running low, and the cheese was almost gone. In the mornings, I had been making pancakes, and a box only lasted for two breakfasts. We were more than halfway through the plastic bottle of syrup. The box of PowerBars that I had brought along had been depleted by the end of the third day. I had packed a big supply of freeze-dried dinners—Texas chili, Thai chicken, and Szechuan beef with mushrooms. This, I thought, would be our insurance policy in case we didn't catch enough fish to sustain ourselves for ten days. But the dinners that came out of the foil packets tasted foul, like gritty mold. I had bought them, at a bargain, in the camping department of a surplus store in Philadelphia. Here on the river, I checked the labels on the foil envelopes but couldn't find an expiration date. I guessed that they must have been sitting in the store for years. The gruel that was produced when I mixed their contents with boiling water had a dusty, bitter taste. It was inedible.

I spread the food out on the ground and took stock. I faced some choices: Either we were going to have catch and eat a lot of fish all the way downriver or we would have to stomach the freeze-dried meals or we were going to be very hungry beginning at the end of Day Six. We had two more days of a full cupboard. The other choice was to shorten our rations. I did have a fair supply of spices and condiments: salt, pepper, ketchup, ginger, mustard, and soy sauce. I resolved to make smaller and more interesting meals, and I hoped that the good fishing would last until we reached Quinhagak. I had a box of hot cocoa packets left. Adam loved hot cocoa. I put it aside as a treat for later in the trip in case the food situation got dire. As I set some water to boil, I thought again of the gun. If I had it, I could poach a grouse on the way down the river. We had seen several of the birds walking among the aspen trees at the places we had stopped. But of course I didn't have the gun. Here was one more reason to regret its loss. The grouse had seemed pretty dumb. Maybe I could club one or two for roasting on a stick.

For the night's meal, I boiled a half pound of the pasta and served more fish. I reduced my portion of pasta and loaded up on fish. I doubled the size of the pot of tea that I had been serving and encouraged Adam to drink up. I didn't say a word about the food situation. Adam seemed fine with what I had put together, and we went downstream a quarter mile to set up camp. It was beginning to rain and the wind was gusting. I went down to the river and pulled four big stones from the icy water and set one on each corner of the tent to hold it in place as we inserted the poles and made our home for the night.

I slept uneasily, dreaming and tossing, and woke early the next morning, before Adam. It was raining lightly. I could see the places where the raindrops had found the tent under the fly and stained the fabric a darker yellow. Some of the rain was gathering on one of the inside seams. The tent seemed to be developing a leak, though I couldn't find the source. I was stiff and I craved a cup of hot coffee, but I was having trouble getting myself out of the tent. At least it was warm in the sleeping bag. It would be cold once I pulled myself out, and there would be work to do. I listened to Adam breathing beside me. I could smell him, and it was a pleasant smell: the oily smell of his hair, the smell of my son. Sleep for Adam was a departure to some foreign shore. Once he was there, it wasn't easy to call him back. His ability to sleep through anything had been a family joke.

I remembered the night I pulled into the driveway back in Maine with Patti and him and Elizabeth asleep in the car. I was the only one awake after the long drive back from a visit to Patti's parents' house in New Hampshire. It was late, and we were exhausted. The kids were in the backseat, Adam in his car seat and Elizabeth curled up in the corner. They had cried and fussed for nearly the entire two-hour drive north on Route 95, and then, with only ten minutes before we reached home, when I had turned off the turnpike, they fell asleep. Patti woke when I stopped the car. "We're home," I said. It was dark and the headlights threw their triangle of light on the lawn, bushes, and house. A light snow had fallen, but it was not enough to cover the grass or the bricks of the walk to the front door.

Patti and I acknowledged with a look that if the kids were to wake up they would begin to cry again and, because they were overtired, they would be miserable and it would take us another hour to quiet them and get them back to sleep. We went into our well-rehearsed moves as parents. We had done this many times before. Patti went into the house to pull the blankets back on their beds and turn up the heat. I scooped up Elizabeth and brought her to her room and then went back for Adam. Elizabeth was seven and Adam was three. Our footprints from the car to the door were visible in the dusting on the walk. I lifted Adam from his car seat and carried him through the front door, like a sack of flour, his head flopped back, mouth open, and arms out to the sides. Stuffed into his little parka, he was as limp as a rag doll. I went through the living room toward the stairs to the second floor.

As I turned to the staircase, Adam's head knocked hard against a wood post. It was a solid hit. *Thwack!* I stopped with a foot on the first stair and checked his head for a cut. A spot over his eye turned red, but he wasn't bleeding. I stood there with him cradled in my arms and against my chest and waited for him to open his eyes and begin crying. His eyes stayed shut and his nostrils moved slightly, in and out, with each breath. He showed no signs of waking up. Mouth open, eyes closed, his chubby baby arms and legs limp. I guessed he was okay, though the red spot was beginning to swell. It was directly over his left eye and under the eyebrow. There appeared to be no serious damage. He looked serene. I continued up the stairs and took him to his bedroom. I put him down on the mattress, carefully removed his shoes and coat, and pulled the blankets up to his chin.

I looked more closely at the bump, which was now red and swollen. Still, he didn't stir. I wondered if I had knocked him unconscious. I stood over his bed for a few minutes, looking at him from different angles. He seemed to be breathing normally. There was no sign of distress. I decided to check back on him again in a few minutes, before going to bed myself, to be sure he was all right. The kids' rooms shared a wall, and both had single beds tucked under the sloped ceiling of the gabled roof. Adam's room was at the front of the house, Elizabeth's to the back. Patti had already climbed into bed, so

I didn't say a word to her about the thwack. Our bedroom was on the first floor, directly below Elizabeth's room.

Even though the heating registers were clicking and I could hear the torch of the oil furnace working in the basement, I lit a fire in the woodstove in the living room. It was a cold night, and the woodstove would help warm the house quickly, especially upstairs where the kids were sleeping. I put a couple of chunks of maple inside the firebox and stuffed some rolled-up newspaper and wood chips under them. I lit the paper and it burst into flame. I waited for the fire to catch hold. I wanted to make sure that the flames were strong and steady and the chimney was pulling up the smoke before I closed the firebox door. Closing it too soon would extinguish the fire. Soon the blue flames spread across the wood and danced upward with the inrushing air, up toward the stovepipe and into the chimney. I shut the firebox door, tightened the handle that controlled the flow of air. The fire crackled inside the firebox, and I could hear the cinders and sparks flying upward, through the black sheet-metal pipe and into the trachea of the chimney.

I knew the chimney, and I could even picture its internal columns of space. It had two flues, and it was fourteen bricks square, eight inches to a brick. I had built the chimney. I had set each brick, one brick at a time, with my own hands. The chimney rested on a concrete footing four feet square and ten inches deep in the basement. The first dozen courses of brick were cockeyed and akimbo because I had mixed the cement a little too wet when I had begun and I hadn't yet gotten the knack of laying one brick flat on top of the brick below. I had started over four times. My education in masonry required scores of brick courses and many vertical feet of chimney before I got the feel of it. By then, the lime in the cement had dissolved the skin of my fingertips and I had to work with latex gloves. The horizontal rows of brick grew straighter as the chimney reached toward the first floor, eight feet above, but it wasn't until I broke through the roofline, thirty feet from the footing, that I was skilled enough to make the bricks and the mortar joints between them straight and uniform. I was learning chimney building as I went. The top two feet of chimney were perfect. At the moment I could claim modest competence as a chimney builder, I was done with the work.

It was a house that needed only one chimney. It wasn't even yet a house when I laid up the chimney. It was a wooden box, framed with posts and beams and sheathed with boards. It lacked windows, inside walls, doors, electricity, plumbing, shingles, or siding. It had no steps outside or staircase inside. The north wind blew in the front and out the back. But suddenly, with the chimney in place, the box had a center, or a heart, and it was closer to being a house. The wooden box with no steps and no doors gathered itself around the new chimney. It was plenty of chimney for the house that would surround it. It could take two woodstoves and fill this wooden box of a home with lots of heat. Instead of a house with one chimney, I was beginning to think of it as a chimney with one house: one family, one chimney, one house.

At first it had been an idea, and then the idea had become the expression of what I had wanted in my life: a family, a house, and a sense that I was rooted in a place. It was permanence. I had felled the trees that became the posts, beams, and boards. I sent logs of white pine to the mill and got back beams as yellow as buttermilk. They turned silver that first winter in the yard awaiting their assembly into a frame. In the summer of 1976, on a day that was fated for powerful thunderstorms, my brother and I finished setting the forms for the house's concrete foundation. By 2:00 P.M., six concrete trucks lined up along the road and a seventh pulled up to the hole in the ground that would one day be the basement of the house. The truck sent the concrete down its chute. We wheeled the slurry in wheelbarrows to the far end of the foundation forms and dumped it in. The walls would be eight inches thick, eight feet high. We emptied the second truck to the sound of distant booms. The booms grew closer and soon sounded like trees splitting. Patti, seven months pregnant with Elizabeth, stood, watched, and worried at the edge of the hole. As the third truck released its load, the sky opened. We couldn't stop the work, because the concrete would harden in the trucks and in the forms, creating a seam between the old and new pours. We kept pouring, pushing and pouring. The rain, coming down hard, collected in the ditch along the standing forms. Then a lightning bolt struck the ground, burned a line to Paul, and lifted him into the air. He came down dazed about ten feet from where he had been standing. The black line in the soil was clearly visible. There was the smell of something burned. At first, he walked with a wobble. We crowded around him and I took his arm. The work stopped and even the driver got down from the concrete truck, but Paul said he was okay.

"What the hell was that?" he said.

"You just got hit by lightning," I said.

We laughed that his hair was curlier—he had gotten a cheap permanent. We went back to the concrete, but the rain was undermining one of the forms, and one of the rods holding together the inner and outer walls of the forms snapped. The form opened and wet concrete spilled out. Now we had trouble: rain, lightning, water collecting in the ditch, and a blown concrete form. One of the drivers got on his CB radio: In minutes, men from around town—from the firehouse, a woods crew, a nearby body shop—arrived and the six of them helped us save the foundation.

One of the men owned an excavating business, and I immediately felt embarrassed because I hadn't hired him to dig the foundation hole. There were two men in town who did this work, and I had chosen the other. I knew this man's name. It was emblazoned on the side of his truck and it went back far in the town's history. It didn't seem to bother him that he hadn't gotten my business. He stepped from his pickup, sized up the situation, and took control of the pour and the other men. He had black hair, a sharp chin, small, dark eyes, and a stooped big body inside green overalls. His hands were big and black in the creases. I guessed that maybe he was fifty or fifty-five. He seemed to know just what to do. He nodded to me but consulted with the man in the concrete truck.

We all came to order behind his authority. He pulled three jacks from his truck, slid down into the wet hole, and used them to push the blown-out form back into place. He climbed out and watched to see if it would hold. It did. He and the others shoveled, wheeled, and hoed the concrete along with Paul and me as the rain came down, and Patti encouraged and laughed with them. The sight of her, with her swollen belly, was not hurting our cause with these men. They didn't introduce themselves to us or make any attempt to exchange names or handshakes. They seemed to know one another, and I gathered that two of them were related through marriage. The talk among us was entirely directions called back and forth about the work. We toiled through the afternoon and into the dark. By then the rain had stopped and the moon was out, so we could see pretty well. I knew they had been examining me all along. I felt the looks under their brows as the work went on. I was a new person moving into town, a news-paper editor from Portland. They were naturally suspicious of Portland—big, bad Portland. So that's where I began with them, as someone to be suspicious of until otherwise proven reliable. I worked along steadily and didn't slacken even when it was possible because of all the help that was there. I deferred to the excavator's judgment about how to handle the problems of the rain and the blown-out form and ran out a steady stream of thanks to him and the others.

But all of this help made me uneasy. These men were tak-ing time away from their own jobs and businesses, and they were missing their dinners. I must have looked helpless to them. I didn't like the idea that I had to be rescued, but I had to either accept the hand they had extended or suffer a disas-ter. Their attitude seemed to be: "These things happen, but next time do a better job of setting up your forms. Anyway, some of us haven't seen each other in a while, and it's been a helluva month for rain." It went no further than that: There were no suggestions of the work they had lost or charges to me for their time. When the day had begun I had been thinking only of building a house, but now I was glimpsing what it meant to be part of a town. This was a town where men put down what they were doing to help another person who was in a tough spot on an August day because he was attempting to pour a concrete foundation with his brother and pregnant wife in the middle of a thunderstorm. I wasn't used to relying on others. There had been very few people I could rely on in my life, and all of them had been in my family. "You need to shake that concrete down good in the corners," the excavator hollered to me. "Use a two-by-four to pack it down. Here, do it like this." I felt the door to the town opening to me.

Patti, Paul, and I worked until midnight, expressed our

gratitude to our new neighbors, and finished up the last bit by ourselves. We drove home to Portland and collapsed. We came back the next day and pulled the forms. We had a foundation. And so it went: Day in and day out, we worked. Patti brought a Crock-Pot of meat and vegetables and plugged its cord into the outdoor electrical service pole we had set up for powering our tools. Late in the afternoon, we all ate beef stew ladled from the pot as we sat on lumber piles. We enjoyed the food, laughed, and assessed our work.

Paul and I laid a deck over the foundation in the fall. In the winter we erected the frame of the house. I had mortised the posts with a chisel and cut the tenons in the beams with a handsaw. I had fitted beams to the posts and made a frame that would support a roof. Then in the spring, with the help of a pulp truck, I put the giant rafters in place. They were four inches by twelve inches of stringy Maine fir and twenty-eight feet long. To set them at their proper angles, I had cut notches—birds' mouths, they were called, because of their triangular shapes—so the rafters would sit flat on the topmost beams of the outer walls and touch their opposite-side counterparts to create the ridgeline. The roof would slope from the ridgeline to the tail of the rafter.

Finally, the frame was done. It was a proud moment. Standing there on the hill, with the posts, beams, and rafters exposed to the sky, the house looked like some big musical instrument, a wooden xylophone or maybe a piano stripped of its cabinetry. With the sun melting the last of the snow under the hemlocks and the damp smell of the earth lifting out of the woods, I stood and stared at the full frame of the house. I walked around it to see from different angles and distances, and when I got back to the front after my third or fourth trip around I simply sat on some board ends and watched it be strong and present as a thing of beauty. The sight of it was thrilling, but I felt peaceful: I had taken an idea and turned it into the timber frame of a twenty-four-by-forty-four-foot center-chimney Cape. It gave me a lot of pleasure to be able to give my wife a house. I had given her a sheet of paper and told her to draw a picture of the house she wanted. She had taken a pencil and a sheet of paper and made the picture, and I had built the house.

A house is a lot of things—shelter, a beautiful object made from wood or stone, and a metaphor for family life. It's also a financial stake in the world. It was my first. At that point in our married life, all we owned was a used car with a heater that didn't work and a cheap upright piano I had bought for Patti with the sale of a freelance article to *The Boston Globe Magazine*. Now we also had a half-finished house. I had begun this project with zero dollars. I didn't have enough money to buy a seventy-nine-dollar power saw. But I did have a plan: Once I had found the land and borrowed the seventy-five hundred dollars from the Press Herald Credit Union to buy it, and with the land that I didn't own as collateral and an earnest pitch to an affable loan officer, I got a building loan from Casco Bank & Trust Co. I showed the loan officer my homemade plans for the house and a picture of the property. He gave me a skeptical look and asked a lot of questions. I answered them all with as much confidence as I could muster. He said, "Okay, I'm taking a chance on you, but yes, we can do this." The loan officer, whose name I can't remember, kick-started my financial life by giving me the wherewithal to build a house. A building loan dispenses money to the borrower (me) for building materials as they are needed for construction. I bought my first batch of tools, including a power saw, and bags of nails and presented receipts to the bank, which deposited money in my construction account. I hurriedly took their reimbursements and paid down the credit card I had used to buy the materials. I did this every two weeks.

The emerging house was the bank's guarantee against my possible default on the loan. Occasionally an inspector from the bank came out to make sure the structure was actually going up and that the bank's money was not paying for snowmobiles, deer rifles, or Caribbean cruises. On the day that the house would be complete, the bank then would turn the building loan into a fixed-rate thirty-year mortgage. I figured this would amount to about $29,000. So, through the magic of credit, I was turning an empty checking account and $36,500 in debt into a house that would be valued (in 1976 dollars) at $45,000. Soon we would have a place to sleep and call our own.

Back then, I didn't have the time or even the inclination to reflect on the deeper meanings of building a house. I was a man on a mission to make a life and find a settled place in the world. How could I have been so oblivious then of the unconscious backstory to the crazed and symbolic project I had taken on? It wasn't the first time in my life I had been guilty of deliberate forgetting. I can see now that I had put my past in a box and put that box in another box and that box in another box until I had hidden it so completely in a corner of my mind's attic that I might not have had any past at all. Looking back, though, I can see that the past was directing me like some hidden gyroscope, bending me in the direction of stability, permanence, and a complete family. These were things I had missed as a boy and determined to get as a man.

. . .

It's starting to take shape," my neighbor Bob Hersey had said that summer, sitting on a rock in the shade. "But I still don't understand why you went to all this trouble. Why not just build it with two-by-fours? It's a lot easier than hefting this big lumber."

"It's going to last, Bob," I said. "You and I may be gone, but this house will be standing."

"It won't be hard to outlast me," he said, laughing.

I had sheathed and shingled the roof. I knew every joist, stud, and floorboard. I had pounded sixpenny, eightpenny, tenpenny, and sixteen-penny nails, and I knew them all, and there were the birch dowels that served as trenails to secure the post-and-beam joints. I had fallen from one of those beams when the work was just getting started and spent six weeks on crutches. I knew the posts that weren't plumb and the window frames that weren't square. I knew that six inches of Fiberglas insulation and four inches of air space separated the ceiling's half inch of sheetrock from the roof's one-inch pine planks. Paul and Patti watched me assemble my obsession: The work went on for three years, after my shift at the newspaper, on weekends, and all my vacation time.

I had built this box of a house with a gabled roof and a thirty-two-foot chimney, and I had put a woodstove in it, and that woodstove gave us heat. My family was warm and asleep. I had taken care of everything. I had even driven them home late at night and brought them safely into the driveway and home. I had carried my children upstairs. I thought of Adam in his bed.

The heat was pouring out of the stove and scorching my pant legs; the fire was chugging just fine in the stove. It didn't need my supervision. I went back upstairs to check on Adam and his head. He was sleeping soundly, on his back as was his habit and as I had left him, his little chest rising and falling peacefully under his blue blanket. He called that blanket with a satin edge his silky. I got so close to look at his head that I feared he would feel me breathing on him. The bump was hardly red at all. There was no cause to worry. I checked on Elizabeth, in the next room. She, too, was sound asleep, in a ball, still in her pink tights. I went downstairs, undressed, and got in bed next to my wife. The stove hissed as the fire sucked in air through its door, and we all slept soundly in the hushed house as the snow began to fall again and the chimney sent its heat and smoke into the night.

7

Adam had begun to stir in his sleeping bag, so I slipped quietly out of the tent. The butane lighter that Denise had sent with us, the one we had almost forgotten, wouldn't light. It was sparking when I pulled the trigger, but it wouldn't hold a flame. It seemed to be out of fuel. I dug around in my pack and found two books of paper matches that I had taken from the motel in Anchorage. They were going to have to last us until the end of the trip. I lit the stove and put the matches in a plastic bag, which I stored inside one of our big "dry bags." I made breakfast from the last of our pancake mix. I cut open the box and scraped out every bit of the flour. When I had a stack of pancakes ready and had warmed the syrup, I stuck my head into the tent and called Adam to breakfast. We ate, packed the gear, and set off again, floating and fishing, and looking for Klak Creek. I still was feeling sick about the gun. It now had been four days and we were maybe thirty miles from Kagati, or so I guessed, and we had not yet encountered the creek. Without the gun, the absence of the creek wasn't as funny as it had been the previous day. Then there was the problem of the butane lighter and the two books of matches and the food.

The country continued to flatten out, though there were still hills—big humps in two shades of green, looking in the mist like the Scottish highlands. We stopped for lunch at an island where we saw enough driftwood to build a fire. We collected a pile of it, and I dug out the matches. The plastic bag seemed to have captured some moisture, and the sulphur tips of the first two matches just smeared on the abrasive. The third one lit. Soon we had a dancing fire. We discovered that there was not a lot of firewood to be found along the river. Most of the woody growth was small shrubs or stunted aspen, and a lot of the wood that washed up on the bars was too wet to burn. We had scrounged enough to get a fire going around the roots of a big aspen tree that must have been deposited on the highest part of the bar months ago by the spring freshet. It was bone white, and dry. It caught the fire of the smaller sticks around it and blazed. We piled on some soggy sticks: A smoky fire would be our bear repellent as we had lunch. The sun came out, and I hung my sleeping bag by the fire to dry. It had become damp from the leak in the tent the previous night. It was a cheap cotton bag and not easy to dry. I also dried the matchbooks and returned them to the dry bag. We had been naming every place that we had stopped for a meal or for the night. Adam picked the name for this place, Dry Island.

I was grilling a char on the coals when I heard the faint hum of an outboard motor a long way off, or at least I thought

I did. I motioned to Adam. He listened and confirmed hearing
it, too.

"We may get that gun back yet," I said.

The hum grew progressively stronger, and in about half an
hour we saw an aluminum skiff with two men, in green ranger
uniforms, coming up the river. There was a man in the stern,
standing and steering a big outboard motor, and another in the
bow, seated. As they approached us, I waved them ashore.

"Heaven must have sent you guys," I said.

The man in the back was burly and big through the chest,
with a shock of thick black hair and a big smile. He looked
Yupik. Up close, the second ranger looked like a Caucasian
teenager or maybe in his early twenties. He was thin, blond,
and expressionless. He had a sharp nose and small eyes. The
big man stepped out of the boat. He had a broad, open face
and keen black eyes. He wore knee-high rubber boots on his
short legs. A black leather holster hung from his belt.

I asked them if they would like some hot tea and lunch.

"Hot tea sounds good," the big man said.

He pulled the boat ashore, grabbing it under the lip of the
bow and hauling it onto the gravel bar, and then the boy
stepped out, too. The boy was wearing hip waders. We introduced ourselves. The big man's name was Frank, and the boy's
name was Kyle. There were handshakes all around. They came
over to the place where I had set up the stove and where our
fishing gear was spread on the rocks. I had made the tea in a
saucepan by boiling the tea bags in the water and adding
sugar. I set out four cups on the stones and poured tea into
each of them. I handed a cup to Frank. Adam and Kyle picked
up their own cups, and we all found a rock, log, or the cooler to
sit on. For four days Adam and I had heard no other voices

than our own. This little bit of socializing was adding some cheer, at least from Frank. Kyle seemed annoyed at the delay in their progress upriver. He kept glancing back at the boat.

"Are you burying your waste along the river?" Kyle asked. "The law requires you to bury your waste."

I said that we were and that it seemed like a good law. It went quiet again, with just the sound of the river behind us, the occasional gurgle or unexplained splash. Frank's eyes were darting around, not at our gear or fire but at the bushes, the trees, the sky, and the river, up and down. He was paying close attention, to what I wasn't sure, but he seemed to be taking in impressions of the place around us. It was as if he was awaiting a change in the weather or the arrival of a bird, or maybe he was just trying to avoid eye contact with me or Adam.

I made a second offer of food and told our guests that I was cooking a char. I pointed to the fire where the fish was grilling.

"There's plenty," I said.

Frank laughed.

"I don't think you're making it the way I like it," Frank said. A smile spread over his wide face.

"How's that?" I asked.

"I like it the way my mother makes it for me."

"What's her recipe?" I asked.

His smile grew broader. "She wraps it in seaweed and puts it in a box in the ground, and then she waits a few months until it ferments. I take it out of the seaweed and eat it frozen with some seal oil."

"I guess you're right," I said. "I don't know that recipe."

He enjoyed the impression his story had made on us and sipped his tea. I let it be quiet for a while, in deference to the goodwill Frank was extending to us with his story, and then in answer to a question I put to Kyle he said he was a wildlife management student at college getting summer work experience in Alaska.

"Jobs are hard to find," Kyle said. "This is good on my résumé."

Frank asked us about how the fishing had been, and I described our recent success with the char and a few pinks. I had a lot of questions for him about the river and the country we were passing through, and it was clear that he knew every twist and turn along the way. He asked us if we remembered passing a particular place where the high right bank of the river was cut away and the remains of a cabin stood on a cliff above the water. I recalled what looked like a single corner of a cabin that had collapsed and burned. Adam did, too.

"That was my uncle's cabin. He jumped in the river there and got killed."

"What happened?"

"He was drunk."

I paused to hear the rest of the story or gain some insight from it, but that was the end of it. The uncle had jumped in the river and gotten killed. He was drunk. Frank seemed to toss it out like a stone into a pond just to watch the ripples on the surface. He wasn't going anywhere with it, and he just smiled.

"That's too bad," I said.

"He was crazy," Frank said.

I asked Frank if he hunted along the river, and he said, oh yes, he and his cousins shot moose and caribou in the fall. The caribou crossed farther down the river. He told us what to look for when we got there, a place where the land sloped down to the river on both sides, making a kind of spout that directed the animals to the one crossing place. He said they were easy to shoot there and that they would be crossing in another three weeks.

I asked Frank if he had a family.

He said that he had a wife and son and daughter in Quinhagak.

"I had another son," he said, "but I gave him to my cousin in Oscarville."

I wasn't sure I had heard that right.

"You gave your son to your cousin?" I asked.

"In Oscarville," he said. "It's just over the hills, the next river over."

"You gave your son to your cousin in Oscarville?"

"Yes," Frank said without revealing any sign that this was the least bit unusual.

This seemed to be another stone thrown into the pond for the sake of ripples.

"Why did you do that?"

"Because he didn't have one and I already had two kids. One was a boy," Frank said.

This seemed sufficient to him.

I couldn't let this pass so easily, yet Frank wasn't giving up any more explanation. I wanted to know more, so I tried to pull it from him.

"Do you see him much?" I asked.

"It's not a far trip," he said, "just the other side of the hills, the next river."

He pointed in the direction of Oscarville.

"How was your wife with that, you know, giving your son to your cousin?"

"She was okay with it," he said.

(I later learned that sharing children is not an uncommon practice among the Yupiks.)

It was quiet for a while, and then Kyle asked if we had kept any fish, besides the one on the fire. He wanted to check them. I told him that we weren't keeping any fish, except the ones we planned to cook immediately, because I didn't want any trouble with bears.

"Are you familiar with the length and bag limits?" he asked.

I said that we were and respected them. Actually, I didn't have the slightest idea of the fishing laws on the river. I decided now was the time to change the subject and bring up my request.

"I wonder if I could ask a favor of you guys."

"What?" Frank asked.

"I left my gun upstream," I said. "Or at least I think I did. It was a bonehead move. Now we're traveling without a gun. Is there any way you could give me a lift upriver to get it?"

Kyle spoke immediately.

"No, we couldn't do that."

Frank stepped on his words.

"Yes, we will take you up. Do you know where you left it?"

He was concerned and sympathetic, and he was clearly pulling rank on Kyle. Kyle dumped the rest of his tea from his cup onto the ground and went to the boat, where he made himself busy. Frank stayed seated with us.

I said that I had a pretty good idea. At least, I thought I knew where I had left it.

After he finished his tea, which he did not rush, Frank said, "Let's go find your gun."

Adam decided to stay with the raft. I worried about him being alone, but he insisted. I told him to keep the fire blazing, which would ward off bears. Off we went, the three of us, up-river, with Frank handling the motor and steering the boat. Kyle was in the middle seat, and I sat at the bow, scanning the shoreline. Frank regularly banged into rocks, and several times the shaft of the outboard was thrown up out of the water. It was a noisy ride, and I wondered if the boat and the motor could withstand the pounding they were getting from Frank's driving. At one point, the boat went up onto a rock and we had to step out to float it off.

We traveled several miles, and I began to look carefully for the slow stream with the tilted big willow. The first time I saw one, I called out to Frank over the roar of the outboard and pointed toward shore. He beached the skiff, and we went ashore. We couldn't find the gun. In fact, it was the wrong is-land. I apologized for the false stop. Frank was easy about it, and we pushed farther upstream. I was astonished at the number of slow streams with tilted willows that came into view. I told this to Frank, and he found it funny. I was getting the feeling that maybe he had left a gun behind at some time in the past. He was being awfully understanding. We stopped a second time and then a third. This was it, I was positive, and sure enough, the gun lay against a rock next to the spot where I had cooked lunch. We all smiled, even Kyle, and headed back toward Adam. On the way back, I thought of another way Frank could help us.

"I have a question, Frank," I shouted over the roar of the outboard.

He nodded.

"We've been looking for Klak Creek. You ever heard of it?"

"You passed it about a mile upstream," he said. "You can't miss it."

I shook my head and muttered.

"What?" hollered Frank over the whining engine.

"Nothing," I said. "Oh, nothing at all."

When they dropped me off at Dry Island, Frank told me to be sure to bring the gun to the ranger shed when we got to Quinhagak. He said he could find some gun oil to take off the rust.

"Dad," Adam said as they motored upriver and went out of sight. "Do you know how lucky you are that you got that gun back? That was a pretty stupid thing to do."

II. GROWING UP AS
A FISHERMAN

We look at the world once, in childhood.
The rest is memory.

—LOUISE GLUCK, "NOSTOS"

This is a memory behind all the other memories: A cold, clear brook flows between grassy banks and among tall trees, and I am standing in a place close to where the brook enters a river. My pant legs are rolled to my knees. The clear water of the brook mingles with the slow, muddy water of the river along a seam in front of where I am standing. I am holding a fishing rod. It is summertime, and the sun warms my face. I am nine years old. I am alone except for the trees and the birds. One bird is calling, a three-note song pure and melodic. *Konk-a-ree!* It teeters in a tree that leans over the brook. It is a red-winged blackbird, and I know its call so well that I assume it is singing to me. *Konk-a-ree, konk-a-ree!* I seem always to see only one red-winged blackbird at a time, so I have come to think of all red-winged blackbirds as one. *Konk-a-ree!* The bird is my friend. So are the trees, the brook, and the green ferns bowing their tips into the water. I am familiar with each of them. My legs are icy cold, and I clench my teeth against the ache in my shins. I feel the stones and sand of the stream bottom pushing into my arches and between my toes. I work my heels into the sand. Behind me, the brook comes down from a hill, and the cool breath of the woods touches my back in occasional puffs. I am at home and at ease. I sense that the place where the two waters touch and mix, the clear water flowing into the muddy water, is trying to tell me something. I can't unlock the meaning, but the sensation of connection and companionship is so strong that even as I am experiencing it I know it will always be important to me. I long for a way to express it, but having none, I flip a silver spinner into the wrinkle pushed up by the two currents. The spinner sinks, and right away I feel a tug at the end of my line. I have hooked a fish.

2

"Timmy, slow down. You'll scare the fish. They'll hear you coming."

"Oh no, they won't. Fish don't hear people coming down a path. I got on my bare feet."

"I'm telling you, they can hear your feet touch the ground. Footsteps go through the ground and they make sounds in the water. Why don't you just throw stones at them? They feel it. They know just where you are."

"No, they don't. You're making this up. I know you're making this up."

"They do. It's just like trying to catch night crawlers in the graveyard. There you are, on your hands and knees after a good rain in the spring, picking your way through the gravestones and the blackness and shining your flashlight on the grass and moving as slow and easy as you can. The crawlers are out of their holes and reaching toward each other's slimy bodies. You're moving along nice and easy, and you're careful not even to put the light on them direct, and once, just once, you set your coffee can down a little too hard, and, *pow!*, they're right back in that hole. Faster than you can grab, or even dig, they're scurrying down to wherever they came from, probably back to the eye socket of some dead man in his coffin."

"That's different."

"How's that different?"

"That's what night crawlers do. They stretch out on the ground and feel stuff. They have feelers in their skin. Their skin is full of feelers. Just like snakes. But snakes ain't fish. Worms ain't, neither."

"How about the bullfrogs you've been trying to shoot off the lily pads with your bow down in DeVoe's Swamp? They hear you coming, don't they? You walk real still when you want to get close for a shot."

"That's different. Frogs got good ears. They got good eyes, too. Big ears and big eyes. You gotta be careful with frogs."

"I'm telling you, Timmy, you got to be quiet with fish. We shouldn't even be talking. We're getting close. Let's walk up nice and quiet. Look how still everything is. Look at that water flowing so calm and flat. It's perfect. Timmy, ain't it perfect? Ain't it beautiful?"

"Sonofabitch, Louis. Can't we just catch a few fish without making it a goddam big deal?"

3

I lived an unsupervised childhood mostly. My brother, Paul, and I had babysitters when we were very young, an odd assortment of my mother's friends or women around town whose availability had been churned up in the female chatter in her beauty shop on Main Street. There were, among others, a fervent Pentecostal who took in foster children for pay, a fat woman who smelled like frying pork chops, and another whom my mother chased out of the house when she claimed to have discovered that the woman had been stealing our sheets and towels. I always thought the woman was innocent and that my mother, who was prone to a quick temper, had another gripe with her that she was unwilling to share with me and Paul. While my mother was possessive of her linen, I'm sure the sheets-and-towels indictment was a stand-in for some other complaint.

One reason was as good as another to my mother. Life was a story to be shaped into something better and more pleasing even as it was occurring. In her memory, events were made to conform to her prejudices. The woman of the sheets and towels was banished, and her tale became part of the story of our growing up. My mother brought it out from time to time with a laugh as an example of the vicissitudes of raising two boys without a father and the patchwork of improvisation and adventure that formed our lives in those years. One of the reasons I doubted the woman's guilt was because, as the years wore on, my mother would conflate the woman of the sheets and towels with the Pentecostal.

"And the whole time that Holy Roller was watching you boys," my mother would say, "she was stealing my good sheets and towels."

I knew for sure that these were two different women. I was getting an early sense of my mother's loose command of reality.

My mother hired these women when we were very small or when she expected to work late at the beauty shop, which was mostly on Thursday and Friday nights when many of her customers wanted to get their hair done for a weekend christening at the Immaculate Conception Church, a dance at the VFW, or a dinner at the Knights of Columbus Hall. There was one sitter whose water broke while she was watching Paul and me at our rented house in Helmetta. Paul and I sat on the steps as she left for the hospital in the back of an ambulance. But from the age of about eight years old I more or less conducted my own life in my own way, without the oversight of a sitter, or a parent for that matter, and mostly that meant finding a way to a pond or stream that held fish.

We lived in a succession of rented houses and apartments in and around Spotswood, a small town in central New Jersey. Spotswood was a Main Street, four churches, two of which were Roman Catholic, a mill that made cigarette papers and sometimes spewed a rotten-egg smell over the town, a clapboard hotel with a lunch counter, a bar and a bowling alley, and a lake, Spotswood Lake. A small river formed at the base of the dam that impounded the lake and flowed in a broad curve behind Gorski's Hardware, past the Spotswood First-Aid Station, and along the cemetery grounds of St. Peter's Episcopal Church. My favorite fishing hole was on that little river, at the place that everyone in town called the Point, a wooded half acre of peninsula behind the first-aid station.

The Point was formed by the convergence of the small river and some stream, not much more than a dead-water, that seemed to originate in a depression where the water table rose up to form a little swamp with lily pads. It slithered and shimmered with tadpoles in the spring and leopard frogs in the summer. From the place where I sat in the grass, at the end of a path that led to the end of the Point, with my fishing rod cradled in the crotch of a sassafras sapling I had planted in the mud, I could see, turning counterclockwise, the white steeple of St. Peter's Episcopal Church, the concrete bridge that carried the road from the farms in Englishtown up the hill to Spotswood's town center, and the back of the cement-block first-aid station. Despite the cars moving up and down Englishtown Road, the Point held trees enough to sustain my illusion of woods.

Three places—the Point, the lake, and the Spotswood Hotel, which marked the town's center—described a thin triangle that was my universe when I was nine years old. I knew every inch of its square half mile: the cracks in the root-heaved sidewalk on Main Street, which I carefully stepped over to avoid seven years of bad luck; the five-cent pinball machine in the sweet shop and especially the smooth silver meniscus on each of its side-mounted flipper buttons and the satisfying clunk of the machine when I won a game; the vestry of St. Peter's Church, where I hung Father Cox's vestments after a service; the gravestones in the churchyard, where I hid small treasures under the dissolving limestone lambs that rested atop the children's markers (these treasures included a penny flattened by the train that ran to Perth Amboy, empty .22 cartridges, a silver bracelet I had found on the street); the chain-link fence in the yard of the Margaretta M. Birchall School, which was embroidered with honeysuckle that I tasted by pinching off the bottom of the flower and pulling out the sweet pistils; the fire station with its deep bays, long gleaming trucks, and crackling radio traffic; the cold stream that disappeared in the upland woods behind the snuff mill; and Gorski's Hardware, where I sold night crawlers that I had gathered with a flashlight in the graveyard on warm wet nights in the spring.

One year I won Mrs. Gorski's fishing derby with a thirty-four-inch chain pickerel I had caught in the river on a weedless Johnson's silver spoon. I carried the giant fish through town like Peter bringing home the wolf. I presented it to Mrs. Gorski, who always appeared quietly and a little mysteriously from the shadows in the back of the store, which led to a kitchen and her gruff potbellied husband. I sometimes caught a glimpse of him, between parted curtains, in the gloom. He wore sleeveless undershirts and had hairy shoulders.

I held up my pickerel.

"Dat's some feesh," said Mrs. Gorski, who was not prone to overstatement.

She measured it with a yardstick and recorded its length in a notebook. I was awarded five dollars' worth of fishing tackle at the end of the summer.

The sum of these places gave my life coherence. I moved about them confidently in the day and in my dreams at night. Asleep, I sometimes felt as if I had been lifted aloft and I could look down on my small world. It was a reassuring map of street corners, big familiar trees, muddy riverbanks, a tall church steeple, and winding paths through patches of woods. Occasionally I ventured out of my three-sided universe. Timmy lived just outside of it in a sandy neighborhood of prewar bungalows about a mile from town. For a year or two he was my best friend, though the only thing we seemed to have in common was the love of the woods.

Timmy's family was Polish, and his father looked like the Soviet ideal of the proletarian hero. He was tall and muscular, his arms showing biceps the size of softballs, and his hair was dirty blond. He had big hands and feet. He came home from work smudged and greasy, and I guessed he worked in a furnace or among roaring machines. He wore a blue work shirt and blue pants and black engineer boots that laced up high. I never heard him speak except once when I stayed for supper and he asked his wife to pass him the mashed potatoes. His request seemed full of intimidation to me. Timmy's mother was garrulous and unafraid of her fearsome husband. Her name was Olga. She was one of my mother's regular customers and always got a five-dollar shampoo and set. She liked it that I was Timmy's friend: I was polite, got good marks in school, and had been chosen to carry the American flag for the Cub Scouts in the Memorial Day parade. I was a good influence. Timmy was a miniature version of his father, pale skinned, with thin, straight hair and hard, round ball-bearing biceps and calves. He used rough language, and he was lawless and often in trouble at school for talking back to teachers or fighting.

He had a tree house in the woods behind his family's house, built in a towering oak. It was ridiculously high, dangerously high, dizzily high, and he reached it by climbing up twelve broken fence slats that he had nailed, ladder-style, into the trunk. They brought him to the first big branch. From there he shimmied and reached from branch to branch, pulling his legs, skinny ankles, and black high-top sneakers up behind him, until he achieved his aerie, a platform of wood planks that he had nailed between two branches, each the size of a man's thigh.

I climbed to it with him once and sat on the boards as the branches swayed in the wind. I wrapped my legs around one of the branches and clung tightly to another and watched the blue sky move through the green leaves. It was an unbalancing and abstracting height, and to know what was up or down you had to rely on a weighted sense of the direction in which you would fall if you lost your grip. The platform swayed a foot or two back and forth in the wind. Timmy peed from the treetops in a gleeful golden arc and showered the earth with the gift of his urine. From our perch we could see the tops of other trees, the backs of birds, the silver brook that curved through the bushes, and the dirt path that led out of the woods to his house. That tree house was a lot like Timmy: dangerous and irresistible. He was the boy who dived from the highest part of the bridge into the river and stood the longest on the railroad tracks when a train was bearing down on us and furiously blowing its horn. He stole watermelons, had a collection of *Playboy* magazines, and shot bullfrogs with his hunting bow. He was the first person to tell me that men and women had sex and how they managed it. The act he described was so preposterous that I told him he was crazy. Did he think I was stupid enough to believe what he was describing? People wouldn't do that. Who would do that? I was disbelieving and scornful and I told him to stop talking, but I knew Timmy to be a cold-eyed realist, a boy who dealt in facts, and the conversation in the treetop that afternoon tilted the way I took in the world. I had already begun to feel odd stirrings within myself. It was frightening to think that Timmy's explanation was the definition of things to come.

Years later, soon after I had graduated from college and long after I had erased Spotswood from my memory and I was visiting my mother in a different apartment, in Hightstown, New Jersey, she told me that Timmy had been killed in a motorcycle accident. I wondered why it had taken so long.

In the summer when school was out, I went to the Point every day. I caught catfish, pickerel, bluegills, and yellow perch. I acquired all of the basic skills that would last me a lifetime of fishing. Sitting under the leggy maples and oaks, I studied the river and its fish. A good fisherman looks for patterns. When there are changes, good fishing or bad, he seeks the explanatory variable: Is the water low, cold, or cloudy, is the sun bright, are insects rising from the surface, are green worms falling from the trees? Does the bait work best when stationary or retrieved? Fast retrieve or slow retrieve? The river gave me a lesson in the value of observation, experience, and practical memory. I was abstract and dreamy in the rest of my life, sometimes dangerously so, but as a beginning fisherman I was an empiricist, grounded in fact. I learned not to repeat what did not work.

My expertise was catfish. To catch a catfish, you first need a good catfish hole, and I had an exceptional one at the Point. Typically, catfish holes are found in rivers or streams with muddy bottoms and moderate currents. The trick is to fish close to the bottom with bait—garden worms and chicken gizzards are good baits. I liked a hook with a long shank, which makes extracting it easier: Catfish have tough, rubbery lips. I also liked to set the hook quickly, soon after the fish picked up the bait, because a catfish will quickly swallow the bait. A catfish declares itself by a pull on the line that is sustained for a second or two as it lifts the bait that hovers near the river bottom. Sometimes a slack line indicates a bite as the fish picks up the bait, and the sinker it is attached to, and moves toward the fisherman. If you wait too long to set the hook on a slack line, the catfish will swallow the bait, causing no end of trouble. A hook is not so easily pulled from the stomach of an angry catfish.

A bucket or a stringer is essential to a catfisherman, because a good catfish hole will give up infinitudes of catfish. My guess is that it was catfish that Jesus had on hand when he was distributing the loaves and fishes. The bread I can't explain. I once caught 117 catfish in one day at the Point. Two other important catfishing tools are pliers, for working out the hook, and a flashlight. The fishing is best at night. The hardest part of catfishing is handling the fish. A catfish has two sharp pectoral fins, which act as side spears. A catfish should be held by slipping the index and middle fingers of the right hand over the right pectoral fin (or spear) and the thumb behind the left pectoral fin. This allows a sure grip on the fish's head, which is broad and shovel shaped, while the left hand wiggles the hook free. A catfish is a sly operator, and a fisherman who lets his guard down will get a painful stabbing from the pectorals' spikes. A catfish's skin is smooth, like gray paper, and scaleless like a shark's, and it should be peeled away after the head and guts are removed. The meat is white. A veteran catfisherman, after a few well-placed incisions, can remove head, guts, and skin in a single motion. In a pinch, a piece of catfish makes acceptable catfish bait. They are not reluctant to eat their own.

I usually caught more catfish than we could possibly eat, so I either released them back into the river or gave them to the husband of a woman who had been one of our sitters. She was one of my mother's friends. Her name was Purina and she wore loose cotton housedresses and shuffled about in slippers that accommodated her misshapen purple-nailed big toes, bent almost at right angles to her bulbous feet. I remember her neat house, the linoleum kitchen, and the knobby texture of the chenille bedspread on which I would sometimes take a nap in an upstairs bedroom. I left a little swirl in it when I got up. Purina's husband was Italian. (Probably she was, too.) I delivered the catfish to him in a tin bucket, and he cleaned, skinned, and salted them and then he clothespinned them to a clothesline. He advanced the clothesline by way of a pulley at his back step as if he were hanging out the wash. The fish made quite a sight: From down the street, they looked like a string of drying handkerchiefs. I kept Purina's husband in fish. My reputation as a fisherman grew.

4

When I was seven years old my father left us, my mother, brother, and me, and I never saw or heard from him again.

I had feared my father. Today, if I sit with the thought of him long enough, I also feel some pity working its way into the shadowy presence that he has become in my memory. Always a shadow, he never becomes substantial or recognizable. He is not corporeal: He is gray, brown, black, and white light compressed into the shape of a man. The pity I feel comes from what I learned later, much later, not from what I knew then.

At the time, I only knew he was dangerous if he was made angry. I was careful not to make him angry. I stayed quiet. I walked close to the walls. I tried not to break anything. I did what I was told. He was a day laborer and a lot of the time he was out of work. So he was at home a lot during the day. I tried to stay outside. He drank, and when he drank he became hard and mean. He drank beer and it is one of the smells I associate with his memory. Most of his hardness was spent on my mother and me. Paul was still very small. My father made threats; he pushed furniture aside, tumbled chairs out of his way. He was obviously unhappy with us. Either from life or an old photograph I remember him in pleated baggy brown trousers, brown dress shoes with leather weaving on the tops, and a sleeveless white undershirt over a flat, hard stomach. He had muscular shoulders, big forearms with clouds of light brown hair, and dark deep-drilled eyes. I remember he once asked me to scratch his back for him as he sat on the front steps of our bungalow on Polonia Street. I used a tooth-brush and lightly worked it around and between his shoulder blades. With forearms on his knees and head dropped down, he said it felt good. It's the only tender moment I can recall between us. He smelled like beer, aftershave, sweat, and ciga-rette smoke. His hair was receding, even then in his early thir-ties, and he combed it straight back. It was thin, the way mine is now.

5

My mother's first beauty shop was in a one-story dilapi-dated shoe box of a wood-frame building on Main Street in Spotswood. It was called Lynn's Beauty Salon. The name fol-lowed the shop through several closures and reopenings, never more than a mile and a half from the place of its first ap-pearance in 1949 on the run-down end of Main Street. My mother furnished her beauty shop with four folding chairs, one of which was backed up to a porcelain sink hung from the inside wall, a card table, which held her scissors, brushes, combs, and towels, and three big posters of women with luxu-rious heads of hair who used L'Oréal hair products. Her hair dryer was a household vacuum cleaner with the hose con-nected to the exhaust. It blew a noisy stream of warm air on the wet heads of her customers.

Later a beauty supply salesman sold her two secondhand dryers with big globes that fitted over her customers' heads as they sat reading women's magazines or filing their nails with emery boards. The hair dryers looked like props from a low-budget space movie. A coal stove in the corner heated most of the shop, though on the coldest days frost formed on the front window. She never paid for her coal, because she cut the hair of the woman who worked at the coal-and-oil delivery business next door. Throughout my mother's life, she bartered haircuts for all manner of goods and services—bedsheets, car repairs, frozen meats, knife and scissor sharpening, winter coats, and accordion lessons for me. A lot of hair fell to the floor trying to give me a musical education, never with any success. Had I not gotten a scholarship to college, I'm sure my mother would have offered the registrar a lifetime of free haircuts.

My mother walked to her shop from our home two miles away, and she worked five days a week and a half day on Saturdays. She came home exhausted. As we got older, my brother and I would unlace and remove her white work shoes and rub her stockinged and swollen feet as she told us about her day: how many five-dollar permanents or ten-dollar hair colorings and who had given her good tips. We lived off her tips, mostly, the crushed dollar bills and quarters that we pulled from the nylon pockets of her white beautician's uniform. We smoothed out the bills and put the coins into paper sleeves.

My mother was the second of four children and the only daughter of Greek immigrant parents. As a Greek girl, she had been allowed no freedom and very little choice. She was pushed into the background; her brothers—"the sons"—had received all of the parental attention and praise. At Orthodox Easter, the boys would be dressed and brushed and shown off to neighbors. My mother would be left at home. This misogyny is one of the dirty secrets of an otherwise rich and proud culture.

My mother's name at birth was Eleni, anglicized to Helen, the most beloved of names for a Greek girl, but she had renamed herself Lyne when she was ten. She wanted a name that sounded more like it belonged to a movie star, something that suggested romance and Hollywood. It was part of a glamorous identity that she was always assembling from whatever materials were at hand and probably an early sign of the fantasy world that so enveloped her life and eventually, by extension, mine. Lyne became Lynne in her adolescence, but by the time she was married and pregnant with me, her first child, in 1950, Lynne had become simply the workaday and burdened Lynn. She was twenty-eight years old by then. The simplification of her name may have reflected a temporary loss of hope and imagination as she struggled through a dangerous pregnancy and a bad marriage. But Lynn it stayed even as her life improved, and Lynn it was until her death. Some things a person never gets over. I always introduced her as Helen.

The beauty shop was at the edge of town, adjacent to the snuff mill. Behind the building that it occupied, the ground dropped away so steeply that posts were required to support the structure's rear corners. There was enough space below to admit animals and small boys, though I don't remember ever having the courage to climb underneath the shop. I do remember, however, scrambling down the hill behind the beauty shop into the woods, descending over leaves, branches, and rocks, running so fast at times that I couldn't keep up with my feet, and moving deeper and deeper through the tall trees to a place where the ground leveled and the ferns were thick and waist high. At the very bottom, there was a stream that came cold and clear out of the woods. It was the place of the red-winged blackbird.

6

My father was a simple man. From what I remember and what others have told me, he was overwhelmed by my mother's stormy temperament. He had been raised by stern and silent Roman Catholic parents, and he was unequipped by birth or experience to deal with the emotional drama of a life with my mother. It would be hard to conjure a woman more unsuited to him than Helen Kallas.

My mother wanted an interesting life, full of surprises and fine things, and she was unyielding in her independence as a woman. She didn't want anyone telling her what to do. This infuriated my father and flummoxed him. My father did not want an interesting life. He hated surprises. He wanted a clean house, an obedient wife, and thirty weeks of outdoor work a year, enough to rent a small house and keep him in beer and cigarettes. My mother opened her beauty shop and brought home money, enough for them to live on. He drank. They fought. He wanted a life on a farm. She was raised in the city and craved its excitement. He liked to sit at the kitchen table with a bottle of beer. She wanted to go dancing. He was quiet, brooding; she was explosive. He liked a neat house; she cultivated a lifelong aversion to any form of house-keeping. He liked the feel of a tool in his calloused hands, a hammer, a spade, a saw; she dreamed of evening gowns, deco-rated rooms, and candlelight. She wanted compliments; he of-fered rebuke and rough language. She wanted to be swept off her feet; he was happy listening to the ball game on the radio.

It was simply unbelievable that these two had found each other.

They never had a truce in their marriage. A battle was al-ways breaking out or about to break out. My mother's weapon was words.

"You call yourself a man. You're no man! Where's your job?"

My father sulked. He watched the black-and-white televi-sion until the screen went blank. He fell asleep in his chair.

For most of my childhood, when they were together, I felt as if I were walking across a pond's skinny ice. I could break through at any moment. There would be no warning, no loud crack that told me to run to shore, just a plunge into cold, dark water, panic, and an inability to breathe. The tension in the house turned to shouting that fast. I was in a constant state of worry about it.

"You belong on a farm with the other Polacks."

My uncle John later told me that my father was Ukrainian, not Polish, but my mother knew how to make her words cut. "Polack" was her shorthand for stupid, dense, crude, and dirty.

A fight could begin over vegetable peelings in the sink. My father's parents, who spoke Eastern European–accented English, had kept an impossibly clean home. His family ate in the finished basement so that the upstairs kitchen would not be messed. He abhorred my mother's disregard for housekeeping. It was an insult to him, a provocation. It was irreligious.

"Why is this garbage in the sink?"

"Because I made your dinner, that's why."

"A fucking pigsty, that's what this place is."

"Shut your filthy mouth in front of my kids."

"Clean the house. This fucking house is what's filthy."

"You want a clean house and you want dinner? Get a job. Act like a man. You're no husband. You're not even a man."

I watched this from under the kitchen table with my fingers plugging my ears.

One year, my cousin John-Louis had come to live with us. I adored John-Louis, who was five years older than I. He was eleven that year, 1957. I don't remember what John-Louis had done wrong to anger my father, but he grabbed John-Louis by the back of the shirt and pushed him into the cellar. My father locked the door. Maybe John-Louis had talked back to him; maybe he had used a tool without his permission or hadn't returned it to the garage. The cellar had wood stairs, a cement floor, and cement-block walls. It was cold and wet and dark in the corners. John-Louis banged and cried to be let out, but my father leaned on the door and said nothing, counting off the minutes of punishment. Five, ten, fifteen minutes, the sentence to the cellar went on and on. My mother screamed and pulled at the doorknob, but my father was too powerful to be moved. She threw herself at him and pulled at his clothes and hair. He pushed her back across the kitchen and she fell against the refrigerator. I crawled to my place under the table. The ice of the pond was giving way under my feet. I could feel it caving, but I couldn't escape and I was falling into the pond. Surely I would be lost under the ice and there would be no air to breathe. I would drown.

The last memory I have of my father is in his DeSoto, picking up Paul and me for a visit during my parents' last separation. The year was 1958. I was seven. I remember the seat upholstery was scratchy (like my father's face those few times when he held me close to him) and the car floated on its springs as we went down the highway. I was in the big front seat. Paul, who was four, was in the back. My father seemed very sad as he asked me how I was. His eyes said I was my mother's child, and not his, and that my loyalty was to my mother, not him. It was clear to him where my allegiance was anchored. I said that I was okay, but as I answered I could see that he was looking through the windshield, down the highway, and far ahead into another life. It didn't include me. I think that's when I began to make my own adjustments as well. I don't remember either him or my mother telling me that he was leaving and never coming back. I was never told there was going to be a divorce. I simply sensed and accepted it. My mother didn't speak of it, so I followed her into silence. I never asked any questions. I didn't want to upset my mother. It became a past that didn't exist. After he left, I appointed myself man of the house and my mother's guardian. I kept the role even when she married a second time. As I grew up, I told people I didn't have a father.

7

In those years, we moved around a lot and for a time we had no place to live. We ended up in a room at the back of my mother's second beauty shop in Spotswood. It was one of two storefronts (the other was a fish store) in a two-story building on Main Street, closer to the town's center and on the other side of the Spotswood Hotel. The room at the back of the shop had a pullout sofa and a sink. It also had a hot plate that my mother used to soften the wax that she applied with a Q-tip to her customers' eyebrows and downy female mustaches. We also heated soup on it. The three of us slept on the pullout sofa, and unfortunately for my mother and brother, I often wet the bed as a boy. So, along with being squeezed onto a thin mattress that failed to pad the sofa's metal frame, we all had to contend with my weak bladder. My mother and brother never complained about my problem, though it humiliated me. In the morning, my mother pulled up the sheets and laundered them and she left the mattress, with big yellow-brown circles, open to dry.

The building that the beauty shop was in was owned by a husband and wife who lived upstairs from the beauty shop and fish store. They rented out the fish store, and they ran their own butcher shop in a cinder-block building out back. The husband was a stout man, a butcher, and his wife was pudgy, with a cinched-in apron around her bulging stomach. Neither was much over five feet tall. They had three children, including a boy my age. They were fussy about their property and suspicious of my mother, who had two children but no husband. They were pious Roman Catholics. We definitely were not allowed to be living in the back of the beauty shop. It's astonishing to me now that we were able to keep it a secret for several months. For my mother, at least at first, it seemed to be a game to keep it from them and funny that we were able to succeed. I was in the sixth grade at school, which was directly across the street. I lived in constant apprehension about the arrangement.

At some point during one of my parents' separations and before we had moved into the back of the beauty salon, another man entered my mother's life. His name was John Kababick. He was a big man with light sandy hair. He had an easy cowboy manner and a bent smile that conveyed charm and a little danger. My mother liked a little danger. She was drawn to men who had swagger and raw manliness. She loved Clark Gable in *The Misfits*. A lot of my mother's ideas came from the movies. Johnny, as we called him, had just gotten out of the Navy. He had a heart tattooed on his right arm and an anchor on his left. He loved music and played the accordion, polkas and an astonishing "Lady of Spain." He sang, too, in a playful baritone after a couple of drinks: "We'll Sing in the Sunshine," "Don't Fence Me In," "Your Cheating Heart." Sometimes he would dance a country two-step, moving those big feet and muscled frame as he grinned and snapped his fingers. I remember my mother's joy one day when she returned from an afternoon with Johnny. He had taken her for a ride in a rowboat on a creek that meandered through the woods between Spotswood and Helmetta. They had packed a picnic lunch and taken a blanket and had been gone for hours. I had never seen her glow the way she did that day when she came back from the trip into the woods.

Johnny seemed to be around more and more, and he gave my brother and me rides on his Indian motorcycle. We sat on the back and held tight to his waist. He had spent much of his boyhood in the woods around Spotswood, and he told me stories of hunting for squirrels with his .22 rifle and trapping muskrats and foxes and selling their pelts for extra money during the war.

One winter, he pulled us on our sleds on a rope behind his car down our snow-covered dead-end street. Johnny brought home stray dogs and cats. He taught one of these cats, a spindly orange creature that he named Red, to retrieve a cellophane cigarette wrapper that he rolled up into a ball and tossed across the living room. Once he caught a big snapping turtle crossing the road and he put it in our bathtub. My mother screamed when she saw it. We all laughed, Paul, Johnny, and I and eventually my mother, too. I was happy that my mother was laughing. I stood to the side and watched her laugh as Johnny pulled his stunts. Johnny seemed always to be broke and often out of work, but he managed to buy us impractical gifts like a parakeet or slingshots. Once he put a puppy in my mom's Christmas stocking. She cried she was so happy. For Christmas, Paul and I always bought Johnny the same thing: a carton of Marlboro cigarettes. My mother called him her Marlboro man. The resemblance was striking. When he worked, he kept a box of cigarettes rolled in the sleeve of his T-shirt.

In the years that he was in my life, up until I went off to college, I watched men and women fall in love with Johnny. He only had to walk into a room, put his big frame into a chair, set his arms on the table, smile his crooked smile, and tell one of his Navy stories or make a wisecrack. My mother fell in love with him. I fell in love with him. All of us had our reasons. One of my reasons was that he took me fishing. I think all of us knew that we would pay dearly for our love with disappointment. He was a heavy drinker when my mother met him and a falling-down drunk when they finally parted.

I knew almost from the beginning that he was unreliable. Even as a child, I had sensed a weakness in him, some failure of character that begged for help. I saw the resignation in his eyes. He was afraid of something—of what I didn't know. It surely wasn't any other man. Johnny was bigger and stronger than all of them. I didn't know how to help him. I wanted to take him aside and tell him to stop drinking. Of course I couldn't. It would have been a rebuke to his standing as a man to have me, a boy, tell him what he needed to do to straighten out his life. Didn't he realize how big and strong he was and how much we loved him? He was our hero, but there was some indefinable tragic quality to his prominent and twice-broken nose, his big shoulders, his swept-back hair and pale blue eyes that wrinkled at the outside edges when he stood in the sun.

8

John Kababick had grown up in Monroe Township, just over the Spotswood line, in a house that was a stone's throw through the scrub oaks and sandy lots from the bungalow where my mother had lived at the time of my birth. It was a dusty little settlement of small homes and pebbled-tar streets that petered out to paths into the pine and oak woods. It was a place where families would keep a chicken coop or a rabbit hutch in their backyards and mongrel dogs strained against their ropes and barked when someone came to the door. Nobody had much money, and a steady job conferred status on a man.

John Kababick's father, a wide-shouldered and slightly stooped man who attended church every Sunday morning in his shiny blue suit, worked for the railroad, as best I can remember. It was some job of substance, that much I recall, as a crew foreman or a station clerk, which, along with his membership in the Knights of Columbus and a lay position at the church, made him a figure of authority. He had big hands, big feet wrapped in white socks and the heavy-soled shoes of a cop on the beat, and a gray crew-cut haircut. He drank Canadian Club whiskey. Johnny's mother was a soft-spoken woman with a long-suffering smile, hair in a bun, and a big kitchen. She had raised two boys and three girls. John was the second oldest and her favorite. Sure, he was a hell-raiser, but that only made her love him more. Occasionally, when John had suffered a setback, at school or at work, she gave him a glass of whiskey to help him feel better.

Johnny's father, also named John, was capable of harsh punishment. He commanded his children with a cat-o'-nine-tails that hung behind the cellar door. Johnny was big, even as a boy, but John Senior was bigger, and his authority, from the railroad, the church, and as head of a Polish family, was overpowering. In Johnny's senior year of high school, he had planned to take a girl from Jamesburg to the senior prom. She was pretty and several rungs up the social ladder. He had rented a tux and bought her flowers. He had washed and waxed the family car. As he prepared to leave the house, grinning in anticipation of the night ahead, his father spoke up from the newspaper.

"Don't take the car."

Johnny had already gotten his father's permission to use the car. It was how Johnny had planned to take his date to the prom. There was no other car to use. Without the car, he couldn't get to the dance. He couldn't pick up his date. By now, she would be dressed and waiting for him.

"But I have to use the car," he said to his father. "Karen is waiting for me to pick her up."

"I said don't take the car."

"I can't go without the car."

"I said don't take the car."

Johnny missed the dance. He was too embarrassed to call his date and say he couldn't pick her up. The following week he quit high school. He just didn't go back. There wouldn't have to be any explanations. On such small moments a life can turn. I have thought about that moment many times as I tried to understand what happened to Johnny in his life. For a long time, it seemed to me implausible that a life could be wrecked in a moment of random paternal capriciousness, especially over the senior prom. I eventually came to see that his father's decision was mean and hurtful, but it was not random: The decision to deny Johnny the car and Johnny's decision not to return to school were, taken together, the compressed and emblematic moment of their lives together. They both were acting in character; the moment bore the stamp of their common life and fate. Sooner or later, Johnny's life would have taken this or some similar turn for the worse.

Quitting school left Johnny without a place to go: no school and no work. He was eighteen years old. He started hanging out at a neighborhood bar called the Casablanca in Monroe. One afternoon, at the bar, he got into a fight with an off-duty cop, a notorious local bully who liked to throw his weight around town. The cop had started an argument.

"Whata you doin' in here, kid? Punks like you oughta get a job."

Johnny ignored him; the cop persisted.

Johnny got up from his bar stool and knocked the cop unconscious with a single blow from his right fist. He walked out of the bar. He was arrested the next day and put in jail. His mother bailed him out. When he appeared before a judge he faced jail time, but the judge was willing to waive the sentence if Johnny enlisted in the service. So, in 1947, he joined the Navy. He took the bus to Great Lakes, Illinois, for basic training. Eight years later, he returned home, bigger and stronger, with tattoos on both arms, a seabag of clothes, and the Pacific Fleet Heavyweight Boxing Trophy. Twice he had risen to bosun's mate and twice he had been busted to seaman for fighting.

I had heard this prom story and its aftermath from my mother many times as I was growing up. It was her attempt at justifying Johnny to me: She traced his problems in part to disappointment. My mother had a well-developed intuition for the insidious power of disappointment to shape a life. But it was disappointment coupled with alcohol that she saw as the destructive combination in Johnny's life. She pointed to his mother as the biggest reason for his drinking. She pushed a drink in front of him, my mother said, whenever life was too hard. So Johnny, in my mother's analysis, was caught between a tyrannical father and an indulgent mother. My mother reserved her most damning judgment for Johnny's mother: "She made him a weakling."

My mother was thirty-two when Johnny returned to Spotswood. He was twenty-six. My guess is that they met at his parents' house: Johnny's sister was a friend of our next-door neighbor, a nervous and religious woman who sometimes babysat for me, and when our neighbor was unavailable to watch me Johnny's sister filled in. So, it would have been natural for my mother to end up in the Kababick house, and Johnny probably would have been at home. It's where his mother wanted him. She doted on him then just as she had before he had left for the Navy. I can say nothing of my mother and Johnny's first meeting except what I can imagine based on the circumstances: She would have been drawn to his manliness, and he would have been drawn to her exotic dark looks. I'm sure he took an early interest in her, though my first actual memory of him surfaces when I was eight years old and my father was already gone.

9

By then, we had moved twice since the first house in Monroe and we were living in Spotswood, on Polonia Street, in a house that backed up to the railroad tracks, and by then, too, he and my mother were close and easy with each other. We were becoming a family, the four of us: Paul, me, my mother, and Johnny. He usually slept overnight on the couch at our house. His head rested on one arm of the sofa, and his legs went up over the other. He slept in his clothes, shoes off, socks on. He worked odd jobs: He was a milkman, drove a bread truck, made up orders at a lumberyard. Sometimes, when my mother was at work at the beauty shop, he brought me with him to his parents' house in Monroe. It seemed to me a little house for such big people, the Kababicks. Inside, there was a roomy kitchen with a low ceiling and a living room where I sat quietly on a couch with a glass of Coca-Cola that Mrs. Kababick had given me while I waited for Johnny to take care of whatever it was that had brought him home. The only sounds in the house were from Mrs. Kababick's nervous Chihuahua as it clicked nervously across the linoleum floor of the kitchen and a gold pendulum clock across the room from where I sat. It whirred under a glass dome: Its mechanism was a carousel with three gold posts that first turned one way and then reversed to turn the other way. It made me dizzy to watch and a little sick. I drank my Coke.

The feature I remember best about the Kababick home was a wood-frame garage that stood apart from the house and at the end of a short driveway. It was nothing more than a gabled shed with two small windows and rough-board siding. The walls were open inside, showing the two-by-four studs, brown as tobacco. Inside, it smelled like wood and motor oil. Looking up, I could see the silver points of the roofing nails that had been driven all the way through the asphalt shingles and the roof boards. It had a sandy dirt floor that was stained black with crankcase grease and a hump between the tire ruts. Johnny had stored his hunting and fishing gear in the garage before he had gone off to the Navy. The first time he took me into the garage, to get a pump for my bicycle tire, I looked around in the dim light and felt a wave of wonder at his boyhood. Among the dozens of old license plates that had been tacked to the walls, I saw his muskrat traps hanging by their short chains, and hip boots, old fishing rods, a pack basket, and a hunting vest and cap hanging from nails pounded into the studs. There was a canoe stored overhead in the rafters. Because it was upside-down, I saw its cane seats. I stood mesmerized and pieced together an idyllic picture of his youth: he and his younger brother, Charles, paddling down a woodland river, checking their traps for muskrats and mink and occasionally reaching for their shotguns to shoot a wood duck lifting from mist on the water.

Some years later, when I was about fifteen, I came across a snapshot of Johnny and Charles, at about sixteen and fourteen years old, with the garage in the background. The snapshot had been hidden in a box of magazines. I recognized the garage from the siding and the small four-light mullioned windows. They were posed on bended knees with shotguns slung sideways and a beagle at their feet. There was a little snow on the ground. The day seemed bright. They were beaming from a successful day of rabbit hunting. They were blond, strapping, and all-American. I could stare endlessly at the photograph. I traced the outlines of their shapes, two boys leaning forward toward whoever was holding the camera on that winter morning. I inspected the background for clues to the moment: Had the snow fallen that morning? Was it still fresh and new in the brambles, cornfields, and hedgerows between the bean fields? What had been the dog's name? There were no rabbits in the photo: Maybe the boys were preparing to leave for a day of hunting and not just getting back. If they were going and not returning, would they drive to their hunting spot?

I felt nostalgia for a boyhood I had never experienced. It was an indefinable and morbid ache for something I had missed or lost and badly wanted: Looking back, I realize maybe it was a place in which to be rooted and a normal life that revolved around a house, garage, and woods and fields. The photo seemed to fill a hole in my heart. At the time, the ache was inexplicable to me. It has revisited me many more times in my life, usually at times of deep loneliness, and it still has the power to bring me to tears.

Over time, I came to dissolve the ache in the details of my own outdoor life, and in nature, and eventually in my family and especially my children. I could never put myself in that snapshot, the third boy standing with the other two, as either a brother or a son, holding my own gun and smiling at the great fun we had had walking behind the baying beagle as we hunted rabbits in the cold air. I did the next best thing as I got older: I packed my life like the Kababick garage. I accumulated fishing rods, shotguns, duck calls, hunting boots, shotgun shells, canoe paddles, decoys, wool shirts, trout flies, tackle boxes, pocketknives, canvas pants, sleeping bags, backpacks, ice augers, tents, geographic survey maps, mess kits, canteens, and snowshoes. Much later in my life, I even kept hunting dogs. I taught my son to fish.

At the back of the garage, I noticed several boxes that rested on a low shelf in the dark triangle untouched by the slash of sunlight that slid between the two doors that hung right and left on heavy hinges. I went over to the boxes and asked Johnny what was in them.

"Old magazines," he said.

I ruffled through them. They were back copies of *Field & Stream, Outdoor Life,* and *Fur-Fish-Game.*

"Can I look at them?"

"You can have them," he said.

I could not believe the treasure I had just come into. They were full of pictures of animals and wild rivers and boys fishing in ponds. I took an armful of the magazines home, and Johnny said he would bring the other boxes another day. There were five boxes in all, with magazines dating back to the 1930s. For several years, those magazines gave me endless delight: I read and reread the articles about hunting, fishing, and trapping in the Adirondacks, on the Minnesota prairie and the

Upper Peninsula of Michigan, and in Ontario, Wyoming, Alaska.

I read about men who chased mountain lions with hounds in Utah and boys who ran traplines along creeks in Kentucky. There were stories of close calls with bears in the Yukon and Cape buffalo in Africa. I developed a love for the aesthetics of Georgia-plantation quail hunting, though I had yet to see a quail or even leave the state of New Jersey, and I thrilled at the long-distance shooting skills of pronghorn hunters in Nebraska. They used what were called long "flat-shooting" rifles. I came to know that there were three types of marlin: black, blue, and white, and that the black was the most prized. I knew the world-record sizes and weights of nearly every fresh- and saltwater species of fish in North America, and I knew the Alaskan moose was much bigger than its counterpart in Maine and the Roosevelt elk was the biggest of its species and could be found only in California. I knew that the giant lake trout pulled from the deep lakes of Manitoba were nearly a hundred years old and that the best brook trout fishing on the continent was in Labrador, Canada. I could distinguish a ptarmigan from a partridge and a lynx from a bobcat. I knew that the best set for a wolverine was a baited cubby and that a fox went to high ground when its suspicions were aroused by human scent.

The magazines, along with a set of encyclopedias my mother had bought from a door-to-door salesman and a white soft-leather Bible that had been given to me by one of our babysitters, were what I read until about age twelve. Then, at the library, I discovered a series of books by Lew Dietz about a teenage boy, Jeff White, who worked as a hunting guide in Maine. I lay on my bed and read them on my back, with my legs and feet up against the bedroom wall. Sometimes I was on my stomach hanging over the side of the bed with the books on the floor. I would read them for hours on a Saturday, lost in the wilderness tales. Jeff White solved mysteries, shot big bucks, and accomplished dangerous backwoods rescues. I pictured myself as Jeff White in hunting boots, wool trousers, and a red-and-black-checked wool mackinaw. I was also a methodical reader of the Bible. I began with Genesis and worked my way forward through the books of Moses and the rest of the Old Testament and then on to the Gospels, the Acts, Epistles, and Revelation. Always I was looking for clues about how to live. My early Bible study fused the lives of Abraham, Isaac, Amos, and Ezekiel, and I developed the idea that the man God was holding out to me as a model was taciturn, long-suffering, polygamous, and frequently hallucinogenic, at least in spiritual matters. Biblical man and God did what they wanted—everyone else be damned. This was a liberating message. From all of that walking in the desert, I deduced, God's man was gaunt and brown. I assumed he was sandal clad and very tired at the end of the day. That's when the foot oil and pomegranates came out and he sat down to admire his sons, daughters, wives, and sheep. Some of his wives wore cymbals on their fingers. For a boy just entering puberty, this held some appeal. The lesson I pulled from it was that the mind of the man who is in touch with God is like an electrical storm: Trees get split, bushes burn, and disfavored tribes and relatives pay a heavy price. I also concluded that a man (or a boy) could talk directly to God and didn't need intermediaries to carry messages back and forth. I began to pray at night. I asked God to fix things so my mother didn't have to work so hard and Johnny didn't drink so much.

But the Jeff White novels were easier to follow than the

Bible and more fun to read. They led me circuitously through the literature of the North American Indians and eventually to Henry Thoreau, who had made his own trip to Maine to climb Katahdin with his Penobscot Indian guide, Joe Polis. Thoreau was a solitary traveler and a careful observer. We had this in common. From Thoreau, I was launched on a lifetime of reading, always trending back to the woods, the waters, and the land: Leopold, Hamsun, Turgenev, Stegner, and Tolstoy.

10

The beauty salon was the last place we lived in Spotswood. By then, we had lived in seven houses or apartments and Johnny was a fixture in our life. The beauty salon was only about a half mile from Manalapan Brook, the river that spilled over the dam at Spotswood Lake, and sometimes I took a shortcut that led behind the butcher shop, down through a field, which also was owned by the butcher and his wife, and into the woods to the river. One afternoon, following the shortcut, I met their son, Donny, in the field. Donny was an odd boy. He was in my grade at school. He walked on his toes in mincing steps. We did not do much together, but we got along all right and I said, "Hi," when I met him in the field. He was alone and he seemed to be amusing himself outdoors, as boys do without doing very much at all. I was carrying my fishing rod.

"Where are you going?" Donny asked.

"Down to the river."

"Is that your fishing rod?"

The question struck me as dumb. He often had seen me

with the rod, and it was nothing special to be carrying a fishing rod. Who else's rod would it be but mine? He reached out to take it from me.

"What are you doing?" I said.

I did not want to let it go and held on. He yanked it, and I pushed him away. He fell on his back even though I hadn't pushed him very hard. He got up, said nothing, and hurried up toward the butcher shop. It was a strange encounter, but I left it at that since he was a strange boy. I kept walking, and when I reached the end of the field I stopped to dig worms for bait. Usually I just pulled up some clumps of grass and searched the dirt that came up with the roots for small pink earthworms. While I was busy pulling the worms out of the dirt, I looked up and saw Donny and his butcher father walking toward me. They were moving fast. Donny's father looked determined. I stood up and watched them approach. What did they want? This was more strangeness. When they reached me, the butcher grabbed me by the arm.

"You're going to learn a lesson," he said.

I was mute. He pulled the belt from his pants. Donny stood there and watched. He was smiling. I wriggled to get away, but the butcher had a firm hold, now on my shirt, and it gathered around my neck as I squirmed. I could not find my voice to shout. I did not know why this was happening, and I did not know what to say. I was wearing a pair of shorts, and the butcher yanked them down. I was standing in my underpants. He brought the belt down hard on my backside. He struck me three times. When he was done, he released my shirt and he put his arm on his son's shoulder and the two of them walked back up the field. I pulled up my shorts. I sobbed. My face burned and I was shaking. I waited until they were out of sight and I ran back to my mother's beauty shop. I told her what had happened.

She was speechless. I could see the anger gathering in her eyes and her tightening mouth. She wasn't saying anything. She didn't move. I wondered why she was not running out of the beauty salon shrieking.

"He hit with you with his belt?" she said, finally.

"Yes."

I could see her mind working furiously, but she was stuck in place. Why, I wondered, wasn't my mother running from the shop to find and confront the butcher? This was more strangeness. Nothing was making any sense to me. I had been unfairly punished, *hit!*, by a person not even related to us, and this called for outrage and retaliation. I knew my mother's code. She would not accept this, not to her Louis. There should at least be a shouting match in which my mother would insult the butcher and make threats, even if they were bluff threats. I knew the potential of her fury when it was kindled. I imagined her waving her scissors at the butcher and shouting, "Touch my son again and I will cut out your heart, you short, fat bastard!"

Instead, my mother's feet were planted on the floor of the rented beauty shop. Her eyes were moving as if plotting a route of attack or escape, but she seemed incapable of moving. Her darting eyes didn't seem to be finding the route she was looking for. She seemed trapped. Every ounce of me was willing her to run out of the shop in my defense. *The man had hit me with his belt.* Finally, she took me into the back room where we had been living and asked me to take down my pants.

"Let me see where he hit you," she said.

I was embarrassed, but I brought down my shorts and my underwear to show the redness on my buttocks. Surely this would be enough to ignite her rage. She seemed at a loss for words and for action.

"I'm going to tell Johnny about this," she said finally. "He'll take care of that little bastard."

I wanted immediate action, but the prospect of Johnny, big, strong Johnny, going after the butcher soothed some of my humiliation. I was willing to wait a little while for justice to be delivered. I fantasized about the ways in which Johnny would confront him. Johnny would let the butcher know that he was going to pay for his meanness to me with a beating or at least the prospect of one. The butcher would plead for mercy. Johnny would let the butcher humiliate himself with his pleadings, and then Johnny would step up to him, hit him hard in the jaw. It would take only one punch. The butcher would be knocked unconscious. Or maybe it would be enough for him just to be forced to beg not to be beaten and then Johnny would just walk away.

In the days that followed, I avoided Donny and took a different route with my fishing rod to the river. I took a path that didn't lead over the butcher's field, the place where I had been strapped, but almost immediately after the incident, and with no warning from my mother, we moved from the back of the beauty shop. My mother found an apartment for us in a nearby city, New Brunswick. I still waited for Johnny's thrashing of the butcher. For a time, I figured it must have happened and nobody wanted to tell me about it. My mom and Johnny were just keeping it quiet from me, I guessed, because it would be better if I didn't actually know about it. It wouldn't be right for a boy to know that a grown-up had thrashed another grown-up. People who were grown-up weren't supposed to fight. But no indirect word of it reached me, and I saw nothing on their faces to suggest that the score had been settled.

My mind worked at an explanation for their inaction: Was it because my mother rented the space for the beauty shop from the butcher or, more likely, that we weren't supposed to be living in the back of the shop and this was his way of showing my mother that he wasn't so dumb and that he knew how to handle her? I came to feel the humiliation more for her sake than mine. The strapping faded into the past without any fight between Johnny and the butcher, and we never talked any more about it. The month after we left the back room of the shop for the apartment in New Brunswick, my mother moved her beauty shop out of the butcher's building and farther down Main Street. It was Lynn's Beauty Salon, number three.

11

I have always been attached to places, fields, mountains, brooks, but my life as a child never centered on a house, at least for very long. We lived in too many of them. For a while, we actually "owned" a home, that is, we paid mortgage payments for as long we could, and when we couldn't pay them, we lost it in a foreclosure. That's what the humiliating fluorescent red sign on the telephone pole out front said: "This house is in foreclosure." I had my own bedroom in that house, but even then I was reluctant to claim it as my own space. My life centered on two people, my mother and brother, and a third, Johnny, for the time he was with us. I can count seventeen different houses or apartments that we lived in by the time I had left for college; nearly all of them fitted inside a circle of central New Jersey that did not exceed twenty-five miles in diameter.

There was the first house in Monroe, then the two bunga-lows on Polonia Street in Spotswood, the three-story haunted house in Helmetta that was built with tilted floors and high windows and meant as a home for the blind, or so my mother had explained to Paul and me, an apartment over a garage run by a family of mechanics in Jamesburg, the room behind the beauty shop, of course, the apartment in New Brunswick, then the big leap to the house down the shore, which my mother and Johnny splurged on ("No money down") soon af-ter they were married, and, after we lost the house, a sequence of garden apartments and a rented house in Toms River. I re-turned to one of those apartments during the Christmas break of my first year at college. I tried the key and it wouldn't work; I pulled on the knob and banged on the door. I cupped my eyes at the front window and saw that the apartment was vacant. There was not a stick of furniture on the bare floors. I carried my duffel to a pay phone and called my mother at the beauty shop where she was working as an employee, since by then she had given up her shop in Spotswood.

"Mom, the apartment is empty. What's going on?"

"Oh, I moved out," she said. "We have a much better place. It's on the same street. I meant to call you. Just walk up the street. You'll see it on the right. It's in Jamestown Apart-ments. We're at Two-forty A. You'll like it."

The moves were often wrapped in drama. We once lived in a second-floor apartment over a mechanics' garage. We reached it by a long set of outside wood stairs at the back of the building. The owners of the building also operated the garage, and they lived in a house next door. They were fastidious peo-ple, Italian-Americans, who even kept a clean mechanics' garage. The landlady was a small, severe woman with purple gums who terrorized her sons and husband with her shrieking. One day, when we were out, she entered our apartment. She must have been horrified. There were unwashed pots in the sink, dirty dishes on the table, and laundry on the bathroom floor. She hoarded her secret until days later. As my mother, Paul, and I came down the back steps, the landlady met us at the bottom.

"You should pay a mind to your housekeeping."

In a flash, my mother saw she had been violated.

"Have you been in my home?"

The Italian landlady walked away.

It was my mother's turn to bide her time. I knew this was going to end badly. Two weeks after our rent had been due and about three weeks after the bottom-of-the-stairs remark, my mother arranged for us to move. She had no intention of paying the rent and no intention of giving notice of our move. On the appointed morning, a moving truck arrived. The sight of it—a big truck that could have carried everything we owned in one small corner—brought the Italian family out of their house and garage.

"What are you doing?" the landlady shrieked. "You owe us rent. We get a month's notice!"

"This will teach you to sneak into people's houses," my mother shot back.

My mother pointed the moving men to our upstairs apartment. The landlady stood in their way on the steps. There was a stalemate. There was shouting back and forth. I stood to the side, out of the way, holding my brother's hand and watching these two fierce women firing insults at each other.

"You deadbeat!"

"Nosy bitch!"

"Trash!"

"Guinea bitch!"

No action seemed possible beyond the exchange of shouted slurs. Then the landlady's husband entered the argument. It was the first male voice to be heard.

"You have to pay the rent," he bellowed.

This was too much for one of the moving men. He judged it a bully's move. It had stopped being about two women. The moving man, a wiry rooster of a guy with a flattened nose, shot forward.

"This lady wants us to move her, and we're here to move her. I'm on the clock. So get out of my way before I make my way!"

He was ready to take on the entire brood of Italian mechanics. His partner, a much bigger and younger man, whose rear-end crack showed above his drooping work pants, followed him up the stairs, and they carried down our few pieces of furniture. The landlady shouted that the police were on their way. Savoring victory, my mother drove off with her two sons. We were gone before the police arrived. I was relieved when we crossed the Jamesburg town line into Spotswood. I figured the police couldn't chase us into the next town. We moved into the back of the beauty salon. The furniture on the moving truck went into storage.

Once in a while, I can dredge other houses from my memory, places where we must have set down for hardly more than a few months. I remember one house because I couldn't squeeze between it and the dense, prickly branches of a big Norway spruce in the yard; another comes back as a memory of me seated on a wide windowsill, looking out on an empty pasture and hearing the sound of a marching band across a long treeless distance. This was in Spotswood, which was still a rural town then with many open fields. I recall getting up from the sill, going outdoors, and struggling to see the band. I remember even climbing and balancing on a fence post to see farther and then walking and eventually running through fields of dry weeds and soybeans and across roads toward the music without ever finding the source of it or without it even getting closer or louder. It sounded like the band at a football game, with drums, horns, and cymbals. It kept playing as a distant marching band, somewhere far off beyond my seeing, but always at the edge of my hearing.

Eventually, dusk and the falling autumn night ended my search. If the recollection of those brass horns and bass drums were not so vivid and the sight of the purple sunset at the horizon were not so clear in my memory, I might have long ago written this off as a dream that powerfully expressed my nascent longing for something beyond the life I was living. I swear that it happened.

In nearly all of the places we lived, there was a framed drawing that my mother brought along and prominently displayed on some table or cabinet. It showed a Stone Age mother in a lion skin protecting her two children against some danger that lurked outside the cave. It must have struck an immediate chord with my mother in whatever magazine she had torn it from. She kept it for a lifetime, and I found it among her possessions after she had died when my brother and I cleaned out her last apartment. It was the image she had of herself: she and her boys against the world. Actually, I think a more accurate image would have been of a mother cat restlessly moving her kittens from a crevice below the porch to a place under a woodpile. But it was an image that sustained her dignity, and it was the truest expression of how I felt about my mother: Her love for me and my brother was fierce. Not a day passed that she didn't tell me I was handsome and smart and destined for something big. I was Greek! (She dismissed any paternal contribution.) One of my teachers in elementary school had told her in a parent-teacher conference, "Your son is college material." She repeated the phrase as if it were a religious incantation. She introduced me to her customers in the beauty shop: "This is my son Louis. His teachers [she already had transformed it into the plural] say he is college material."

So, in the middle of all this tumult that was my childhood, there was powerful love, my mother's love for me and my love for my mother, brother, and Johnny. It was a buffer against the storm that continually swirled around my life.

Why did we move around so much? In part, it was because we were often broke and unable to pay the rent. In that situation, either my mother concocted a dispute with the landlord and stormed out as the aggrieved renter, full of righteous indignation, or we loaded our car in the middle of the night with our possessions and drove off in her Ford Fairlane convertible before we could be caught.

I can only infer from these quick departures that there must have been times when we were without much furniture. We were portable. But the reasons for our transience went deeper than lack of money. My mother seemed to invite tumult in her life as if it would stir up some interesting drama. My mother was always seeking something more in her life, and I'm not sure I can give it a name. It was, I think, some vague, sad, and impossible piece of the heart roughly bounded by respectability, love, and excitement. These were strong impulses, not always consistent or understood, hard to resolve into anything sensible, and they plunged my mother deeper into her life of fantasy. These were the three abstractions that were at work behind most of her decisions and actions.

Her engagement in life was, more or less, the fusion of disappointment and imagination. A new apartment represented a new beginning, a new canvas that she could paint her dreams on. It always seemed to include new furniture bought on credit: a sofa in a rich floral print, a wall sconce made to look like the handiwork of a Spanish goldsmith, curtains with elaborate drapes and valances. A nice apartment gave her respectability; she seemed to get her excitement from men; love was what she had for her sons, unbounded love and pride.

As a consequence of buying objects (sofas, curtains, carpets) that would give her respectability, and our generally precarious financial situation, Paul and I had become experts at foiling bill collectors. The most persistent were from the Beneficial Finance Company. My mother would borrow money from them for a bedroom set or a sofa and be unable to pay the bills as they came due. After two months of nonpayment, the phone calls would begin. Paul and I knew the voices and approaches of the collection agencies and made up stories about how the family that had been living there had moved to Australia or had been taken to jail because of a terrible murder in the neighborhood. If the bill collectors came to the door, as they sometimes did, we played dumb and gave false names and said the people who used to live in the apartment seemed like such nice people. They didn't seem at all like the people who wouldn't pay their bills. Could we offer a cup of coffee? One bill collector, a man with a fleshy face and circles of sweat showing under the arms of his short-sleeved white shirt, threatened to stay until my mother showed up.

"We'll see if she pays," he said.

My eight-year-old brother sprang at him, driving his head

and arms into the man's big stomach. The man staggered backward and went away.

Another man who regularly came to our door was a life-insurance salesman. He collected two dollars toward two burial policies that my mother had bought. She lived in fear of the shame of dying without money for a burial. The salesman was polite, and if my mother happened to be at home when he came, and sometimes he came early in the evening when she was back from work, he was pleasant and deferentially formal with her, which pleased us because he was handsome and wore a suit. My mother flirted with him slightly. He was American. We lived in an ethnically prismatic world. People were Italians, Jews, Irish, Germans, Polacks, or coloreds. This man was what we called American, the kind of person we saw on television, and this elevated him in our eyes. I appreciated the respect that he showed my mother when she gave him a check or an envelope with the two bills in it.

"Thank you, Mrs. Ureneck."

"Please call me Lynn. Can I give you a cup of coffee or something to eat?"

"No, I really have to go. But thank you. I will see you in a couple of weeks."

I still have those policies, blue formal documents in plastic cases, among her old papers. My brother and I cashed them when she died. They were worth six hundred dollars each. The money went toward her funeral.

My mother's imagination was not limited to the magic of an apartment's ability to confer a new and better life. Sometimes she would tell me that her dream was to open a fancy tea shop, where high-class women would come in the afternoons for tea and delicate pastries. I had no idea who these women were or where they could be found, and I'm not sure my mother did, either. We didn't know any of them. They weren't the women who came into her beauty shop. My mother, I think, must have picked them out of magazines and movies. Maybe they were the well-dressed women she had seen as a child in Newark having lunch in Bamberger's Department Store during their daytime shopping trips. She imagined the tea shop's décor in detail: white wicker tables, delicate bone china tea service with red-and-blue patterns, lace tablecloths, bouquets of flowers, porcelain knick-knacks, antique clocks, art on the walls. I listened many times to her describe this dream and I could see that talking of it lifted her spirits, so I would join in and try to make suggestions on how we could raise the money for the business and sell extra items, muffins maybe, to make it more profitable or extend it into catering.

All the time that I was listening to her and offering her encouragement, I was thinking to myself, We don't know where next month's rent is coming from, and my mother is dreaming of opening a fancy tea shop.

The realization of my mother's impracticality and her annihilation of reality caused me pain, but I was unwilling to burst the bubble of her fantasy. It made her happy. I suggested maybe we should add fancy breads as well as muffins. It would boost our profits.

So, for me, our houses and apartments were simply bookmarks, reminding me of particular chapters in my childhood and helping me keep my personal chronology straight: I lived in the house in Monroe after being born in Middlesex General Hospital; my father left for good when we lived in the first house on Polonia Street; Paul nearly cut off a finger climbing through the broken window of a locked garage at the second house on Polonia Street, which was when Johnny began living with us and where I fell asleep to the sound of the Perth Amboy train tapping the tracks, which edged our backyard; I was at the pinnacle of my catfishing expertise when we lived in the back of the beauty shop; the furnace grate burned a waffle pattern into my pink soles one winter in the house in Helmetta, the house where the babysitter had gone into childbirth; and I bought my first fly rod when we lived at the apartment in New Brunswick.

12

It was there, on a worn patch of grass between buildings in a complex of "garden apartments," that I taught myself to cast a fly rod. I was ten years old, and it was the summer of 1961.

The grass would have to suffice: The nearest water was a stream behind the apartments that was littered with shopping carts, car tires, and refrigerators. It flowed over a rust-colored bottom and disappeared under Livingston Avenue in a concrete pipe. There were no fish in it. It was too noxious even for mosquitoes.

I had saved the money I had earned from delivering the daily and Sunday *Newark Evening News*. With my first paycheck, I bought my mother a blue nightgown at Korvettes. With the money I saved from my second, third, and fourth paychecks, I bought an eight-foot-long medium-weight Fiberglas fly rod at a sporting goods store in North Brunswick. It cost twenty-two dollars, a princely sum in those days. I walked to the store on a Saturday and examined all of the rods in the rack. Working from what I had learned from the outdoors magazines, I picked out one that was the right size and weight for trout. I had never seen a trout except in the photographs of the outdoor magazines. They looked to me like living rainbows, beautiful, fragile, and reflecting back the light of a mountain brook.

Following the directions in a little book that came with my new rod, I practiced my casting. The booklet showed a hip-booted fly fisherman, in a sequence of panels, against the face of a clock: The rod was raised from the three o'clock position to the twelve o'clock position, and the line unfolded in a tight loop behind the fisherman, and then the rod was brought forward to the one o'clock position, and the line shot forward to lie flat on the water. It was a motion in four beats, accomplished with a stiff wrist and anchored elbow.

On summer nights, I practiced my casts until the yellow fly line was invisible in the darkness. One-two-three-four, up-back-forward-down. I became a proficient fly caster. As I stood on the patchy urban grass, cocked my elbow, and brought the rod through the casting positions, I pictured myself on a clear mountain stream, coaxing a wild trout to my delicate fly, probably a No. 16 Fan-wing Coachman tied with green peacock herl and the barred breast feathers of a male wood duck.

The apartments' superintendent, Mr. Klaman, stooped through his rounds of the buildings twice a day, weighted down by his keys and responsibilities. He shook his head and waved to me: "How's it going, Mister Fisherman? Catch any big ones?"

Trout are not anything like catfish. Catfish and trout occupy opposite ends of the fishing spectrum. The difference in status terms is roughly the difference between teaching at an Ivy League university and working the back of a garbage truck.

I had mastered catfishing, and I had moved on successfully to catching perch, pickerel, sunfish, and even the occasional calico or smallmouth bass. To catch a trout was a calibrated ascension of finesse, by degrees of magnitude, from chicken gizzards as bait, to shiny lures that wobbled and spun when they were retrieved, to flies that alighted as gently as goose down on the mirror surface of cold, clear streams. Some fishermen, I saw from the magazines, caught trout on spinning rods and even used worms, but the best fishermen, the ones who moved in the elite world that I wanted to move in, used fly rods and forswore bait as an abomination. They fished the legendary rivers of Montana and Idaho and the Adirondacks. They were the poets of the outdoors. I knew their names by heart: Ted Trueblood, Ed Zern, Art Flick, and the granddaddy of them all, Theodore Gordon, who made fly-fishing an American sport. Like Emerson, who had implored poets to write in their American language, Gordon had encouraged innovation and tactics for American rivers and streams. It was Gordon who brought the fly onto the water's surface Before Gordon, flies swam underwater. He created a new genre: the American dry fly. It was all done with feathers, hair, and tinsel tied to a very small hook to look like an insect drying its wings and about to take flight.

This was fly-fishing, and I dreamed of catching a trout. The line between nature and art in my life was already beginning to dissolve. Fortunately, I was as interested in reading as I was in fishing. I really had nowhere to fish, but I had plenty of magazines and lived not far from the public library.

I didn't yet own any flies, though I had consumed the literature on them. It hardly mattered. I was learning one of fishing's most important lessons, that fishing reaches perfection in one place only, the imagination. Fly-fishing is an idea. Here was a pursuit that invited abstraction, and into this world of anticipation and pure thought I drifted with my fly rod. I entered a better life, one that was free of trouble and conflict. It was both aspiration and escape, the twin themes of my life. I could not have been happier, laying out the line and aiming for dandelions in the scruffy grass.

That same summer, I bought a fishing vest, the kind with twelve pockets to hold boxes of flies and accessories, a landing net with a clip that fitted on my belt loop, and a pair of green hip boots. I wore this uniform as I practiced casting among the garden apartments. I can only imagine what residents of the squat buildings thought when they looked out of their windows and saw me in the urban twilight as they sat down to their suppers of meat loaf or stuffed cabbage. Nearly a year passed before I got to use the rod on water. The chance came when a friend's father took us to Farrington Lake, in nearby Milltown. I impressed them both by bringing along a fly rod and catching sunfish on a hook wrapped with green thread and delivered with pinpoint-accurate casts.

I lived two lives, as a fly fisherman and bait fisherman.

Johnny was not a fly fisherman. I didn't even speak to him of fly-fishing. It was something I kept to myself. It would have been like admitting to an interest in ballet. When he and I went fishing, we used a hand line, which was a ball of heavy cord tied off at the end with a sinker and a hook. We baited the hook with night crawlers, swung the line lassolike overhead, and threw it into the water. We had a place—about a twenty-minute drive from the city—where we could almost always catch catfish or yellow perch. It was near the outfall of the Kimberly-Clark paper plant in Old Bridge, where the water was warm and plunged from one of the mill's giant pipes. We would catch a stringer of catfish in an hour or two, carefully clean them by splitting their gray bellies and removing the entrails, and take them home and cook them in flour, salt, and pepper, setting them, when done, on newspapers to absorb the hot fat.

13

As a boy, I was always clipping the "tips" columns from the outdoor magazines I got in the mail and putting them into scrapbooks (how to build lean-tos, track a big buck, skin an elk—all the stuff a boy in a New Brunswick apartment complex needed to know). I pasted the clippings onto notebook paper and put them into a three-ring binder. I kept the binders in a box in my bedroom. One part of the outdoor magazines, in particular, fascinated me: the back section of classified advertisements for hunting and fishing lodges. They showed men posing with giant muskellunge or big-antlered deer. I wrote letters to many of the lodges and collected their return letters and brochures.

Dear Sir, My name is Louis Ureneck and I live in New Jersey. I am a pretty good fisherman. Would you send me information about fishing in Labrador? I am interested in fly-fishing for trout. What species of trout are in your area? What flies do you recommend? Please include your rates and directions for getting there. Sincerely, Louis A. Ureneck

One year, I guess I was about thirteen, Johnny saw me with a magazine. He asked what I was reading. I told him that I was looking at the ads for fishing lodges.

"We should take one of those trips," he said. "Maybe to Canada."

I could hardly believe what I was hearing. Was it possible, we would actually go to a fishing lodge?

Why not? he answered.

Yes, why not?

I saw pictures of boys and their fathers in some of the ads. Why couldn't that be us holding those strings of big pike or lake trout?

Why not?

Johnny opened the door with his question, and I rushed through on a mission of planning and information gathering that lasted for two months. I wrote to lodges, state fish and game commissions in Maine and New York, and tourist bureaus in Ontario and Manitoba. I collected maps and borrowed books from the library.

I made lists of lodges and copied the dates of fishing seasons. I compared prices and calculated driving times. (Johnny never had a reliable car, so this was crucial information. We would have to drive there. I worried that his car wouldn't make it to Canada. In fact, I wasn't even sure a person could drive to Canada. Maybe the roads stopped at the border.) Eventually, I settled on the Adirondack Mountains in New York. The lodges there were the most practical because they were the closest to home. They cost the least, too.

I had everything planned to the smallest detail. I shared the information with Johnny one night. He looked it over and smiled.

"Yeah, these all look good," he said.

The time drew near for us to mail in a deposit. I had been hoping that he would know this and that I wouldn't have to actually say it out loud. Finally, with time running out, I spoke up.

"It says we have to send in money for a deposit pretty soon."

He looked at the letters and rate sheets.

"Why don't you keep looking? Check them all out. See if there's anything closer, something that costs less."

We were not going to take the trip. There was nothing that was closer or cost less. The trip, at six hundred dollars, was beyond our means. I was angry for letting myself think the trip was possible. It wasn't just the money that stood in the way. It was our inability to do the things that regular families and fathers and sons did. We didn't plan anything; problems always interceded, car problems, work problems, drinking problems, money problems. We were different from people who went on vacations. These were the people who owned station wagons. We didn't go on vacations. The best I could hope for was a day trip to the Metedeconk River, where we barbecued hamburgers and hot dogs on the brown, silty sand, put out a couple of traps for blue-claw crabs, and swam in the muddy salt water. Those trips were fun, but they represented the tight boundary of what was possible. There wasn't going to be any wilderness fishing trip for us. I packed up all the papers, brochures, and maps in a big brown envelope and put them away in the back of my closet.

The loss of the trip made me realize something: We were stuck in place. The recognition of the limits of how we were living jolted me: I began to think more seriously about a different life. I wondered what it would be like to leave home. The interesting life that I had vaguely felt loomed somewhere ahead of me, shapeless and indistinct, was going to require a plan. I imagined myself in college, though I had only a postcard picture of what was meant by college. I had never been to a college, and except for my teachers who had gone to a state teachers college I didn't know anyone who had gone to college. I imagined college as a cluster of ivy-covered buildings that held laboratories. What little I knew about colleges had come from the television quiz show *GE College Bowl*. I watched it every Sunday and answered a lot of the questions put by host Allen Ludden. I was good at geography and biology. I called out the answers ahead of the college boys in their sport coats and crew cuts. Johnny, if he was in front of the television, would look at me, amazed. I decided I would become a scientist. I would be a man of considerable reputation whose work studying animals took him into the woods for research. I went to the public library and found that this job was called wildlife biologist. I began making more lists, this time of colleges and universities and books that I should read.

Johnny never brought up the trip again, and neither did I.

14

Once in a while, Johnny would decide that he was going to take me fishing "down the shore." That's how New Jersey people refer to the line of beaches and bays from Sandy Hook to Cape May, "down the shore." These trips were always an adventure because of the cars Johnny owned. For a while he had an English Ford, old and broken-down, which he had won in a barroom arm-wrestling contest. This is how he came into things. The car was barely big enough for him to fit in the seat behind the steering wheel. It had a clutch and hand throttle and a half backseat. The top folded down. The plastic rear window had been repaired with duct tape. The top had to be manually folded and lifted back. He called it his Hungarian

Cadillac, a typical bit of self-derision that was an allusion to both the pretensions of refugees of the Hungarian uprising in 1956 who had been resettled in central New Jersey and his own Eastern European background.

The car's starter, on the floor, usually didn't work, so one of us would have to get behind the wheel while the other pushed it down the street. At about 5 miles an hour, the driver, usually me, because I was lighter, even though I was three years shy of my driver's license, popped the clutch in first gear. The engine would choke and the car would buck and sputter, but it was enough to get the four little cylinders under the red hood firing continuously so that the car lurched forward and under its own power. The person who did the pushing, usually Johnny, had to run ahead to the door on the passenger side and hop in while the car was rolling. It would cough, hack, and spit for a mile or two, and then it would just cough. The driver had to be careful to gun the engine while stopped at a red light to prevent the engine from stalling. Somehow, it got us to our destination, even on the cold mornings in March when the flounder were running in Raritan Bay.

I remember one place that we fished, near the town of Keyport. It was remarkable because it was more or less an industrial waterfront. We traveled on Route 1 toward Sandy Hook, which marks one of the busiest shipping corridors in the country, the entrance to New York Harbor. We turned off the highway, lined with motels, gas stations, crab-and-fish stores, cheap restaurants, and bars, and followed a dirt byway downhill to an unpaved parking lot and rock jetty. Johnny was careful to park the car on the hill so he could jump-start its engine if it stalled. A river came in from the left and sent its green bubbled water surging against the rocks and into the bay. Spanning the river was a railroad trestle, which could pivot to allow barge traffic to pass, and a stand of old pilings that described an ancient pier. A few rotten boards still held to the old pilings. Seagulls screamed. I placed myself between the jetty and the trestle, downstream from the pilings, where the pebbled shore sloped to the waterline. The bottom was muddy sand and gravel, and it fell away gently from the place where the waves were lapping my boot tops. It was a good spot for flounder. Flounder are caught in the early spring when it is cold and windy, and I remember using my numb fingers to impale bloodworms onto my hook. Bloodworms are nasty creatures, long and turgid, with barbed retractable mouths. Flounder hooks are long to hold plenty of the bloodworm, and they bend to make a narrow gap, which can fit into a flounder's petite mouth.

Johnny would stay with me for ten or fifteen minutes at the waterline, to make sure I was settled, all the time leaving the car running, and then he would say, "I'm going to drive back a few miles to pick up some things. Do you want a soda?"

"Sure, a soda would be good."

"I'll be back in a while."

He would be gone two or three hours, and I knew he was at one of the bars we had passed along the way. It was an understanding between us: He said he was going to pick up some things, and I knew he was going to a bar to drink. I was okay with the arrangement. I got to fish and get some time with him in the car. I caught flounder, if they were running, and explored the rocks and shoreline for bottles or shells that had washed ashore if they were not. I waved to the bargemen as they went by and to the occasional powerboater who was headed up the river. I contemplated the flight of gulls, examined the speed and direction of the tide and the waves that moved against the current, and I studied the synchronicity of the schools of small fish that darted along the shoreline. I also prospected the tidal margin for flat palm-sized stones among the seaweed and skipped them across the tops of the waves. Even though I was cold in my jacket and sweater, three hours passed quickly.

When Johnny returned, ruddy in the face and smelling like beer, I would hop in the car with my rod and my catch and open my jacket to the warmth that was blowing from the heater that rattled on the floor. I pulled my feet out of my boots and wiggled my toes to get the feeling back. On the way home, Johnny would suggest that we grab something to eat. We would stop at one of the crab-and-fish places, which resembled a roadside farm stand, and get smoked whiting to eat on the way home. The fish man would take three or four of them, with their heads still on and their skins smoked golden brown, and wrap them in stiff waxy paper, fold over the ends, and seal them with pieces of masking tape. I opened the paper in the car and pulled the sweet, oily fish from the bones, gobbling it ravenously. I washed it down with the birch beer Johnny had brought me back from the bar in one of those cardboard containers that were used in those days to sell beer in New Jersey on Sundays.

We were still living in New Brunswick during this period, but Paul and I had continued to attend school in Spotswood until someone ratted us out and we were called to the principal's office and told to say where we lived. I spoke for the two of us.

"We live with our mother, who works across the street."

I was twelve, and already I knew the art of ambiguity to

evade a question. The principal saw what he was up against, so he dismissed me and Paul back to our classes. The jig was up. We had to leave the school in the middle of the year. We entered the Lee Avenue Elementary School in New Brunswick. I was in the sixth grade; Paul, in the second.

15

A pivotal event in the life of my mother and Johnny came when he joined the merchant marine. The job promised good pay and regular work: something that had eluded him until then. In the mid-1960s, the American economy was humming and the Vietnam War, which was building toward its peak at the end of the decade, required the transport of enormous quantities of supplies, from ammunition to food, across the Pacific Ocean. The shipping industry was busy. Johnny had loved the Navy and could use his service time to get seaman's papers. Even though the job would take him away from home for months at a time, my mother saw the work as a path to a better life for both of them.

Johnny had been out of work a lot; he had held seasonal construction jobs or factory jobs that didn't seem to last. He would be working along fine for a while and then his spirit would seem to give out and he'd miss a day or two of work, and this would set him on a downward track of disappointment and torpor, and he would begin drinking and sleeping. But those were dead-end jobs, and the merchant marine seemed to confer status. It required union membership. A steady union job would be a big step up for us. My mother gave Johnny the money to join the union, which turned out to be a complex series of transactions involving friends and crooked business agents and gifts of bottles of whiskey. She also gave him money to buy the clothes and gear he needed to ship out. He wore a jacket, white shirt, and trousers and shiny black shoes when he went to the National Maritime Union hiring hall in Manhattan. We beamed at how handsome and neat he looked when he left the house to catch the bus to New York.

His first trip was a success. He was gone six months, working on a freighter that carried military cargo to Da Nang, a main staging area for the war. He came back with his pay, and he handed it to my mother. It was an envelope full of hundred-dollar bills. Merchant seamen were paid in cash. The tears welled in my mother's eyes when she held the money, five thousand dollars, in her hands. Fifty one-hundred-dollar bills. It was more money than she earned in a year. It was about this time that I think she first gave serious consideration to marrying him.

My mother asked my opinion before marrying Johnny. This did not strike me as unusual at the time: My mother consulted me on many of her decisions and often shared her feelings with me, loneliness, joy, discouragement, anxiety. I was twelve. We sat in the living room of the garden apartment in New Brunswick and talked it over. I was in a chair; she was on the couch. She told me she wasn't going to marry Johnny unless I said I approved. After wrestling with the question, I told her I thought it was the right thing for her to do. I thought it would make her happy. Three months later, Paul and I stood by her side on a spring day in 1963 as a minister married them in the garden at my uncle's house in Watchung, New Jersey.

My uncle John, my mother's oldest brother, was a successful executive. He wore a suit and tie to work at Bell Laboratories. I marveled at his prosperity and his life in the suburbs. He had a house with paintings on the walls, extra bedrooms, a swimming pool, and a big lawn. The wedding party gathered on the lawn. My mother wore a pink dress and hat, and Johnny was in a blue suit. The minister asked, "Do you, Helen, take this man, John, to be your lawful wedded husband?" I stood next to my mother. My legs felt weak. One last time, I quickly ran through the reasons for and against the marriage. On one hand, Johnny had brought fun into my mother's life with his motorcycle, his jalopies, and his stories of travel in the Navy and, at the moment, he had a good job. He was earning money and giving it to her. On the other hand, his previous jobs usually ended in disaster and a lot of times he came home drunk or not at all for days. She was bolting her future, and ours, to a man who reminded me, in ways that I wouldn't even whisper to myself in my deepest thoughts, of the unreliability of my father. I worried that I should have stopped her before things had gone this far.

My mother had always said I was a worrier, and standing there in my new brown suit and shiny shoes I certainly was worried. I looked around at the people in the garden, my uncles and cousins, and my new relatives, big-boned people with blond or light brown hair. Polacks, my mother would have called them if her anger had been aroused. Now they were family, new aunts, uncles, and cousins. The wind lifted slightly across the long sloped lawn, and the women in sleeveless dresses crossed their arms against its coolness. When my mother had asked for my opinion of the marriage, which was really her way of asking for my permission, I had resolved that this was what she wanted, a husband. For that reason, so that my mother might be happy, I stood quietly in support of her decision when she said, "I do."

I was the son, but I was also the father giving away the bride. I hoped she would be happy and find security and be able to work less and enjoy more of her life. My mother kissed her new husband, who looked dashing, and I hoped the good feelings would last. Maybe we would all live happily ever after. I came to see clearly much later that what my mother wanted more than anything else was support and encouragement and, since she had gotten neither from her parents, she had hoped to get them from a husband. For the second time, it was to become a misplaced wish.

Later that summer, to celebrate their marriage, Johnny and my mother gave themselves a gift. They bought a house down the shore. I learned of this when I returned from two weeks at Boy Scout camp in the summer of 1963.

"We have some good news, Louis," my mother said.

I knew this could mean only one thing: trouble. We were on the move again. The peace that I had brought back with me from the lake at Camp Sakawawin evaporated in an instant.

I didn't know what to say.

"Is there any fishing there?" I asked.

Johnny assured me that there was.

The house was newly built, a double A-frame with a steep roof that descended almost to the ground. It was preposterously out of place among the small wooded lots and modest ranch and split-level homes. It belonged in a Swiss resort or an amusement park. It was exactly the kind of house that would appeal to my mother's desire for something different and something special. In terms of respectability, it was her grandest gesture yet. No apartment could stand up to it.

It was on a double lot on a street that had been laid out for development in a section of piney woods and marshes near the northern end of Barnegat Bay in Ocean County. The development had a name: Silver Bay. This sounded suspicious to me even before I got there to see it. I later learned that the name on the old maps was Mosquito Cove. One end of the street, which was named for the developer's son, Aldo, was wooded and marked off in low-priced quarter-acre lots; the other end had higher-priced waterfront lots. The "waterfront" was not natural: It had been created by filling in marshland and then digging "lagoons," long, straight canals that connected to the bay. It was an ingenious idea, worthy of a Florida real-estate scam: It increased the amount of waterfront property tenfold. God knows how many ducks, turtles, raccoons, and fish lost their lives to the bulldozers and muddy fill that covered the Barnegat marshes.

The wooded end of the street held maybe a dozen houses with sparse struggling lawns and split-rail fences. The sassafras-choked sandy spaces between the houses grew bigger as the street reached toward the lagoons. One entire lagoon was houseless. These were the early days at Shangri-la at the Shore. Our house was on the wooded end of Aldo Drive. Behind our house was a field, which contained the remnants of a chicken farm, and behind the field there was an undeveloped tract of woods, mostly sassafras, oak, holly, bramble, and scrub pine. Across the street, in front of our house, was more piney woods and marshland that had been scored by a grid of bulldozed dirt roads. The trees flew dozens of fluorescent surveyor's ribbons. The signs up and down the street advertised: "Easy Payments No Money Down." The general impression was of a backwater being pushed reluctantly into "waterfront vacation living."

Our "development," which was what this emerging collection of houses was called, was on the edge of the Pine Barrens, a swathe of sand and scrub pine that cuts across South Jersey. I spent a lot of time in the Pine Barrens. I hunted and fished. I went into the woods because they were beautiful and peaceful and they seemed to understand and accept my solitude. I had developed the habit of being alone: I had been a nervous child. As I entered my teenage years, I drew inward and kept my own company. Solitude works just fine for a boy who loves the woods. You can fish alone, hunt alone, and just walk through the woods alone and be engaged in a conversation with yourself and your surroundings.

You ask yourself, "What made that hole or burrow?"

A set of tracks and stray pieces of black and white hair tell you it was a skunk.

"What is that sound in the tree?"

You look up to see a porcupine chinning himself slowly up the trunk.

"Is that the sound of feeding ducks or a pond full of frogs?"

The clap of wing beats when you approach the marsh grass gives you the answer.

The woods were clean and always new—washed by rain, blanketed by snow, or pushing up new green shoots. The woods were for me a deliverance from the everyday world of argument and discord at home. They also planted in me the notion of metaphor, though I didn't know the word then, a way of making sense of ideas, people, and emotions: the spider's web, the spreading tree trunk, or rivulets that gather to make a stream. They were patterns that embodied logic and beauty. Impressions that had flooded down on me could be made sensible in the woods. Nature, for me, became a way of thinking about the world.

16

It was probably around this time that the ideas of fatherhood and fishing got mixed up in my mind.

"Louis," my mother said. "I think Johnny would like it if you called him Dad. He thinks of you as his son, and he'd like you to think of him as his father."

This didn't sound like my mother. I think she was speaking for Johnny. For nearly a year, life had been going smoothly for us. Johnny had a job, he and my mother were now married, both of their cars were running, and we owned a home. We had our first washer and dryer, which for us, as former apartment dwellers, seemed a symbol of our new economic status. All of this prosperity seemed to derive, indirectly, from the war in Vietnam, which was paying Johnny handsomely. Maybe my mother and John felt that natural next step in our rising fortunes was for me and Paul to regard John as our father and the way to make that happen was for us to begin calling him Dad. Or maybe Johnny felt that way and my mother went along with him. Maybe if we were a family with a mom and dad and two boys, we could extend our luck. But this didn't feel right to me; in fact, it felt unnatural and wrong.

"Dad."

It was such a big word. I couldn't remember ever having used the word. I had successfully pushed back the memory of my real father. I honestly didn't know what I had called him. My mother, brother, and I never spoke of my father. I didn't want to upset my mother.

"Dad."

To speak the word now would somehow rattle that older memory. I wasn't eager to do it; it seemed risky. Maybe it was a buried loyalty to Eugene Ureneck; maybe it was my unconscious desire to avoid disturbing the dead. To me, Eugene Ureneck, my father, might as well have been dead. I don't know. It just seemed wrong. I adored Johnny. I craved the minutes and hours he spent with me. But there seemed to be some step missing between what I felt for him and calling him my father. The distance between him as my mother's boyfriend and him as my father seemed a long way to travel, and my mother's imprecation to use the word "Dad" didn't seem sufficient to help me jump that chasm. To just begin using "Dad" without some understanding between us, or without some deep talk about it, would be fake. I admired Johnny, and I didn't want to introduce a lie between us. That's what it felt like to me, a lie. He wasn't my father. I told everyone who needed to know, if the subject arose, that I didn't have a father. It even made me uncomfortable that my mother was working this out between us, Johnny and me. If he wanted me to say the word, why didn't he ask me? Besides, I didn't remember him ever calling me Son. Why did I have to go first?

I carried the burden of the request for weeks. I looked at it from many different angles, and I paid close attention to my friends when they talked to their fathers. Did they say "Dad," or "Father," or "Pop"? How did they say it, at the beginning of a sentence or at the end? Was it, "Dad, can I stay out late tonight?" or, "Can I stay out late tonight, Dad?" All of this was very consequential to me. I also had to admit, at least to myself, that I was reluctant to use the word because I felt like it would change my place in the scheme of things. I lived with a lot of independence, granted by default by my mother, and the entrance of a father into the picture might close that down. I resented the idea of it.

The other problem of accepting Johnny as my "dad" was that it required me to give up some of the claim I had on protecting my mother. I wasn't sure this was a good idea. I thought of myself as more reliable than either of them. I struggled with her request.

One day when Johnny and I were fishing at one of his secret spots on a creek not far from our new house, I tried to use the word on him. We were fishing for blackfish, a cousin of the grouper, a heavy-scaled fish with fat lips and teeth for crushing its favorite food, crabs. It is a big fish, running to six pounds, and it was a fish that Johnny liked to catch because it was delicious when baked in the oven with onions. We were sitting on the bank of the creek. It was beginning to get dark, and Johnny was smoking a cigarette and watching his fishing line where it went into the water. He had brought along several bottles of beer. He was drinking from one of them. After a while, I pulled in my line and decided to rebait my hook with another crab. The pail of crabs was next to him, and since I couldn't reach it without getting up, this seemed the perfect time to try out the word.

I could say, "Can I have the bait, Dad?" Or, "Dad, can I have the bait?" Or, "Johnny, can I have the bait? And by the way, do you mind if I call you Dad?"

I kept formulating different ways to push the word out of my mouth. It felt like pushing a big box off the back of a truck. It was too heavy to budge. Each formulation sounded worse than the next. This was too much for me. A dad was equivalent to a mom, and my mom was the most important person to me in the world and I knew how important I was to her. She was there for me, in her own way, at least emotionally, the way the sky was always there for me when I looked up. Johnny wasn't. He could be gone tomorrow. I just wasn't ready to call him Dad, and I was sure I would make a mess of an important moment if I tried. I would embarrass us both.

Maybe we would get there one day, I thought, but we weren't there yet. Something more would have to change between us, and as I tried to think of what it might be it occurred to me that it would take some act of reassurance on his part to make me feel that he really was my dad. What would it take for Johnny to make me believe he was going to be my father? It would have had to be something big, like protecting me against some big danger. Or maybe it would be a God-be-my-witness promise that he would stop drinking. That's it—no more bottles of beer in the refrigerator, no more containers from a tavern on Sunday, no more shots of Canadian Club. We all wanted that.

Then I thought of something else he could do: He could go back to Spotswood and thrash the butcher. That would do it: I would hug him afterward and say, "Thank you, Dad, my new and most honorable father. I'm glad you kicked that son of a bitch's ass. Now I shall kick the ass of his son, and the memory of this shall live forever in the annals of Spotswood."

None of these things happened, so I continued to think of Johnny as my mother's boyfriend and a kind of super-big-brother-and-almost-father. I know this disappointed him, but I just couldn't do any better.

Johnny took his gift for adventure into the merchant marine. We got letters from him telling us of his travels. He was on a ship in the Caribbean when President Kennedy ordered a naval blockade of Cuba during the missile crisis. "If war breaks out," Johnny wrote to us in his careful script of printed letters, "all of us onboard are going to go to the side of the ship and throw our coffee cups at the enemy." He sent us letters from Africa. He had shipped out on a freighter from Brooklyn that had unloaded its cargo in Angola, then proceeded up the Congo River to pick up mahogany logs for the trip back to the States. It was a time of the unrest, and his letters told us about the heat, the black nights on the river, and the dangers they had been warned against onshore. My mother would read the letters first, and then she would hand them to Paul and me to read together. They always spoke directly to my mom, beginning: "Dear Lynn," but they contained asides for me and Paul about what Johnny was experiencing or what we would do when he got home. I carefully peeled all the foreign stamps from the envelopes and put them in a scrapbook.

"Tell Louis," he wrote to my mom in one of his letters, "that I am getting stamps for him in all of these countries, and that another guy and I were fishing off the back of the ship when we were anchored in the river and caught two big bass on bait from the kitchen."

Johnny was at home at sea, but he also came back each time with forebodings about the dangers of these trips. He wasn't his easy self when he returned. He seemed troubled, worried, and reluctant to return. He was losing his confidence. Each time he came back, he also drank more heavily, and the amount of money he brought home to my mother was decreasing. After one long trip, to Australia, with presumably a big payoff, he came home broke. He had no money at all. His brother had met him at the dock in Staten Island, and the two of them had gone to the Monmouth racetrack and lost Johnny's entire four months' pay. It was money my mother had been counting on to pay the mortgage. My mother commenced a verbal assault on him that stretched over days, and then she stopped talking to him. He barely defended himself and stayed drunk for most of a week.

During his time at sea, I had allowed myself to begin trusting him. Our communication was through letters: my letters to him and his letters to my mother that contained messages to me. He said we would go fishing and hunting when he returned, and he encouraged me to be good in school and good to my mother. "Take good care of your mother, Louis. I will be home soon." In one letter, he even asked my mother for our forgiveness and understanding, my mother, brother, and me. He named each of us. He was expressing contrition for his drinking without using the word. He said he would do better and that we should have faith in him. I had a map on my bedroom wall, a big Mercator projection of the world, and I marked the course of his ship on it with pins and little flags as we received his letters.

He came home with trinkets, souvenirs, stamps, paintings, handbags, and carved figures, and in the beginning of his stint in the merchant marine he and I did go fishing and hunting in some nearby towns. But each time he returned, he seemed more damaged and farther down the road of his alcoholism. I wanted badly to save him; he seemed to be asking to be saved. Was that the reason he was telling us that it was harder and harder for him to ship out? It was obvious that he shouldn't be drinking and that he had to find a way to stop. I couldn't find a way to say this. All of us saw it, but none of us could speak of it. He was collapsing and my heart was breaking. We all were watching this, and he was beginning to turn mean as he collapsed. In her disappointment, my mother began attacking him the way I remembered her attacking Eugene Ureneck.

One thing that I knew that I could do for Johnny was make him a good cup of coffee. He loved coffee and drank gallons of it. It was a habit he developed on the merchant ships. Seamen worked a schedule of four hours on duty and eight hours off duty, around the clock, so they were constantly moving between sleep and work. They made the pivot with caffeine. They came to rely on their cups of coffee, taken black in a heavy mug, to get them through their daily and nightly routines, and they knew a good cup of coffee from a bad cup. Coffee was my way of bribing him out of bed on mornings when we were supposed to go fishing.

I remember one morning in March in what was probably 1965 that was like so many others: I woke early, at 6:00 A.M., and stepped out of bed and into my dungarees. I went downstairs to the kitchen and pulled out the makings for coffee: the tin percolator pot from under the sink, the can of coffee grinds from the cupboard over the sink, a jar that contained dried chicory and a box of salt. Johnny had said the secret to a good cup of coffee was chicory and a little salt. I rinsed the pot and scrubbed out the brown residue from the previous batch and cleared the spout of old grinds. I filled the pot with cold water. Johnny had told me that it had to be cold water to begin with. I rinsed the basket and stem that would stand inside the pot, and I made sure the glass bubble on the pot's top was clean. I squeezed the flat handles of the can opener, and its flanged jaw bit into the edge of the coffee can. It released its vacuum with a gentle *pfffft*. I cranked the can opener around the circle of the coffee can and I threw the jagged disk top that came off into the trash. I measured eight tablespoons of coffee into the basket and added a ninth "for the pot." I put a sprig of chicory and a dash of salt into in the basket with the grinds.

Another of Johnny's secrets to good coffee was to put a few broken eggshells in with the grinds. He said they made the coffee less acidic. I had saved a few from the day before. I set the perforated cover on the basket containing the grinds and carefully put the stem and basket into the pot. I pushed the cover with the glass bulb onto the top. I turned on the gas and waited for the first perk. I didn't want the water to boil over, because that would push some of the grinds out of the basket and into the water of the pot. A perfect cup of coffee didn't contain grinds. I wanted to make the perfect cup. At the first *plop,* when the coffee moved up the stem to the glass bubble, I turned the heat to low. I looked at the clock. The coffee should perk for exactly eight minutes. I had managed to turn the making of coffee into a ritual nearly as elaborate as preparing a mass.

As I watched the clock, my mother came into the kitchen. She worked on Saturdays, a half day.

"Why are you up so early on a Saturday?"

"Johnny and I are going fishing," I said.

"Be careful," she said. "Don't take chances near the water."

I set out three cups, one for Johnny, one for my mother, and one for me, and poured the coffee. It filled the house with a warm roasted smell. I had opened the door to the bedroom Johnny was sleeping in. It was the extra bedroom and not the bedroom where my mother had slept last night. He had been drinking the previous night, and getting him up to go fishing would be difficult. I hoped by opening the door I would make the smell of the coffee find its way to his nose and that the muted bustle of me in the kitchen would begin to wake him. I carried the coffee in to him in a mug and set it on the table next to the couch. He was still asleep, with an arm thrown over his head. He snored when he slept.

"Johnny," I said. "Here's a cup of coffee. It's fresh. I just made it."

I waited, but he didn't move.

"Would you like a cup of coffee?" I persisted.

He lifted his arm from his head and opened his eyes. They were rimmed with red and bloodshot.

"Leave it next to the bed," he said.

"We were going fishing today," I said.

"Give me another hour to sleep," he said.

I knew from many previous mornings trying to wake him that the request for an extra hour of sleep was not a good sign. A delay could mean that he would spend all morning in bed. I was going to try to not let that happen.

"Okay," I said. "I'll be back in an hour. I'll be back at seven."

I went back out to the kitchen to drink my coffee and watch the clock. I was going to give him just a half hour before returning.

"Is he getting up?" my mother asked. She was about ready to leave for work.

"He says he wants another hour," I said.

My mother looked disgusted. She was, after all, on her way to work. She got up from the table, where she had been eating an egg that she had fried, and went to the room where Johnny was asleep. I wanted him to get up, but I didn't want an argument to erupt between my mother and him, so I wasn't sure how I felt about her going to the room.

"Louis is waiting for you to get up," she said. "You said you were taking him fishing. The boy is waiting for you to take him fishing."

"Leave me alone, for chrissake, will you," I heard him say.

"Look at you," she said. "You're a disgrace."

My mother came back out and finished her breakfast.

I heard John get up and go into the bathroom. The water was running in the sink, and the toilet flushed several times. My mother left for work.

"Call me at work," she said.

In the years that Johnny's drinking worsened and as our financial situation deteriorated, my mother became more and more anxious. Her old defiance was in tatters. She was always asking me to call her at work, when I left for school, got home from school, arrived at some destination. She had frequent premonitions of car accidents or drownings. I said that I would call her. She told me again to be careful. I heard her drive off. Eventually, Johnny came out of the bathroom, in pants and a T-shirt, in bare feet. His hair was tousled and his eyes tired.

I poured him another cup of coffee.

"Where should we go?" he said.

"Maybe that place where you said the flounder were running," I said.

"Okay. Why don't you warm up the car and get the rods?"

I was elated. I had already pulled the rods and tackle box together. I had even strung the rods with hooks and weights. I put them in the backseat of the car, their tips sticking out the rear window. I took his keys from the ring by the side door and went out to start the little English Ford. I depressed the clutch, pulled out the choke, and stepped on the floor starter. It turned over, coughed, and started up. This was a good sign: We weren't going to have to push it down the road. I sat feathering the accelerator long enough to consider it safely running and not likely to die when I stepped out of it. I went inside, made another pot of coffee, and filled a thermos jug. Together Johnny and I went out to the car, and he suggested that I, who was then thirteen, back the car out of the yard and drive it down the street to the main road. I was happy to comply. I liked to drive, and the offer meant he was in a good mood. It appeared that we would go fishing on this day after all. We switched seats at the main road, and off we went.

17

It turned out to be the last time he took me fishing, back to the river at Keyport. Johnny shipped out again, but his drinking worsened. He came home and went back to working odd jobs in the area. He would be okay for a while, then would begin drinking again. My mother was increasingly anxious and strung out. Most of their fights were out in the open, but there was something else that was going on. At first it eluded me; then I pieced it together from the fights that they had late at night after I had gone to bed. There was a battle raging over their inability to have a child together. It was now becoming clear to me why my mother had mysteriously spent two nights in the hospital a month earlier. I hadn't been able to get a clear explanation from her. "Female problems," was all that I could draw out of her. This was unusual. My mother had always shared everything with me. She had finally found the place where she would draw the line of talk with her son: a miscarriage. One night, this new battle between them erupted into the open during a particularly vicious shouting match: Johnny spit out something about her not being able to make him a family; my mother shot back that the problem was that he wasn't man enough to make a child.

They both were in deep pain and I tried to break up their arguments, but I was unable to pull them back from their attacks on each other. I tried. Johnny told my mother he was leaving. I begged him not to.

"You can't leave," I said. "You're part of this family."

I blamed myself for this. I thought, Maybe if I had called him Dad there wouldn't have been this need for a baby. I stood there and watched Johnny walk out the door. I saw the lights of the car as he pulled out of the driveway. The house was suddenly quiet, and my mother sat at the kitchen table just looking at her hands. My mother had small, strong hands that were permanently stained with hair dye and peroxide.

I stood next to my mother.

"What can I do for you, Mom?" I asked.

"I'll be all right, Louis," she said. "Don't worry. I'm tough. I won't let him talk to me like that."

I knew she was a wreck. Paul and I went to bed, relieved that at least for now the battle was over.

Several hours later, around midnight, I was awakened by a loud crash. I felt the entire house shake. I couldn't imagine what had happened. Was there an earthquake? I pulled on my pants and ran downstairs. I saw a car's headlights shining in the front window. I looked out and saw that Johnny had driven the car into the side of the house. He was getting out of the car, and he was stumbling. The front of the car was crushed on one side. My mother came into the living room, from her bedroom. She told Paul and me to get to our bedrooms. We went to the stairs but no farther. We stood next to each other, fearing what would happen next.

Johnny came into the house, and my mother began screaming at him.

"Leave me alone, will you." His words were slurred.

He dropped into a chair at the kitchen table. She stood over him.

"What the hell is this?" she screamed. "Are you trying to kill us? Look what you've done to the house. You're scaring the kids. You wrecked my car."

She kept it up. I wanted her to stop. I thought we should get out of the house.

"You could've driven that car right into the kitchen. What if the boys had been in the kitchen? You could've killed us. Look at the car! Look at the house! Look at what you've done!"

He stood and grabbed her hard by the arm

"Shut up!" he shouted at her.

She shook loose from his grip and went to the telephone. Johnny just sat at the table, in a stupor. She got off the phone and began screaming again.

"The police are coming. You could have killed us."

The police came. They knocked once and just walked in. I saw the guns in their holsters, and one of them was holding a wooden baton. They saw Johnny at the table with his head down, and without even asking any questions, they stood him up, pulled his arms around his back, and handcuffed him. He offered no resistance. One of the policemen took Johnny out to the police car while the other asked my mother to calm down. The blue lights of the police car spun round and came in through the window. They swept across the kitchen wall. The policeman came back into the house. He asked my mother to explain what had happened. He wrote it down.

Then he said to my mother, "We're taking him in."

He gave her a piece of paper.

"This is my name. You can call this number in the morning."

The two of them went out to the police car and pulled away, the blue lights still spinning. I was sure the neighbors had seen what had happened.

My mother sat at the table. She kept smoothing the tablecloth in front of her and working her hands.

"Why don't you boys get back up to bed," she said.

"Can I get you something, Mom?" I asked.

"No. I will be all right."

Paul and I went upstairs to our bedrooms. We didn't say anything to each other. I laid out my clothes for school the next morning and thought about what had just happened. I felt sorry for both of them: Johnny's drinking was the source of the problem, but my mother's screaming was making it worse. They were going round and round and kept hurting each other. I couldn't see how it would end. I read a little from my English textbook. We were studying *A Midsummer Night's Dream*. I got to the part about the play in the forest, stopped reading, and went to check on my brother. Then I went to sleep, too.

Three days later, after Johnny promised a judge that he would attend AA meetings, my mother bailed Johnny out. They didn't speak to each other for days.

The arrest chastened Johnny. He acted contrite around the house. He cooked our meals and sat quietly in front of the television set. He stopped drinking for about two weeks. The incident, though, broke something inside my mother. She was perpetually anxious. Johnny wasn't drinking, but he wasn't working, either. We fell behind on the mortgage payments. After several warning letters from the bank, a sign was stapled to a pole in front of our house. It declared the property to be in foreclosure. We had tried everything to avoid it: I had an aluminum rowboat that my uncle had given me; it was my prized possession. I went fishing with it in the bay. My mother asked me if we could sell it. She looked embarrassed. I said yes. We put a classified ad in the newspaper and sold it for one hundred dollars. It left us about two hundred dollars short of what was needed. Finally, we got a letter that gave us the date by which we would have to be out. If we continued to occupy the house, the letter said, we would be removed by the sheriff. We packed the car with boxes of dishes, sheets and blankets, pots, and our clothes. A friend with a pickup truck helped us move the furniture. We moved into a garden apartment, in nearby Toms River, close to my high school. I was a junior by then.

The loss of the house made it clear to me that we would never have a normal life. My mother's anxiety worsened, and she closed her shop in Spotswood. She took an hourly job as the manager of a beauty shop in Lakewood. She was depressed over the loss of the house and her beauty shop. I tried to cheer her up by spending nights with her watching television or going out to dinner in a nearby diner down the street from the apartment. Slowly, she seemed to make a recovery. Johnny was still with us, and he was drinking in spells. He would be dry for two months, and then he would come home drunk. He would be gone for days, but he was no longer violent. He slept off his drunks in their bedroom. I saw that I couldn't help him. I set my mind on getting into college: I filled out the applications that I had sent away for and applied for financial aid. I felt guilty for wanting to leave my mother; I could think of nothing else but getting out of Toms River, away from New Jersey, and into college. I was accepted by the University of New Hampshire. I won a Pell Grant, a scholarship for students whose families had low incomes, and another scholarship from the New Jersey Department of Education. I declared my major (wildlife biology) and chose the least expensive dormitory on campus, Engelhard Hall. It had been thrown up after World War II to accommodate the flood of veterans. I shared a room with two boys from rural New Hampshire. I was lean and tough and on my guard, and to them I talked funny. Another boy,

Frank, a football player from Chelsea, Massachusetts, gave me my new nickname: Jersey. Frank would say to me, "Hey, Joisey, you need more time with the ladies." I liked Frank and palled around with him, but I also bought a book, *How to Speak Better English*. Soon when I wanted a hot drink in the morning I ordered a "coffee" and not a "cawffee," and "wawt'r" became "water." When I went back to New Jersey that summer, my mother said, "You sound different. You're beginning to talk like you're from Boston." Secretly, I was pleased with my progress. In high school, when most of the boys I knew greased and combed their hair straight back, I parted mine high on the left and pushed it flat across my forehead without a wave. I thought it looked more "collegiate." Losing my Jersey accent was one more step in making myself into a college man.

In my sophomore year at college, my mother, Paul, and Johnny moved to a rented house about a mile away from a second garden apartment. It was a small wood-framed house with a backyard. It was old-fashioned, with a pantry next to the kitchen, and homey. I saw it over Thanksgiving break and liked it. One night during the winter, my mother called me at my dormitory pay phone to tell me that Johnny had fallen asleep on the couch with a lit cigarette and burned down part of the house.

"Everybody is safe," she said.

Johnny was spiraling downward. I went home for the summer, to the small house, which had been repaired but still smelled smoky. I worked a construction job. Housing developments seemed to be going up everywhere. Johnny hardly got out of bed during the day. One day, in August, he left the house on a Saturday afternoon. He didn't have a car; he just walked out. He didn't take his clothes; he didn't say anything: He just didn't come back. One day passed, then two days, three days. We didn't know where to look for him.

"He's gone," my mother said.

She was sad, but she was also relieved.

I returned to college in September and tried to put my mind to my studies. By then, I had changed my major to English. I had become absorbed in the study of literature. I had fallen in love with the poetry of John Milton in a class taught by an elderly southern professor with great enthusiasm for *Paradise Lost*. I committed Milton's "Lycidas" to memory. It was the first poem I memorized. It was a sad poem, and its beauty and wistfulness appealed to me. I worked forward, chronologically, and packed in courses on the Augustine poets, the Romantics, the Victorians, and finally a glorious graduate-level course on the modern novel. I discovered Henry James, André Gide, Albert Camus.

About a year later Johnny and my mother were divorced; my mother had completed the papers and action in his absence. My mother heard through the grapevine of friends from Spotswood that he had moved to Florida, where he was living with a woman and working construction on the new Disney World that was being built there. Then we heard that he was sick, problems with his heart. Then we stopped hearing anything.

Twenty years later, when I was married, living in Maine, and had my own children, my mother called me. She was sobbing.

"What's the matter, Mom?"

"Johnny's dead," she said. "His brother, Charles, just called me. He had a heart attack."

Johnny's brother told my mother that he had already been buried, at sea, by the Navy. The arrangements had been made by his mother. There was no funeral. Once again, we were left with a void. This time even his body was gone, deep in the ocean somewhere.

For the first time, I told Adam and Elizabeth about John Kababick. They were eleven and fifteen. I sat them down and explained how he had been part of my life when I was a boy.

"He had been like a father to me," I said.

And then I sat down and cried.

III. BACK ON THE RIVER, IN THE RAIN

The Middle River gave us good fishing. In fact, it was the best fishing I had ever experienced. We encountered our first pod of pink salmon, toothy little bastards with mean eyes that fought like tomcats. We also began picking up torpedo-shaped silvers. They struck only the egg-sucking leech patterns. They hung in the back eddies and sloughs, out of the main current, and in the deepest water. I caught the first rainbow trout of the trip and the second and third ones, too. The first was a massive and royal fish, nearly two feet long and as fat as a September cucumber. The weather was awful, moving between a heavy mist and a steady downpour. It was the kind of weather Maine lobstermen called snotty. We were too busy catching fish to care.

By now, we were on a diet that was almost exclusively fish and unsweetened tea. I was losing weight; I felt the pounds coming off. My whiskers, unshaven for nearly a week, had begun to show as a beard. I had caught my reflection in the skillet one morning as I scrubbed it clean and was amazed to see that my beard had come in gray. I didn't recognize myself. When had I gotten this old?

The rain and dampness penetrated everything. The cardboard box of salt in the gear bag was limp, and the salt itself had been made lumpy by the moisture. The rods, the stove, the tent bag, the fly boxes—everything was wet and dripping. We were deeply settled into a familiarity with our gear and the daily packing and unpacking, cooking and eating, and the fishing. At the end of the sixth day, with fifty miles of river behind us, we set up camp on a big broad bar across and just downstream from an elbow bend in the river. It was a haunted-looking place with chest-high willows and two big aspen trees lying on their sides, root systems intact, which had been dropped by some earlier flood. They were draped with dead grass, also pulled up and swept downstream by the current. The river water was black, and it swirled angrily around the bend.

For a stretch of about fifty yards it made whirling funnels that moved in the current, their vortexes appearing and disappearing and getting swallowed in the downstream rush. It was unsettling, even scary, but we decided that we had to take it for our camp since we might not find another for a long distance. Together we set up the tent, shaking it hard like a bedsheet between us to remove the beads of water before laying it flat on the ground, inserting the poles, and pulling tight the fabric that would be our shelter against the foul weather.

Sometime in the middle of the night, as I had been moving through anxious dreams, a vague discomfort had begun to make itself felt down my right side. It winched me up from subterranean sleep. I was drifting in the weightless space between sleeping and waking, not quite one and not the other, either. My dreams had evaporated with my ascent toward waking, and I knew that they had been unpleasant only by a slight residual feeling of alarm. In recent years, I had grown used to coming awake and feeling jangled in the nerves.

The bag I was sleeping in was a cheap model from Kmart. Made of nylon, cotton, and polyester stuffing, the bag, a thin blue-quilted rectangle that wasn't quite long enough for my body, was probably intended for a children's summer sleepover in a suburban backyard. Maybe two five-year-olds were supposed to sleep in it or one twelve-year-old and a teddy bear. I had bought it years ago, when the kids were small, for a family outing. I had judged that this toy bag would be adequate for me in Alaska, one more sign of the mania of economy and desperation that had gripped me in the run-up to this trip. I hadn't anticipated that Alaskan temperatures would drop much below forty degrees in late summer, and if they did I had figured I could put on extra clothes. I hadn't counted on nearly all of my clothes being wet. It was a good thing I hadn't planned the ascent of a Nepalese mountain as Adam's graduation gift: I might have picked up the belaying lines at the True Value.

I tried to get warm in the sleeping bag, but when I grasped it to pull it closer to my neck and chest, the way a baby tugs at its blanket, I found myself with a handful of wet fabric. The bag had been a little damp, near its bottom, from my unpacking the previous night when I let it drop to the ground, but now it was sopping wet, dishrag wet: wet enough to squeeze out water. I cursed my inability to pull together the two hundred dollars to buy a good bag. Unconsciously I wiggled away from the wetness, hoping to find enough dry space to resume my sleep. The wetness pursued me deeper into the bag. I tried rolling away from it, but when my hand came down on the tent floor it landed in a pool of water.

Now fully awake, I reached down into the bag to determine how wet it really was, and I found that it was soaked for most of its length down one side and across the middle. I opened my eyes and felt for the flashlight I kept behind my head. I could hear the rain. It was coming down rhythmically, with an occasional drumroll. I shined the flashlight to investigate. The tent was leaking along a seam directly over my bag. In steady drops, the water was falling from several places along the line of stitches. I put on my glasses, which I also kept behind my head, and saw the threads and the needle holes they passed through and the drops of water gathering before they splashed down. I slithered out of the bag and, stooping under the low ceiling of the tent, took off my pants, which had become wet along the left leg. I opened the bag completely and folded it inside out, trying to give myself a narrow dry space on which to lie and sleep. This was not so easily done in the tight half sphere of the tent. I was trying not to wake Adam.

The water had collected in small puddles on the floor of the tent where I had been sleeping. My moving around had only made the bag wetter. We were on a slight slope, and Adam was on the uphill side. The water was dripping above my bag, and it was puddling on my side of the tent. I passed the light up and down the length of his bag. It was bone-dry. Having pulled his head inside the bag, he was invisible except as a long mound. His bag was a deluxe extra-large down-filled mummy job with a water-resistant surface. I had bought it for him at L.L.Bean for a trip he had taken in high school to the White Mountains. Had his side of the tent been leaking, chances are the bag would have simply shed the water and kept him dry. He was sound asleep. If I could have found a way to get even partially comfortable in the wet bag, I would have slept through the dripping and dealt with the problem in the morning. I was that tired. I decided to check outside the tent to see if a fix was possible. I had to take some action to stop the dripping or at least get dry and find some way to catch some sleep.

I unzipped the tent flap and stepped out into the night in my rain jacket and undershorts. Here was a sight for the cover of *Fly Fisherman* magazine: the American father in his skivvies trying past midnight to fix a tent that had sprung a leak. This was what it was really like to fish in Alaska. I peeled off my socks and pranced barefoot in the dark over the wet stones to a plastic dry bag and dug around for pants, shirt, and socks. I quickly put on the pants and shirt and covered myself back up with my rain jacket. I kept the socks in the pocket of my jacket: Socks that were dry were too valuable to expose to the weather. I investigated the tent and saw that the storm fly was sagging and soaked. It looked like a limp, wet sheet strung between two clotheslines. The rain was finding its way underneath and saturating the tent on my side, which was catching the force of the gale. There wasn't much to be done now, in the darkness and wind. I surveyed the campsite. I could see about one hundred feet into the darkness. Even at 1:00 A.M. in the rain, enough light seeped from the horizon to keep the night from going completely black, more like the heavy shading of a No. 2 pencil than a piece of charcoal. The edges of the willows and a couple of stunted birches appeared in silhouette, but the land beyond, the tundra and the distant mountains, was lost in smudge. I shined the light on the river. It had risen a few inches under the hard rain. When the wind gusted, the river looked as if it were being sprayed by a garden hose. I turned the light on the raft and saw that water was gathering in the bottom and a fly box floated in a pond of black water at the stern. The bushes on both sides of the raft drooped under the weight of the wetness and the pounding of the rain. The campsite seemed forlorn: the stove, a pot, bags, rods, all dripping wet.

I had started back toward the tent, picking my way carefully, when I caught something sharp under my foot. I hopped on one foot, once and twice, and then slipped on the wet stones. I put out my hand to break my fall and came down hard on it. My thumb jammed against a rock. I felt the pain all the way up my shoulder. I just stood there in the rain thinking I would vomit. I put my thumb into my armpit and squeezed hard to try to relieve the pain. I went back to the tent, my thumb hot and beginning to swell.

Inside, I folded my bag, with some dry fabric faceup, giving me something to kneel on. Now what? I couldn't sleep sitting up because there was nothing to lean against, and I couldn't lie down. Adam's side was still dry, and he was invisible inside the big mummy bag. I couldn't keep kneeling like this. It seemed to me that his bag would be big enough for two of us, and now that I was dressed in dry clothes, the thought occurred to me that I could get inside with him until morning. It would be tight, but it would be dry and we could both get a night's sleep. There seemed to be no other choice. I was exhausted.

"Adam," I said. "Adam."

I was calling him from that far shore that he traveled to in sleep.

"What?" he barked.

He spoke without taking his head out of the bag. He was perturbed at having been woken up.

"The tent's leaking. My bag's soaked."

"Yeah, so?"

He wasn't going to make this easy for me.

"I need to get into your sleeping bag with you."

"No way, Dad," he said.

He didn't move. Letting his father into his sleeping bag was an intimacy he wasn't going to allow. There was no way that he was going to let me, with my father-stink, into his sleeping bag next to him. I had come to the wrong place for a favor. He didn't even pull his head out of the bag to gauge the extent of my predicament.

"I'm dressed, and I'm dry. Come on; there's room enough for the two of us."

"Forget it."

He burrowed into his bag, his first movement since I had awakened him, pulling the top tighter down on his head. This was his signal that he wanted the conversation to be over. I persisted.

"Adam. I'll be still, and we can both get some sleep. I've got nowhere to sleep."

"No way. You're not getting in my bag."

His voice was resolute, and I wasn't going to be able to plead my way into his bag. The only way into the bag was going to be by force. I would have to pull it open and fight my way in. This was one more expression of his unrelenting anger, and I felt powerless in the face of it. I was still capable of taking him in a fight if it came to that, and surely it would if I tried to shimmy into the bag. There would be a wrestling match, and we would rip the bag and knock down the tent and there would be blood and more anger. Had it really come to this?

I sat back on my heels and tried to find some way that I could remain in the tent and sleep. Leaning against the wall of the tent was out of the question. The tent fabric would leak if I touched it, and it probably wouldn't support my weight anyway. Exasperated, I left the tent, taking the shotgun with me. If a bear wandered into camp, I didn't want to greet it unarmed. I put on the dry socks, pulled on my waders, zipped my rain jacket to my chin, and lifted its storm hood over my head. I searched the sodden scene for a plan: It was too wet to build a fire. Could I tip the raft and use it as a shelter? No, it was too heavy to pull from the river by myself. There were no trees big enough to offer a canopy from the rain, and even if there had been, the rain was so steady and deliberate, the leaves and branches would have made a leaky umbrella.

In waders and rain jacket, I was basically watertight, but I was tired and craved sleep. I walked around, checked the campsite, and saw a rock that I could lean against. The ground was flat. I sat down, sidled into place, and pulled the drawstring on my hood tight so that only my eyes were exposed to the weather. I might as well have been inside a ziplock bag. I shivered and hunched my shoulders. The rain was hitting me from behind. I was cold, and I was miserable.

The trip had definitely hit its low point. I was sitting on the ground in the pouring rain, cold and aching for sleep. My son had refused me space in his sleeping bag. My sleeping bag probably would be wet for days. It would take hours of rare and precious sunlight to dry it. I had exhausted my stash of dry clothes. It had been raining off and on for days, and it probably would continue to rain until the end of the trip. I felt wet down to my soul. The trip was a mistake, I thought. My persistence in putting it together, without enough money and without Adam's support, had been an act of stupidity. I had been a fool to stick with it. For three years I had been packing peanut butter sandwiches and counting my change in the morning to decide whether I could afford the bus to work. How did I expect to afford a trip to Alaska? I had been out of my mind to bring us here. It had been unrealistic from the start. It was just plain dumb.

I knew that there was love and hurt on the other side of Adam's fury, but I didn't know how to reach it. At first, I had tried to get there through talk; that hadn't worked. Then, I had hoped that the passage of time and steadiness and understanding would diminish it. That also failed. Everything had failed, and my son had sent me out into the rain.

The only thing he wanted from me was the one thing I couldn't give, and that was the return of his family. I had wanted a family, too, and I had wanted to give to him what I hadn't gotten as a boy and I wanted this desperately, but instead I was inflicting on him the pain that had been inflicted on me. Given my failure as a father, wasn't his anger justified? What possible response could I make but contrition? In the face of my failure, the only reply seemed to be forbearance and patience and the acceptance of the barbs of his anger until it had spent itself. Then we could start over.

Of course, there was more: I had learned a long time ago that human relationships were fragile and that even the bonds that were supposed to be the strongest—parent and child— could be broken. Hadn't my father left me? And what about Johnny? Hadn't he been willing to just walk out, too? So, below the guilt there was also this: By putting myself first and seeking a divorce, I had put the relationship with my son at risk, and I feared that unless I made a superhuman effort to hold on to him, I would lose him. Not that I would walk out on him but that he would walk out on me. This had always been in the background for me. That the people who were closest to me in my life would leave me, that I would be abandoned and alone. There was hardly anything I wouldn't do to prevent it, including sleeping in the rain.

My breath filled the jacket and soon began to warm my neck and chest. Well, that was a little better. I was tired enough to sleep sitting up. What the hell, I thought, this is one more disaster in a long line of disasters. It almost made me want to laugh: a fatalistic laugh. At least it wasn't likely to get any worse. This was rock bottom. Sure, I was miserable, but when it came to adversity, I had a world-class ability to suck it up. Wasn't this one of my few good attributes, the ability to suck it up? As they said about boxers, I could take a punch. It was a compliment to punch-drunks and losers. I was a loser. Maybe I had been trained for this; it's what everything else had prepared me for: taking a punch.

When I was a kid, I remembered boxing in a friend's basement. I was a gangly boy and my weight was a long time catching up to my height, better in the classroom than the football field. I had gone out for the cross-country team, the odd-ball club for boys who were smart loners or couldn't make the football team, and from there, with only mediocre results as a long-distance runner, I went out for the track team the following spring. It was a more respectable setting. I ended up hanging out during the season with another boy, Jimmy Baldwin. Jimmy was a smart aleck and sometime bully and the best quarter miler on the track team. He actually won his races against other schools. One day, we ended up at his house after practice, in the basement, where he pulled out two pairs of boxing gloves. He and I decided that we would set up a ring with some rope and box two-minute rounds. We would time them on a big clock that hung on the wall. He was smaller than I was and fast, very fast, and as good at boxing, I was soon to learn, as he was at running the quarter mile. His jabs, quick as a snake's tongue, kept finding their target: my chin, my nose, my eyes. In the third round, my nose and lip were bleeding. His jabs were fast and mean. I was strong but slow. He was on his toes; I was flat on my feet. In the fourth round, my left eye closed. We had no referee, and I wasn't going to stop, not if I could stay on my feet. I was too proud and too angry to stop. Each blow to my face hurt, and each made me angrier and more steadfast. I brought my forearms up against his jabs and looked for a chance to take my shot. When I threw a hard right, he slipped his head out of the way and hit me with a combination: right fist, *pow,* left fist, *pow.* My head swung back, dazed.

The idea of the rounds disappeared, and we just kept fighting. Mostly, it was a matter of Jimmy pummeling me. But an odd thing happened: Out of my right eye I could see fear in his eyes. It wasn't fear of me. It was fear of the mess he was making of my face, of the blood, torn lip, and swollen left eye and my embarrassing and stupid stubbornness to keep fighting. I could read his mind: This dope doesn't know he's beat. Jimmy didn't know how this was going to end or when it would end. Would it ever end? He couldn't put me away, and I wouldn't quit. He kept doing his damage. *Pow!* My head snapped back. *Pow!* again. There was no one to stop the fight. We had forgotten to decide how long this would go on. It was becoming a fight that would last until one of us gave up and said, "Enough." My pride wouldn't let me give up. I could see the pleading in his narrowing eyes: For God's sake, give it up. I kept coming at him. Finally he said, "That's it." It was a sorry performance, but it taught me something important about myself. I had a skill: I could take a beating and stay on my feet. Jimmy Baldwin could outrun me and outpunch me, but he couldn't knock me off my feet. He couldn't make me give up. I was not a quitter. A night in the rain was nothing compared to that mauling in the basement.

The rain seemed to be letting up. I closed my eyes and tried to find a way to be comfortable. I kicked my legs back and forth to push the rocks out of the way, plowing two shallow trenches with my heels so I could sit and lay my legs flat. I worked my seat into the ground. With the gun across my lap to keep it off the ground, I put my hands into my sleeves and folded my arms across my chest for warmth. My shivering had stopped. The rain dripped from the bill of my hood and landed in my lap. I leaned back against my rock and dropped my chin to my chest. In this way, with my son snug in his dry bag and me fifteen feet away and sealed in a rubber suit, we spent the night of Day Six.

In the morning, I was sore and not at all rested, but I had actually gotten through the night. The storm had stopped sometime while I slept. As I stood up, I pushed my hands into the small of my back and tried to straighten out. I felt like a jackknife with a rusty hinge. I went to the stove and heated a pot of water for tea. Adam emerged from the tent, smiling from his good night's sleep. He put on a look of surprise. His face went long, and he lifted his eyebrows.

"What? You slept out here in the rain?" he asked.

"Yeah, I slept out here. Most of the damned night I slept out here in the rain. Where did you think I slept?"

I didn't look up from the steaming pot.

"What was that like?"

Was he asking because he was embarrassed at casting me out, or was this false curiosity, a lame attempt at empathy? I couldn't tell. At this point, I didn't care.

"What do you think it was like," I said. "It was pretty damned awful."

Then, I think not to allow me the moral advantage that suffering confers on a victim, he said with a note of sarcasm, "Why didn't you just stay in the tent?"

I was angry and unwilling to engage him any further. I gave no answer. I was completely and utterly at one with my martyrdom.

"You should have stayed in the tent," he said, ensuring that he would have the last word. "At least you would've stayed dry."

IV. MARRIAGE AND DIVORCE

When we moved to New Brunswick I bought the fly rod and taught myself to use it on the grass between the apartment buildings, but I had lost a place to fish. The brook, the lake, the Point—all of it was gone, back in Spotswood. In the city, I explored the neighborhood around our apartment, went to the bowling alley down by the railroad tracks, rode the city bus to the movies, and hung around Jack's Sweet Shop across from my new school, Lee Avenue Elementary. The teenagers who sat in the wood booths at Jack's played "The Lion Sleeps Tonight" over and over again on the jukebox. It was the big hit in 1961.

Fishing had filled every day of my life, and now it was gone. I needed something to take its place. One Saturday, after the matinee got out at the Rivoli Theater, I was walking around downtown looking for something to occupy me. I saw a stone church, St. Paul's, on a crowded side street. I recognized the red, white, and blue shield of Saint George next to the front door. It was an Episcopal church. The church in

Spotswood, where I had sung (badly) in the junior choir and studied the catechism with Father Cox, was an Episcopal church with the same red and blue shield. I took a closer look at the sign that listed the times of the Sunday services. The next morning I showed up at church. I liked the hushed space. Red and green light from the stained-glass windows fell onto the wood pews and the floor. I followed the service from a back pew. I went again the following Sunday. After five Sundays, I asked the priest if I could be an altar boy. He seemed delighted.

So, every Sunday morning after delivering my newspapers to the apartment buildings and three-decker houses in the neighborhood, I rode the Livingston Avenue bus downtown to the church. I went through the chevron-shaped wooden door on the side and into the vestry, where I put on my maroon and white robe. My job was to attend the priest at the 8:00 A.M. and 10:00 A.M. services. I moved silver boxes and chalices, starched linen napkins, and brocade prayer cushions as the priest stepped, sang, chanted, and knelt his way through the service.

At the end, he walked to the back of the church and intoned his final blessing to the congregation of mostly old women: "May the peace of the Lord that passeth all understanding be with you and among you always."

The words were my cue to snuff the candles with a long brass stick. It's obvious now, though it wasn't then, that altar boys and fly fishermen have a lot in common: In church, the collect always precedes the reading of the Gospels, and in the liturgy of fly-fishing the sequence of mayfly hatches follows an unvarying sequence: first the quill Gordons, then Hendricksons, pale evening duns, and then the light Cahills. There is a right way to hand to the priest the books and objects he uses to conduct the service, and there is a right way to tie a clinch knot and a Bimini twist. Religion and fly-fishing offer certitudes in a disorderly life.

After the service, I helped the priest remove his layers of heavy silk vestments in the sacristy and I pulled off my own robe and hung it in a cedar wardrobe. Then, on some sunny mornings in the warmer months, the priest and his wife invited me to breakfast in the church's little courtyard.

It was a flower garden, crisscrossed by a brick walk. It was closed off from the city on two sides by the church and the rectory and front and back by a gated stone wall and wooden fence hung with blue and white morning glories. It was an island of serenity in the city. These breakfasts were among the happiest hours of my childhood. We sat at a small round table, the three of us, with a white linen tablecloth, white dishes with delicate roses painted around the edges, two forks at each setting, big and little spoons, a silver sugar bowl, with its own tiny spoon, a pitcher of cream, and cut flowers from the garden in a vase. There was a plate with butter and another with cream cheese, and strawberry jam and marmalade in small matching tubs. I had never tasted marmalade before. At home, the kitchen table would have had crumbs and dirty dishes, mail going back several days, newspapers, and maybe, at one of the corners of the tablecloth, which needed a good washing, a comb and scissors that my mother had used to cut someone's hair for extra money one night during the week. Breakfast would have been fried eggs, pork roll, and hard rolls. The church breakfasts were an escape into heaven-on-earth. To this day I can taste the sweet acidic bite of the marmalade on the tip of my tongue. Orange marmalade and a benign English God have since been joined in my mind as the very definition of a civilized life, and there are passages from the Book of Common Prayer that can bring tears to my eyes:

> Almighty God, unto whom all hearts be open, all desires known, and from whom no secrets are hid: Cleanse the thoughts of our hearts by the inspiration of thy Holy Spirit, that we may perfectly love thee, and worthily magnify thy holy name; through Christ our Lord. Amen.

I carried the order and grace of those church-garden breakfasts as a submerged dream into my later years, and it was with me when I was married in an Episcopal church in Portsmouth, New Hampshire, in 1974.

2

After college, I had gone to work as a newspaper reporter for *The Providence Journal*. At work, I read the police blotters in a half-dozen small towns in South County and filed three-paragraph stories about summer arrests and local burglaries. In my basement apartment in Providence, I read my way through nineteenth-century Russian literature. I bought my books in the city's used bookstores, which were numerous in my neighborhood around Brown University. My greatest discovery was Konstantin Levin in Tolstoy's *Anna Karenina*. Levin appealed to me immediately. Dostoyevsky had prepared the ground with his stories of lost souls and redemption, and Tolstoy, in my reading, followed him with a vision of love and faith in the Russian countryside. Oh, how I was drawn to Levin, sensitive, tortured, and earnest Levin! He was a man of great feeling who was close to the land. His sensibility seemed formed by books, fields, and the poor and unimportant people of his farms and villages. His heart was open and kind. He was the man I wanted to be. I wanted to swing a scythe and sweat among hay fields under the Russian sun. Once again, I was reaching into a book for a guide to life and inhabiting the persona of a fictional character, this time a shy and bookish Russian landowner. In an odd way, I was doing what my mother had always done—I was escaping the world around me and substituting something more interesting.

I may have wanted to be a latter-day Levin, but at the time I was living more like an angst-ridden Raskolnikov in my belowground two-room apartment on the city's East Side. The old lady who managed the big old house that had been chopped into apartments lived in the front apartment on the first floor, and an Indian graduate student lived down the hall from her. I didn't know the others who lived in the building. On some weekends, I drove down to New Jersey to visit my mother. Sometimes I drove up to New Hampshire to visit friends from college. I didn't know how to make a life in Providence. I was restless, lonely, and anxious. After a year as a reporter doing good work, I decided—on the spur of the moment—to resign. I went to New York City to ship out as a merchant seaman. Looking back, I can see that it was a preposterous move: I had a good job, a very difficult job to get and one that I had liked doing. It had given me the money to buy books and magazines, and in some minuscule way it made me a "writer." I told my editors that I was leaving because I wanted adventure and to write a novel. I put this in a carefully crafted letter of resignation. They were astonished and passed my letter around. I told my few friends that because I had worked through high school and college I had never had a chance to travel. I wanted to give myself that chance. I suppose this might have been partly true. I packed a seabag with clothes and books and shipped out first on an old converted freighter carrying coal to Belgium and second on a containership to France and Spain. I worked the four-hour shifts, drank enormous amounts of coffee, and read my books. I found myself among rough older men who drank heavily and were cut off from the world. In the first ten minutes I was on the first ship, at dock, a knife fight broke out between a steward and a seaman in the mess. At first, I couldn't understand why everyone was rushing around and pushing one another out of the way. Then I saw one of the men holding a penknife in front of him as the other man backed his way through the hatch. It was over in seconds. I stayed away from both of them for the whole trip. On my second trip, I wrote a short story about a young man who ships out as a merchant seaman and one night, while in his bunk with the radio on, he talks with his cabinmate, an older black man, about their life plans. The cabinmate says he is going to take his earnings, return to Memphis, and a buy a shrimp boat that he plans to name the *Harriet Tubman*. The young man in the story says he plans to take his money and buy a farm in Maine. I called the story "The Voice of America." So, while I did actually end up doing some writing, I don't think I really grasped the meaning of my decision to leave *The Providence Journal* and ship out until I returned to New Hampshire to visit a friend after the Spain trip.

I ran into my former journalism professor Donald Murray on the street in Durham.

"Of course you went into the merchant marine," he laughed drily. "It's all about your paternity, isn't it?"

I was struck cold. I hadn't thought of that: Was that what

it really was about? Were the novels of Joseph Conrad and plays of Eugene O'Neill, which I had been carrying around in my seabag, and the writing I had been doing really just a cover? Was my real purpose to follow the trail of John Kababick back and back until I understood what had happened to him and me? I struggled with what Don Murray had said for days. What the hell was going on with me? Was I so unaware of my own motivations that I had thrown away a good job to blindly and unknowingly solve some childhood mystery? I felt like I had awakened in a strange place with a fractured sense of who I was and what I was doing. None of this was making any sense.

About a week later, the friend from college I had come back to see told me he knew a girl he wanted me to meet. I agreed, and she and I had a drink together in Portsmouth. Ten months later we were married.

Patti was pretty, with brown hair cut above her shoulders, high cheekbones, and almond-shaped eyes. She was working as a waitress and going to school part-time at UNH. She cooked me a delicious dinner of scallops and mushrooms in her apartment. She introduced me to her father, and he and I went oyster fishing on Great Bay.

I still was rattled by Don Murray's comment, and I began to see a return to the merchant marine as foolish and even dangerous. My life was ahead of me, not behind me, and certainly not with John Kababick and the merchant marine. It was time for me to start building my life: I had a good education and the *Journal* wanted me back. I had to get back on track. Marriage seemed the logical next step. Patti and I talked about a life together. We both wanted a home, and I liked it that her family seemed close to the earth and had simple values. Her father was a part-time lobsterman, and her grandfather had been a university horticulturalist. Patti liked to garden and cook. This felt right. I was beginning to write a story in my head about her and her family, some of which was true and some of which I imagined, that was persuading me toward marriage. I talked about where I would work. She wanted to stay close to her hometown and resisted a move to Providence. "All the way to Providence?" she asked. So I went to the nearest decent-size city, Portland, Maine, and found a job as a reporter in September 1974 at the *Press Herald*. I worked the 5:00 P.M. to 2:00 A.M. shift covering police and fires. Three months later, we slipped rings on each other's fingers in St. John's Episcopal Church.

3

I had married to make a life, a stable and sensible life. I had work to do: I carried the aspiration of my childhood more strongly than ever. I wanted to write and I wanted to be a newspaper editor. As I moved through my twenties, that hidden gyroscope was at work. I bought a manual typewriter and set up an extra room in our second-floor apartment in Portland as a writing office. In the first years, Patti and I were absorbed in the struggle to get started as a couple. Our only asset was the Volkswagen van with a broken heater that Patti had brought into the marriage, but I had a decent job and the prospect of a good future. I threw myself into my work at the newspaper and as a freelance writer and then into the building of our house. Elizabeth came along in the third year of our marriage, Adam in the seventh. By the time Adam was born, I was editing the *Maine Sunday Telegram,* the state's biggest newspaper. Soon I was in charge of the city's morning and evening papers, too; all of them published from the same newsroom by the same company. I was earning a good salary.

In the middle years of the marriage, we were living in New Gloucester, I was commuting to Portland to work, and the kids attended schools in town. The bus stopped at the bottom of our long dirt driveway. We had made ourselves into Mainers. We were members of the New Gloucester Congregational Church and New Gloucester Food Cooperative. Patti volunteered as a writer and editor at the town's free weekly newspaper. We had three dogs, a horse, a turtle, two hamsters, a car, a pickup truck, and a horse trailer. I had built a barn the year we got the horse. In winter, the kids slid down the long saltbox slope of the barn's roof and into a pile of snow.

I came home from work at night, dinner was on the table, and when I got ready for work in the morning I went to my dresser in the bedroom, where Patti had neatly tucked clean socks and underwear for me. This was nothing short of a miracle: I had grown up with so few clothes, and sometimes in apartments without washing machines, that I sometimes had to pull underwear from the bathroom hamper in the morning and sniff it to see what was wearable. Now, as a rising editor, I had a dozen dress shirts, four pairs of good slacks, two sport coats, a blue pin-striped suit, pair of black shoes, and a dozen ties.

My neighbor Bob Hersey died three years after the house was done, and I went to his funeral at the little evangelical church in town, and the sawmill owner who had turned my logs into boards was killed when logs rolled off a truck in the mill yard. His chest was crushed. He had been an independent cuss of the first order and powerfully creative in his profanity: It ranged from assertions about the anatomy of the Virgin Mary to the attribution of barnyard deviance to lazy tradesmen in town. When encountering foolishness of one sort or another, he had the New England habit of blasting out the name of the Lord with the addition of a middle initial: "Jeezus H. Christ!" His funeral was at the same little church, and I attended it, too, and offered my condolences to his big and tearful sons. I had never seen a family so torn up by grief. After the service, I recalled the work he had done for me and thanked them for it. One of the boys put his muscled arms around me. In a town where most of the men worked with their hands, often in the woods, I wore a tie and went to work in Portland. It was important for me to be there. I had become a person of some standing in the town.

Our trouble as a couple came to the surface when the day-to-day struggle of making a life ebbed and the kids began to grow. The house was built, my job was secure, and with simple survival no longer the goal, I began to crave a bigger professional and creative life. Both Patti and I wanted to be settled; the ambition for a bigger life was mine alone. She was happy with the present: a home among familiar neighbors in the country, a big vegetable garden, a place in the town. I wanted something else; I was always reaching for a more interesting and substantial future and for achievement. For me, life was a ladder and I had to keep climbing it: city editor, managing editor, editor in chief, invited speaker, published writer. Achievement was my insurance policy against a slide into the past I was trying to put behind me.

One night, the conflict came into focus when I said I felt that I just had to move from our house in the country, the one I had built. I wanted to move to Portland or maybe even New York or Washington. Patti did not want to give up the life she had: It was her anchor. Where did this leave me? I asked. "I feel trapped," I said. I heard myself screaming. The argument moved from the living room to the bedroom. I was in a rage. I could not budge her. She was not going to move. I screamed louder. When the argument was ended, or at least temporarily exhausted, my voice was hoarse. The children were upstairs, silent in their rooms. I was horrified at myself. It was a scene that could have been taken from my childhood, and I could have been one of the children cowering in the bedroom. I went upstairs to reassure them.

"Mom and Dad are just having an argument," I said. "All grown-ups have arguments. We'll work it out."

This was not what I had wanted in my marriage. This was *exactly* what I didn't want.

There were more arguments, and they lasted longer. I grew angry, sullen, and distant. I was like the photo that comes out of a shaken camera—a double image of an out-of-focus figure. There was me and there was the person the conflict in my marriage was turning me into. I was irritable, and I stayed away from the house. My stifled ambition made me work harder. I moved farther and farther away from my wife, and she away from me.

One of my resolutions growing up was that I would never be divorced. It was okay for others, and often I had met couples who I thought would be better off divorced. I was liberal and understanding on the subject when it came to friends, and not uncommonly, and without the slightest bit of irony, I would say to my wife after a party or picnic on the car ride home, "You know, the ——s, I think they would be better off apart. They're always bickering, and they bring out the worst in each other. I don't know why they stay together." But divorce just wasn't for me. It had seemed as implausible as deciding to become a Hindu or move to Bulgaria. I had not built the possibility of it into my life.

I had entered marriage, at twenty-three, with little knowledge of myself and how to be married, and now I was in my midforties, in a state of growing awareness. I was torn between two absolutes: keeping my family together and answering the call inside myself to keep opening up my life. I commenced a struggle to know what I needed to have and what I was willing to give up. It's as if I had put myself on a fast of bread and water, except that the diet was anger, anxiety, and introspection. Soon everything that was excess fell away. Emotionally, I was left with bones, ligaments, a little muscle, and skin. In the end, to gain myself, I was willing to give up my marriage. But I would have to struggle a lot longer before I reached that conclusion.

4

The smooth surface reality of my life cracked in October 1996. At the age of forty-five, I lost my job at the newspaper in Portland, where I had worked for twenty-two years. I was the editor in chief when the end came—decent pay, a little prestige, a company car, a 25 percent match to my 401(k) savings plan. New managers came in, and I went out. It's the new American story. One day you're a hero; the next day you're meeting with an employment counselor at your former employer's expense and trying to rearrange your identity.

Like most middle-class parents, I had a steady stream of bills and a mountain of future obligations. There were tuitions, and my mother, then in her seventies, had moved from New Jersey to Maine to be near my brother and me and her grandchildren. She had been married and divorced one more time by then, and she was trading haircuts for Reiki sessions and painting lessons in her new apartment in Portland. She relied on me for her rent. I was prosperous enough to easily pay it—while I was working.

The image of a clock ticking down on my severance package was never far from my thoughts. The first week I was out of work, I wrote notes to my former colleagues at the newspaper thanking them for their contributions during my editorship, which brought generous replies. Like an old athlete with his clippings, I read them over and over for comfort, and then for four months I hung around the house, read books, napped, took long walks, and worked the telephone for a job. Eventually, I found one, at another newspaper, in Philadelphia. It was a generous offer at a good paper. There was the prospect of serious advancement and important responsibility. I began making plans to leave Maine. All of this was about as easy as being pushed from a moving car.

Sometimes a single domino in your life falls and it begins a sequence of actions that ends in an event that you never could have seen. The loss of my job was that domino.

In February, my brother, Paul, drove me down to Philadelphia.

Paul had still been living in New Jersey, in Long Branch, not far from where we had grown up, when I called him first to be my best man and a year later to help me build the house. In the twenty years since then, he had made a life for himself in Maine and started his own family. The car he had volunteered to drive me to Philadelphia in was a van: He now had six children.

"Hey, man, it's a new chapter," he said.

His voice was upbeat: It was telling me that he was happy to help and I should take heart. He was bucking up his big brother.

We had packed into his van a mattress, bedding, clothes, some pots and pans, a box of books, a lamp, and an over-stuffed brown chair that I liked to sit in to read. Paul and I headed south. We arrived in Philadelphia after midnight, parked on the street, and carried my stuff into the building and up to the fourth-floor apartment I had rented sight unseen. Paul spent the night with me in the empty apartment and headed back the next day.

My plan was to start my job, at *The Philadelphia Inquirer*, learn the city and the suburbs, look around for a house to buy, and then bring my wife and son to Philadelphia in the late summer. Elizabeth was in college. In other words, Patti and I would pick up where we left off. This was the plan even though, by then, we were living separate lives, despite sleeping in the same house, sitting across the dinner table each night, and watching our children at recitals and swim meets. She had retreated into her life, and I into mine.

Remarkably, this had happened without the slightest acknowledgment between us. Our connection was our children and our history together. Mutual memory is a powerful glue. I contacted a real-estate agent.

5

"Are you happily married?"

The question had been put to me by a woman in her early forties whom I was about to have dinner with. Her name was Sara and she was a reporter for *The New York Times*. Several months earlier, she had interviewed me over the telephone from her office in Boston for a story that she had been working on in Maine, and then, some weeks later, after a second phone call, we met at a reception of journalists at Harvard's Nieman Foundation. We had dinner after the reception, at a restaurant in Harvard Square, and talked late into the night.

I went back to my room at the St. Botolph's Club in Back

Bay. The room, up four flights of stairs, was spare and dull in contrast to the talk at dinner, which was exciting, even thrilling. Sara struck me as sophisticated and empathic. She had dark eyes and dark hair that was cut into a bob to her chin. She pushed her hair behind her small ears. We talked about newspapers, reporters, and editors we knew in common, the beauty of New England, running along the Charles River, which she said she loved, sailing, the story she had been working on, my search for another newspaper job, and our families. We both seemed to know everything ever written by E. B. White and had practically memorized his essay "Once More to the Lake." I told her that I knew the lake and had actually fished in it. Sara was unmarried, so she told me about her parents, who recently had sold their home in Pennsylvania and retired to North Carolina. The evening passed in the blink of an eye.

On this day in September, I was back in Boston as part of my job search. I looked her up at the *Times*'s bureau office to say hello. We decided to grab a quick dinner in downtown Boston.

As she was working on her story for the next day's newspaper and I sat and waited for her to finish, she turned to me and said, "So, tell me, Are you happily married?"

I looked at her blankly. What kind of question was that to ask me? I didn't know how to answer it, and I was annoyed at her audacity in putting it to me. Was she mocking me or trying to embarrass me, or was she just being way too nosy? I didn't feel that I owed her an answer, despite the intimacy we had developed over our previous dinner, and I didn't want to be pushed into supplying one. I kept looking at her and throttled my irritation. I could have gotten up and left right then, but I didn't. I wanted to have dinner with her. She sat in her seat, turned away from her computer screen, waiting for me to respond. Finally I gave her an answer that was neither a yes nor a no.

"So, you're not," she said.

I mumbled more meaningless words.

We went to dinner at one of those linen-napkin and mahogany-paneled taverns that signify old Boston. After dinner, I returned to my cell at the St. Botolph's Club, but her question stayed with me as I looked out the small window to the vines on a building next door. I had never taken the disappointing tangle that my life had become and drawn it up into a single big question that could be answered with a yes or no. I knew I had felt apathetic about my future and mostly indifferent to my day-to-day life for some time and I was aware of being lonely, but I never had gone so far as to make a judgment about my marriage. I had accommodated my dissatisfaction and accepted it. There was no reason to ask the question. I certainly wasn't going to make any changes.

6

I spent the first spring and summer in Philadelphia living alone. It was an escape from the conflict that I had been desperately inhabiting. The shouting had stopped between my wife and me some years earlier. It had been replaced, in more recent years, by a quiet resignation that was a crueler form of conflict. Now that I was alone, the conflict disappeared. My resentments faded. It was easier to breathe. I seemed more alert to little things, a bird that landed on the windowsill, the rattle of the commuter train passing over a nearby bridge, the way the sunlight fell on the wood floor and up the white wall of my loft apartment.

My job was to assign reporters to city news and edit their

stories. It was enjoyable work. My apartment was a twenty-minute early-morning walk up Race Street to the *Inquirer*'s big white tower on North Broad Street.

The city showed me a new spring. I knew the springs of New England by heart, from the appearance of the broad green leaves of the skunk cabbages along the swollen streams to the first tweets of the peepers' songs at dusk. New England springs came on fast, often not even waiting for the snow to melt around the trunks of the trees in the woods before delivering a warm summer day in May. The Philadelphia spring was slower, more relaxed. It strolled into the city and lingered, slowly nudging out winter and not hurrying in summer. In the vacant lots and along the railroad tracks, paulownia trees showed heavy purple blossoms and the ginko trees put out flowers and foliage with a deep fecund smell of vegetative sex. The grass was green in March. The trees were alive with chirping birds. I was beginning to feel alive, too, in the discovery of my new home in this city that felt a little left behind and shabby.

I spent most of my time alone. It reminded me of my first year as a reporter in Providence. I recalled, with nostalgia, what it was like to be at the beginning of one's adult life when everything seemed possible. In this bubble of time in Philadelphia, between my old life in Maine and the expectation of its resumption in months to come in Philadelphia, I was experiencing a release and intimations of something new. But I had to be honest: I wasn't at the beginning of my adult life. I was well into it and quite possibly past its midpoint. The shape of my life had already been set. I was married. I had children. This period was at best an interlude that would end when I picked up the thread of my responsibilities. If it was a spring, it was a false spring.

I called my wife once a week and made small talk. I never whispered a word of the change that was coming over me. We had stopped sharing our interior lives a long time ago. I started another phone-calling routine: I began calling my mother, and I blabbed to her incoherently about my feelings. I was still close to my mother, and it was her nature to be direct. Nearly every phone call I made to her was the same: "Mom, I'm feeling a lot of stress. I'm not sure what to do. I don't want to go back to the life I had been living." She listened sympathetically and expressed her support and concern, but she held back from pointing me in a direction, not yet anyway.

I had to make a decision about the future, and I began to fear its outcome. I obsessed about it. The urgency of what lay ahead burst the bubble of my make-believe interlude. The agony of thinking through my next steps took over nearly every minute of my day, and if I strayed from the obsessive stream of thought, the faintest suggestion of family or marriage—the sight of children coming out of a school, an item in the paper about some celebrity couple breaking up—snapped me back. The more I thought about it, the more urgent the problem seemed and the more impossible a solution.

I wrote long notes to myself on legal pads, and I began to look at the sources of my unhappiness and drew up detailed chronologies of the problems in the marriage. I was afraid of where all of this was taking me. I felt like a man who was considering a crime he knew he would ultimately commit despite the certainty that he would pay a heavy price. I would sit for hours in my brown chair in the apartment and run through my thoughts and feelings. I repeatedly replayed scenes from our courtship and marriage that had left me feeling misunderstood, disappointed, or unloved. At times, I didn't know whether I was remembering problems or constructing fictitious ones that I could then stew about and use as excuses for the feelings I harbored. I was a wreck.

My job required that I be "on top" of the news at all times, so I would set my radio alarm to the city's twenty-four-hour news station. I would wake up to the blaring headlines and traffic reports already exhausted. I was exhausted through the day. At work, I felt a powerful urge simply to go to sleep. Sometimes, at my desk, I would tear up without warning. One moment I would be typing a list of the day's news stories, and the next moment tears would be streaming down my face.

I had to acknowledge that at some deep level I had been preparing myself for the breakup of my marriage, yet every ounce of me was saying, You cannot do this. You will hurt yourself and your family. You have lost your mind. Your family is everything to you. The other editors on the desk, a woman in particular who sat across from me and who I later learned had gone through her own divorce, saw my torment and covered for me when I couldn't function. The city editor, an urbane man in his early forties who had been welcoming to me since I had arrived at the paper, took me aside and asked me what was happening. I told him.

He gave me the name of a therapist.

"Why don't you make an appointment? And let me know if I can help," he said, putting his hand on my shoulder.

7

Later that spring, I was walking near Washington Square Park in Manhattan with my uncle John. I had come into New York from Philadelphia to talk to him about the struggle I was having with myself over the separation. My uncle John, who was seventy-five, had been married four times. His fourth marriage was the one that had worked: It had lasted twenty years, and he and his wife, Judith, were happy together. John had known me since I was a child and had always encouraged and praised me. I knew that he would have my best interests at heart. In the last year, when I had trouble paying my bills, he and Judith had offered me the money to meet Elizabeth's college tuition. I didn't accept it, but the offer meant everything to me. I explained my dilemma to him.

"You have to think about what's going to make you happy," he said. "You have one life to live. Look at me. I wanted each one of my marriages to work out. I never wanted to be divorced. But I wasn't happy. It took me a long time to find the right person."

We walked a little farther, passed the sidewalk booksellers who gather around NYU, and he said, "What can make these situations really complicated, and hard, is when there's a third person involved. So, you have that going for you."

We took a few more steps.

"Actually," I told him, "another person is now involved."

8

It had become complicated. I was lost and anxious, and I felt like a man without balance or sight who has to slide his hands against walls to find his way out of some terribly confusing and unfamiliar place. I knew what I wanted, but I wasn't sure I had the strength to achieve it. Once, as a child, I had gone into a "fun house" at Seaside Heights. Dark passages snaked through tilted rooms where the floors rotated and the walls fell away as you leaned on them, making it almost impossible at times to move except slowly on hands and knees. That's what I felt as I went from room to room in my apartment. I got up in the mornings and commanded myself to shower and dress and leave for work. I told myself to walk and to eat. I fantasized an escape from my dilemma by planning a life in some cheap corner of Europe, though I never answered the question of how I would earn the money to sustain my escape.

At this point, I was close to a collapse.

The core of my anxiety was the conviction that all of the pain and damage that had flowed from my parents' divorce would rise up again, in my life and the lives of my children. I had spent my adult life eradicating what had felt to me like a curse that had come down through my mother and father. Divorce meant abandonment and the shame of being different from everyone else. It meant not being able to pay the rent, not having a house, not being able to take a vacation, not knowing when the world would collapse, and not being able to rely on your parents. It had fallen to me to bring this curse to an end. There was only one cure: a lasting marriage.

At night, I lay on my back before falling off to sleep and pieced together the history of the marriage, from our first meeting in the bar in Portsmouth to the present moment. Each night, I would repeat the history from the beginning and add more details. They demonstrated either the hollowness of the marriage or my faults as a husband. I was looking for a place to put blame—on Patti or on myself. Usually, I put it on myself and these nightly meditations were periods of neurotic self-flagellation. Finally, after falling asleep, I would dream of being alone in some city, homeless and penniless and without even a person to call for help, not even my brother or mother. The setting for the dream would be a dingy bus station or a soup kitchen. In another dream, I was an old man, living alone in a cabin in the Maine woods in winter, awaiting my death in a brown chair as the room got colder and colder. At the end of the dream, I was near death, numb from the cold, and alone.

At this stage, in my evolution as a man moving toward divorce, I was just about out of my mind.

At some point, from the sheer exhaustion of indecision, I decided I would tell Patti that I wanted a separation. I wasn't going to ask for a divorce because I didn't want to be divorced. I didn't want to continue in the marriage, either. I wanted the interlude to go on and on. I told myself I wanted more time in which to work out my feelings and get to a place of clear thought. The decision to separate was a resolution that I wasn't sure I could turn into action. To someone who hasn't been through a decision so fraught with conflict this must sound ridiculous, confused, irrational, and craven. It was probably all of that and more. I was allowing a war to be fought out inside of myself: Different parts of me wanted different things. I needed some higher part of my consciousness to take control of the conflict. I thought I could gain this with some time.

My plan, once I had made the decision to ask for a separation, was to hold on to the intention of it and set myself in action, like a man who decides that he will just walk off the end of the high-dive. Maybe I would be able to carry it out, maybe not. I wouldn't know until the moment came. Finally, one weekend in summer, I returned to Maine and told Patti that I wanted to live apart, at least for now. I followed the steps I had laid down for myself, almost as if I had blocked out the movements on a stage. For some reason, I decided I wanted to tell her in the car. We didn't drive anywhere: The car was parked on the street in front of the house. I was sick in my stomach and in my soul as I was doing it. The world seemed to be flying apart and it took an act of will just to keep myself upright.

The same day, I took Adam for a ride. He sat in the front seat with me. As we drove along, I told him that I was going to live apart from his mother and that I didn't know what the future held for her and me.

"Are you going to get a 'vorce?" he asked.

"I don't know yet what's going to happen."

I kept talking, but he covered his ears. I said that his mom and I would continue to talk to each other and try to work something out.

Later I told Elizabeth, but the pain of it was so severe that I have obliterated it from my memory: I cannot remember the details.

It was the worst day of my life.

I felt like I was a madman who was moving from room to room and shooting people and that I was watching myself in slow motion. I felt like I had been drawn into a killing spree and was powerless to stop. Blood was splattering the walls. People's faces were contorted in pain. I couldn't bear my own words and my own presence, and I was appalled at what I was doing, but still—like an executioner—I continued to move through rooms killing people who were begging for their lives. Their faces said, Please don't pull the trigger. Why are you doing this to us?

I slept a little—very little—that night at my brother's house, and then I went back to Philadelphia. I had created a separation. I told myself that what I had done was simply to buy time until I could sort out my true feelings. It was an act of cowardice and procrastination. I still had not accepted the fact of a divorce even though I had set it out as the probable course.

The separation detonated a bomb in the family. Elizabeth grew depressed and stayed in bed with a knotted stomach. Adam retreated into himself and hardly spoke. Patti was furious. She went back to cigarettes and began chain-smoking.

9

At the time, Adam was between his freshman and sophomore years of high school. He had been attending a Catholic high school in Maine. It had a good reputation for solid academics and outstanding sports teams. He had connected with one of his teachers, a young Jesuit priest, who taught classical languages. Adam was a good student in Greek and Latin. Three years earlier, I had spent a year at Harvard on a journalism fellowship and Adam had come with me. Together we had lived in a small apartment on the campus, and he had helped me each night with my study of ancient Greek. He had held the flash cards as I practiced my vocabulary late at night in our little kitchen a block from Harvard Yard. The result was that he had learned nearly as much Greek as I did—maybe more. The knowledge he had picked up had made him a favorite of his Jesuit teacher. But Adam never quite fitted himself into the life of the Catholic school.

The culture of the school was built around its playing fields and sports teams, and while Adam was athletic and for a time was among the best swimmers his age in the state, his athleticism was oddly noncompetitive and largely focused on technique and individual performance. He disliked the bully-

ing that went on between the school's strongest and weakest
boys. Adam went out for the football team and lasted one
game. In the opening kickoff, he threw a block to protect his
team's runner and the collision with the opposing player sent
Adam flying. He limped off the field. It was the end of his
football career. There was an undercurrent of intimidation in
the halls and locker rooms, and the boys who were at the top
were the ones with thick necks, buzz cuts, and stubble on
their chins. Football players ruled the school. By the end of
his freshman year, he was sullen and unsure he wanted to return. He only had one or two close friends and spent most of
his time by himself at Portland's municipal golf course.

Of course, he was facing a bigger and harder decision than
whether he should return to the Catholic high school, and
maybe that's where his mind was working as he released
himself, unconsciously, into the rhythm of his golf game. He
played endless rounds, hitting long drives, chipping effort-
lessly onto the greens and sinking putts. With his parents
apart, it was obvious that he faced a looming choice: Would
he stay in Maine with his mother or move to Philadelphia
with his father? I can't think of a crueler choice to put to a
child. He faced two parents, two cities. I knew that this kind
of choice would be overwhelming for any young person. For
Adam it might be impossible.

In June, I drove up to Maine for the weekend and stayed
with my brother. Adam and I played golf. He liked being on
the golf course and it was a place where we could be alone, so
I chose it as the place to talk to him about the near future. The
grace of his club's arc at the tee and the solid and sure way it
came down on the ball made it seem that he was free of tur-
moil. I knew better. He was quiet. Silence with Adam was a
sure sign of trouble. My guess was that he had been using the

game to still his mind and somehow work out an answer to the dilemma he faced about where to live.

We hit from the first tee and talked about his game. Somewhere around the fourth hole, with no one behind us, I raised the matter of the coming school year. We stopped and looked at each other.

"You can come to Philadelphia, Adam, or you can stay here in Maine," I said. "Of course, I would love to have you come to Philadelphia, but I want you to know that I will understand if you decide that you can't come and you want to stay here in Maine."

My heart was twisting as I said the words. I was trying to strike a balance between opening my arms to him and exerting unfair pressure to come with me. I couldn't bear the thought of not having him with me. I knew his mother would have the same feelings. There was no good way through this decision.

"I want to look at the schools, Dad. Then I'll decide."

"Okay," I said. "That sounds like a good idea."

We played through and I kept hacking shots into the trees. I hated the game: It was unforgiving and the slightest distraction of mind seemed to send the ball off in the wrong direction. Adam continued to hit long straight shots that landed on the greens.

In July, I took my two-week vacation. Adam flew down to visit me in Philadelphia. I had made appointments for us to visit several private schools. I also had made plans for us to go fishing. I put the fishing first. We headed west, to the spring creek and corn country of Central Pennsylvania, where we caught the biggest rainbow trout of our lives. We spent a day on Spruce Creek, an astonishing stretch of water that bubbles out of the region's limestone bedrock and produces trout outrageously out of scale to the stream's modest width and depth. We slept in cheap motels, drove through the rolling wooded hills of Central Pennsylvania, with its gritty small towns, and ate dinners at roadside hamburger stands. It was an awkward period. We kept our talk on the surface, and I never got into what was happening between his mother and me and what was happening inside our family even though it was on both of our minds. At times, I felt as if I were a thief on the run and that I was keeping my crime a secret from my son. The feeling of being on the lam was worsened by the sad and worn-out coal country of Pennsylvania. We returned to Philadelphia and began looking at schools.

There was a Quaker high school, Germantown Friends School, that offered a program in classical languages. We visited it together, and Adam was interviewed by the admissions officer. She was a no-nonsense woman who asked me to wait in the reception room as she and Adam met privately in her office. The school's campus was a tight cluster of old brick, wood, and sandstone buildings, including a Friends Meeting House, in Germantown, a decaying section of the city. The admissions woman said the class that Adam was applying for was full but that the school would consider his application. She was doubtful, though, that he could be admitted. He would have to be accepted, and then there would have to be a cancellation from another student, one who had already enrolled. Adam told me that he had decided that he would live in Philadelphia if he could get into the school. In other words, he found a way, wisely, to turn the decision he was being forced to make into a choice between schools and not parents. The time on the golf course had been well spent.

I wanted desperately for him to be admitted. It would seal his move to Philadelphia. I sent the school a letter about

Adam and enclosed copies of the photographs he had been taking during the last year.

The letter said, in part:

> Adam is on a journey of learning and development that thrills me to watch. Two nights ago in the car, on the way back from the Jersey Shore, he began talking to me about problems in the world, problems such as ecological damage and population growth, and he wondered out loud if human life had meaning in a universe without God. He was struggling, in his own way, with the problems of the modern world. We talked of Socrates, and his conception of God and a soul, and the importance of living a Good Life. I told him that Socrates encouraged us all to avoid living the unexamined life. For me as a father, I see a son who will take a good education and integrate it into his life. All parents wish for the aspirations of their children. In that I am no exception. The exception, I think, is Adam.

Twenty long days later, I received a letter from the school's admissions director: "I am delighted finally to be able to accept Adam . . ." He was the last student admitted into the class of 2000. In September, Adam moved to Philadelphia.

10

A columnist at the newspaper whom I had come to know and had confided in gave me the name of another therapist, and I scheduled an appointment. In the world that I had grown up in, therapy was for rich people. They went to psychiatrists because they didn't have mothers, fathers, brothers, sisters, or uncles they could talk to about their problems. Psychiatrists were the medical equivalent of poodles: an indulgence and a joke.

I was adjusting to the idea of seeing a therapist because it was becoming clear to me I couldn't solve my problems on my own. I was drowning and desperately needed help.

When I arrived at the therapist's office on the twelfth floor of an aging building in downtown Philadelphia, he met me at the door. He was maybe fifty years old, thin, dark, and impeccably dressed. His hair, which was receding at the temples but full over his forehead, was a kinky high pompadour. He gave me the impression of an exotic bird out of an Audubon sketchbook. I introduced myself and explained why I was there, and he replied that he would see me for one session and then we would decide whether there would be more sessions. It was clear, though, that it was *he* who was going to decide whether there would be other sessions. But first, he said, he wanted to be paid. I wrote him a check, and he led me into his inner office, the place where we would have our "session."

The room's furniture was ornate and arranged against the far wall, and hung from the ceiling was a collection of birdcages. He left the room, and I was alone. I looked at the birdcages. One looked like an antique, another, made from bamboo, looked Asian, and another was gilded with delicate filigree. They were suspended there like some unexplained metaphor. Surely this must be some commentary on unhealthy relationships or emotions that couldn't escape or maybe feelings that couldn't be admitted. I tried to puzzle it out, and I was beginning to feel that the therapy session had begun even before the therapist had entered the room. When he came in, he sat down and fixed his eyes on me. They were like tacks. He asked me to tell him what was wrong. I said that I didn't think I wanted to be married any longer.

"That's an unusual way to put it," he said.

I explained my life. He stapled his gaze on me. When I was done, he said, "You are afraid. You have to learn to face that fear. You have to walk into that fear as if you were walking into a wind. The other thing is this: You cannot decide whether you want to be married while you are seeing someone else. The matter becomes too complex. You can make an appointment for another session if you like. Think about what I've said."

I left and chose not to make another appointment. I wasn't prepared to end my relationship with Sara.

The second therapist I saw was in New York City. Sara sent me to her. Her address was on the Upper East Side of Manhattan. I had never been to that section of Manhattan before and was surprised to find myself among liveried doormen, aging fashionably dressed and unbelievably skinny women taking the sidewalk in long strides, and young black women minding white children wearing pinafores in the park. This was definitely not my world. I came to the therapist's building, near the East River, rode the elevator to the fourteenth floor, and walked the carpeted hallway to her office. New York has always seemed sinister to me: cruel, complicated, and corrupt. I wondered what went on behind all of these narrow doors with numbers affixed to them. I entered her office to a waiting room hung with photographs and paintings and knocked on an inner door. It opened, and I was met by a tiny woman, in her eighties, with bright blue eyes. She was smiling warmly.

"Come in; come in; please come in," she said. She had a German accent.

This is too much, I thought: I'm seeing a psychiatrist with a German accent. We both sat down. She was wearing a blue batik blouse, white pants, and sneakers. Her sneakers didn't reach the floor.

"Now, Mr. Ureneck, tell me, what's going on?"

I told her. I think I talked for a long time. I was conscious of telling a long story. When I was done, she looked at me, puzzled. It was a look that seemed to want to screw something out of my head. The room was quiet. She tilted her head and knit her brows. She seemed to be looking inside of me.

"Tell me more about your mother."

I complied, and again I felt as if I were going on and on.

"Yes, I see; I see," she said when I was done and after the room had gone quiet again. "Now, here's what I would like you to do. I want you to say the word 'divorce.' "

That seemed an odd request. I was silent. I tried and while I could hear the sound of the word in my mind, I could not get my mouth to form it. I was locked up: It was as if I were being asked to put something dirty in my mouth.

"Can you say the word 'divorce' for me, Mr. Ureneck?"

"I'm having a little trouble with it," I said.

"Yes, I can see," she said, laughing sympathetically.

She struck me at the moment as a sprite. I tried to smile. The old woman's eyes were bright as lights, and she moved in her chair, which was big and made her small body seem even smaller. She brought her spotted hands together. I felt strongly that she wanted to help me.

"Well, now," she said. "What I'd like you to do today is spell the word 'divorce' for me. Can you do that?"

With some effort, I uttered each letter distinctly. *"D-i-v-o-r-c-e."*

"Oh, good!" she exclaimed. "That's excellent. Now, I think we've done enough for today. We should meet again. When can you come back?"

"Next week," I said.

"Good. I will see you again next week."

I took the train back to Philadelphia. I felt like I had met somebody who could help me. I napped until I reached 30th Street Station.

V. MIDDLE RIVER

A good backcast is the prerequisite for a good
forward delivery.
— THE NEW ENCYCLOPEDIA OF FISHING

On the morning of Day Seven, the sun came out.
Adam and I were catching nearly all of our salmon on
a big fly that had a head of fluorescent red chenille and a fluffy
purple body. It was an ugly and preposterous creation of dyed
turkey down, black thread, and chenille wrapped around a
weighted long-shank streamer hook about two inches long. It
was a popular Alaska fly and meant to imitate a river leech
that had fastened itself to a big salmon egg. By now, through
countless snags on rocks and sunken tree limbs and the back-
and-forth whipping of hundreds of casts, we were down to
two of the purple flies and one of them was showing serious
wear. We had other patterns, some of them equally absurd in
color and flash, that sought to provoke a salmon strike. Pacific
salmon flies are not the delicate Back East creations tied on
tiny hooks light enough to float on the surface of a still pond.
They are the floozies of fly patterns, flaunting their pink and
green feather boas. But it was this red and purple concoction

that was getting the strikes. I carefully deconstructed the mangy fly, unwinding the thread and chenille and then winding them back more tightly and tying the thread off with one half hitch and then another. It wasn't a bad job of on-river first aid. I held it aloft for Adam's inspection and approval.

"Not bad," he said. "That one's yours. I'll take the other one."

We were moving through a straight section of the river that tunneled between high banks. The grass of the tundra plain floated higher than our heads, so that the horizon line, were I to envision one, would have hovered halfway up the gravel bank. We couldn't see what was beyond the grass-fringed banks—hillocks, mountains, a herd of caribou, or maybe John Wayne chasing a band of Indians? We were caroming down an underground river that appeared to have been channelized between tall levees by the Army Corps of Engineers for maximum flow and navigation. It was a straight pipe of rushing water.

Looking up, I saw blue sky between pillows of gray clouds that were gathering their strength for yet another assault, and looking down, I saw crystal green water and a bottom of white and gray stones, tresses of river grass, and distorting swirls and eddies that occasionally revealed the torpedo shapes of big rainbow trout. Ghostlike, they held in the lees of rocks or thatches of sticks and branches hung up on the bottom. It was difficult—no, it was impossible—to determine the depth of the water: Three feet? Six feet? Ten feet? It was like trying to guess the thickness of green glass. The water pulled the light out of the sky and sent it back in shards and fluted columns, mottling and distorting what struck me as fissured and flowing jade. There was the gravelscape of the shifting river bottom, and there was us, in a bulbous raft, and, in between, the rushing water, each a world moving at its own speed toward the sea.

The sun felt good on my shoulders and face. Last night had been a nightmare and a low point, but steadily, right from the beginning of the trip, really, I had felt myself making a recovery. The physical exercise, especially in those sections where the river spread out and lost its depth, forcing us to hop out of the raft and push it downstream over the rocks, was putting something back into me. What can I call it—a sense of myself inside my body? The anxiety that had been my shadow was lifting, and I was beginning to accept the enjoyment of the trip for myself. I was just taking pleasure in the sun. In these past few days, I had been taking pleasure in lots of small things: tying a new leader to the end of my fly line, setting up the stove, sitting to rest at the end of the day after a meal, examining the small blue flowers that grew among the stones along the river's edge, keeping our gear clean and in order, making sure the raft was pointed downstream.

I didn't feel a stranger in this landscape. I felt at home and that I belonged. It was that old and inexplicable companionship of trees, grass, and river. Among them, I felt what others must feel in museums or churches: There was beauty in the shapes and patterns and color, a harmony that fitted all the pieces together into a natural divinity. The unspoiled and uncompromised landscape suggested to me the beginning of things, without judgment yet quietly aware of my presence. The water floated my raft; the wood in the campfire warmed my hands; the hawks saluted by lifting off their perches in the trees as we passed by. There is a common strain in all of nature, I think, and the man who learns woodcraft in the Wisconsin woods will find that he has comrades on the African veld, and the fisherman who throws his net from a reed boat in the Indian Ocean has a brother in the herring fisherman of New England. They are related by the life of the planet, its pulse and respiration, and the inexplicable magnificence of so many things working together to create an intricate system of miraculous and connected life. We who are fishermen are both witnesses and bit players in that marvelous poem that is the natural world.

I had always turned to the woods for comfort and healing, though I hadn't been aware at the time of what had drawn me there as a boy and then a young man, but nature had been a balm in my life—a quiet place and a healing force—and again, on the river, it seemed to be infusing me with confidence and strength. I was feeling more myself there in Alaska. The landscape swept by and I listened to the soft whispering of the water brushing the banks.

In the early years of my marriage, before I had begun the house and then after I had mostly finished it, I often took Saturdays to myself and spent them in the woods. In the spring or summer, I would go fishing; in the fall or winter, hunting. It gave me a lot of pleasure to walk among the trees and let my mind wander over the surface impressions of the tree trunks, rocks, and hills: I enjoyed their shapes and colors and textures and took my thinking no deeper. For a long time, I thought of those days as wasted time, a profligate throwing away of precious hours that could have been put to more useful purposes. On a warm day in October, with Patti at home, I would go off with my shotgun and a pocketful of birdshot with the avowed purpose of shooting a grouse. I would walk some woods path or follow a brook. I might find a stone wall and sit with my back against the mossy stones and nap, awakening now and again to the chatter of a red squirrel. I can see now that all that weekend loafing was a convalescence and my therapy was the dry smell of woods duff, red leaves falling from swamp maples, the wind in the tops of the trees, and the pleasing sight of green clusters of pine needles against a blue sky. This was my sanitarium, and with the knowledge that at home I had a family that relied on me, that was safe, fed, and happy, my nerves were knitting themselves together and my inner self was gaining strength. The family at home—Patti cooking or working in her garden, the kids amusing themselves in the house or yard—hovered at the edges of my thoughts and was an important part of these days for me. This seemed like a life.

Yes, it felt like a life, but I suspected even then that it wasn't going to be my only life. I had always been an apprentice to life, and I suppose I had an apprentice's view of the world, which was that work, study, and experience led, step-by-step, to mastery. I had mastered fly-fishing, timber-frame house construction, and newspaper editing. Each of these pursuits had taken me deeper into an idea that I had held dear and as an amulet against meaninglessness. The fishing was the pursuit of order and beauty, and the house was the pursuit of rootedness. Even newspaper editing at bottom was an idea with me: It appealed to me mostly as a way to participate in the place that I had committed myself to, Maine, and to reflect the best values that it represented: practicality, understatement, tolerance, independence, and a strong sense of the land.

When I had redesigned the newspaper's typography, the first thing I did was drive the designer I had hired to Sabbathday Lake to see the chairs that the Shakers had made.

"I want the newspaper to reflect the attitudes that went into that chair," I told him.

"What are those?" he asked.

"Well," I said, "it begins with simplicity and ends in an elegance that is both holy and useful."

There was a long pause. "I'll see what I can do."

I had become a husband, father, editor, home builder, and fly fisherman, but still, I was restless. What was it that I really wanted to master? I wasn't sure, but I sensed that I was answering some call planted by my mother to be the most that I could be as a person ("This is my Louis. He's college material!") and it was tied up with books, ideas, nature, and beauty. I knew that I was only happy when I was making something, so I had to find something new to make.

The feeling of having failed also was lifting and I began to think again about my happier times as a boy. Yes, there was lots of trouble at home, but I had learned to survive and ultimately to get the things I needed in my life. On my own I had gotten my fishing rod, and I found a way to get rides to the lake and Keyport to go fishing, and I had gotten myself to church and to the public library. All of this had sustained me and made me happy. It had allowed me to make myself into a person. Sure, I had gotten through some tough times by leaving my body when the screaming or the drinking started, but I had never left my life. Always there was a plan for work, college, reading, or fishing—I just had to work it carefully through the chaos around me. My brother had said to me once when we were adults, "Louie, we learned how to survive." He was right—that's exactly what we had learned, and we both were pretty good at it. Floating on the river, I thought of what our childhood had taught Paul and me. I made a list in my head. We had learned

- To cook simple meals
- To do our own laundry, sometimes in the sink
- To stay away from John Kababick when he was drunk
- To work

- To scrounge
- To hold up in stressful situations—yelling, fighting, bill collectors, foreclosure
- To defend ourselves in a fight
- To grab an opportunity when it came along
- To sacrifice for each other
- To forgive
- To improve our lives
- To hope

Okay, there were some things I hadn't learned. I hadn't learned how to be angry inside my family growing up. There hadn't been room for me to be angry as a child—what was I supposed to do, leave home at age twelve? Who would take responsibility for worrying about the catastrophe of our lives if I hadn't taken it on? I was the designated worrier. My experience at home trained me to work through and around adults whose lives were one unbelievable crisis after another. I never learned to say, "This madness must stop. This yelling and this drinking must stop. Do you realize you are wrecking my life?" Instead, my response went in exactly the opposite direction: Rather than get angry, I came to understand the torment of my mother and Johnny. I loved them, and my empathy for them deepened. I had listened to their stories and watched them inside their families among their parents. I knew how their lives had been shaped and what they had suffered, and I had stood next to them through disappointments and humiliations. Anger requires judgment, and I could not stand in judgment of them. I loved them. I wanted us to be a family. As a boy, I cleaned the house, cooked the meals, lifted Johnny out of the bushes, counseled my mother through her decision to get married. I suppose these feelings exist for many children who grow up in homes with an alcoholic. The family becomes their responsibility; everyone's pain and problems become their pain and problems. In time I managed my physical escape, but when I did leave, it was with the embedded conviction that relationships were fragile. In my marriage, I didn't feel that I could demand what I wanted. To do so would have meant risking its end, and risking my marriage seemed to be inviting back into my life all the despair and anxiety I had left behind in my childhood. Divorce was a curse. So this was what had happened with me and Patti: I had been unwilling to risk the marriage with an ultimatum for change until the moment I had decided it was already over. I was ready to move into a new life; she was not. Neither of us was right or wrong. Patti had brought her own hurts from childhood into the relationship. In the beginning we had helped each other, but over time we simply had healed in different ways and directions. By the time I was ready to demand what I had wanted (that bigger life), far too much damage had been done to make saving the marriage possible. For the boy who had grown up with ambition and became the man who didn't know how to get what he needed from his marriage, divorce was one more act of survival.

Why had I thought of that now? Maybe nature was connecting me to other times and other feelings from my past. My essential self was getting nourishment. This was ground explored by my old friend Mr. Wordsworth. I had discovered him in Hamilton Smith Hall as a college sophomore, an accidental outdoorsman with whom I felt an immediate kinship. He had traveled with me as a beat-up book on many trips.

But for those first affections,
Those shadowy recollections,
Which, be they what they may,

Are yet the fountain-light of all our day,
Are yet a master-light of all our seeing . . .

Yes, WW understood. This must have been what he felt in the Alps or among his beloved English lakes. My body felt good. My arms felt muscled and strong, and I felt lighter. The skin of my face, under my beard, had been tanned and tightened by the sun, wind, and rain. I was beginning to feel leathery.

For some reason, as Adam and I glided down the river I remembered a giant oak tree in the woods where I had hunted as a boy in South Jersey. It was a monumental tree. Twelve feet around and easily a hundred feet tall, it had massive candelabra limbs that swung out and up from its knobby trunk. Its base, which seemed to gather its size and strength from giant roots that lay like cables in all directions, was as immovable as a granite outcrop, but the branches at its top swayed in the wind. The tree was home to dozens of gray squirrels. It was a village of squirrels; a city of squirrels; no, it was a metropolis of squirrels. Their nests were dispersed among the branches, and they chased and chirped among the leaves, corkscrewing around the limbs and then stopping short in their prayerful positions, front feet touching under their chins, tails arched like shepherds' crooks. I could watch them endlessly as the sun filtered through the cross-hatching of branches, leaves, and twigs. At some point, I had resolved not to shoot squirrels from that tree, and I took my pleasure instead from sitting below it and letting the lowering and still-warm sun of autumn bathe me in its warmth.

Yes, it was the same warmth that I was feeling at that moment in Alaska, from the same sun, a few seconds older on the clock of the universe, and it was the sun, I guessed, that had brought up the memory. I had been younger, seated under that tree, than my son was at this moment in Alaska, seated in the raft. I looked at him and thought of myself. It was at times like these that I had felt released from time and memory seemed a pond that I could swim around in, a deep, grassy farm pond. I could go down to the dark, mucky bottom or up to where the water was full of light.

My mind seemed let loose, and I was shuffling through memories with no rhyme or reason. Elizabeth was born early on a Thursday morning. It had been a long labor for her mother. I had looked out the high window of the hospital room. The sun's first light made the redbrick buildings glow as red as embers. I had never seen red like it before. The light seemed to come from within bricks as if they contained fire. Maybe it was the fire of new life in the world. Always when I thought of that morning, those redbrick buildings and the morning sun came back to me, and the world had felt new in a way that it had not before or since. When Elizabeth was four, she climbed to the seventh step of the staircase each night: pajamas, blond curls, laughter, pink feet, white toes pressed to leap. One and two and three and jump! "Weeeeeeeeeeeeeeee." Into the air and into my arms. "Again, Daddy!" "No, Elizabeth, no more. Time to go to bed." Giggles. "Daddy, one more time." Daddy. Daddy. Daddy. Daddy. Daddy. "My tummy hurts, Daddy. Can you make it stop hurting?"

Daddy.

I was swimming now, stroking hard into the past through the pond weed and gliding between dark and light.

As I absently worked the oars of the raft, Adam had returned to the bow and was casting.

I was in another world when I heard a holler and looked up and saw his rod dive toward the water. We were moving downstream, and the rod tip followed the tight line that was slicing through the water from the rear of the raft. I figured the line was snagged on the bottom. In a second, the line, tight as a banjo string, would snap and the cost would just be a lost fly. No big deal. The thing to do was point the rod at the snag so the line tugged against the reel and didn't bend and snap the rod. Instead, to my horror, Adam sat on the edge of the raft, swung his legs over, and hopped into the river. He did this in one quick continuous motion, in the blink of an eye. I was speechless. He bobbed and then stood up to his sternum in the rushing water. I could see that it was pushing him downstream, and he turned sideways to reduce the hydraulic force on his body.

The current was too strong for him to resist or hold the bottom with his feet. He held his rod high in the air and began playing a fish. It must have been a good fish, too, because the rod was turned to the shape of a U. The raft with me in it quickly left him behind. I knew the danger in these situations.

In water this deep, the body's natural buoyancy makes standing in the river difficult, especially in a swift current. It becomes impossible to keep one's feet on the bottom. The water lifts the fisherman, and he feels himself coming off his feet and soon he is moving with the river and his boot tips are barely touching the bottom as he is pushed to deeper water. The current knocks him over. His legs go to the surface. His waders fill with water, and he is pulled down, headfirst. It becomes impossible to stand or to swim or to right one's self. Many fishermen have drowned this way. I could remember situations in which I had been lifted by the water and was able to bounce on the tips of my toes to shallower water where my weight brought me back to solid bottom. But I hadn't been in current this swift. I felt a surge of panic. I was rushing downstream helplessly, and there was Adam, almost midstream, hooting and hollering, rod held high.

I changed my position in the raft, facing rearward, so I could pull hard on the oars. I tried to row upstream. Coming back as hard as I could on the oars, pulling strokes in rapid succession, I thought I could hold the raft steady in the current. In this position, maybe if I held here midstream, he could back his way down to me and grab the raft. The river would push him to me. I couldn't see him because my back was upstream, and I just concentrated on the job of rowing hard against the current. I pulled with all of my strength and feared snapping the oars.

I looked over my right oar and marked a bush on the bank. I wasn't able to hold my position against it: The apparent movement of the bush upstream told me that I was slipping downstream. I wasn't going to be able to keep the raft in place until Adam reached me. It simply was not possible: I couldn't pull hard enough.

I quickly turned to look back and saw that the distance between me and Adam was yawning. I remembered the anchor in the bow that we had made by filling a bag with stones. I threw it over and when it hit bottom the raft spun around. I played out the line and tied it off on a ring on the gunwale. The raft slowed, but it didn't stop. The stone anchor was dragging along the bottom. There was too much current. I could actually hear it banging on the rocks in the river. I had no other choice now but to try to get the raft to one bank or the other as fast as I could. There was no guarantee that Adam would be able to reach me even if I did, but the farther I slipped downstream the bigger our problem became— supposing that he wasn't going to be upended by the current or fall into a hole.

The river was deep right to the banks, and even if he found footing he would have a lot of trouble reaching me downstream. The river swirled against the high banks. I pulled toward the right bank and fastened my sight and every bit of my willpower on a willow bush that was poking from the base of the bank. If I could get to it and grab it, I could hold on to it until Adam reached me. With some effort and working with the drag of the anchor, I brought the raft to the bank just ahead of the bush. I stood up and grabbed the spindly trunk, pulling myself in closer and holding tight to the thickest part of the bush I could reach. I feared it would rip from the bank. The raft was pulling out from under me.

Throughout this effort, Adam continued playing his fish. He was paying no attention to me or the raft. He had sidled along to a place in the river that was only waist deep, and this had saved him from being tipped by the current. It was a miracle that he had been able to find a place to stand among the slippery rocks and deep, pocked bottom. He brought the fish to his side and he lifted it for me to see. It was a big char. He was laughing and grinning. I was furious. He worked his way through the heavy water to the bank about thirty yards upstream from me and picked his way toward the raft.

"Damn it, Adam," I said when he reached me. "I don't want you to ever do that again. You got that? Never again. Do you hear me."

He looked shocked. His expression went from surprise to defiance. I was not going to have any of it, not now, and I looked him directly in the eyes.

"You could have killed yourself jumping from the raft like that. That was stupid, just plain damned stupid."

"I'll do whatever I want," he said.

His eyes were blazing, his head thrust forward. The anger in both of us was at the boiling point.

"I'm telling you, I don't want you jumping out of the raft like that. It's stupid, and it's dangerous. I won't have it."

I threw down the oar I had been holding.

"I'll do what I want," he said. "Who are you to order me around?"

"I'm your father, that's who the hell I am."

"You have no right to tell me what to do."

We had reached a moment of truth. We had approached this ground before and he knew that he was placing his challenge to my authority on moral grounds—that I lacked the standing to say what was right or wrong. We both knew that the unstated indictment was that I was a hypocrite. He was shoving a stick into a festering wound. The pain went right to my heart. He was standing in the water still, with a hand on the stern of the raft, and I was in the rowing seat. We looked directly at each other. For so long between us, everything had been filtered through the feelings that had arisen out of the divorce and we had been unable to interact without our words and actions touching back to it. It bent everything in its direction. Even this remonstrance against a dangerous act on the river could not be dealt with for what it was but instead became another pretext for the deeper conflict that was smoldering below the surface.

The confrontation no longer was about jumping from the raft. All of it was swirling around us now—my disappointment that he wasn't enjoying the trip, my feeling of lost esteem in my son's eyes, and the frustration that he didn't know who I was or what I suffered. On his side, there was the hurt and disappointment over the disruption of his life and shattering of our family unit, the loss of me as the perfect father, and the substitution of me as liar and a cheat. Three years of mutual hurt that had never fully found their way into words were telescoping into a single moment on the river: rage, sadness, disappointment, and all the unresolved arguments, confrontations, and unanswerable questions. It was all rising up like a thundercloud.

I had felt all of it before, but up until this moment I had always collapsed under the weight of it. I had lacked the courage to hold my ground. I didn't want to lose my son. This time would be different. What more was there to lose? I had earned his enmity and sacrificed my authority as a father. There was nothing left to do but push farther ahead, through all of this hurt, and reclaim whatever I had left of myself as a person. I didn't want to make this confrontation about more than jumping from the raft, but it was too late to untangle it, and maybe I shouldn't even try to untangle it. He had jumped from the raft, putting his life in danger, and that was wrong, and he had spoken back to me, his father, and that was wrong, too. I let my words tumble out.

"Adam, you're acting horribly. You've been acting horribly the whole trip. I'm tired of it."

"I will do what I want. Don't try to run my life," he shot back. "You have no right."

I ignored the stick jabbing my wound. I had moved into unexplored territory. My words weren't being thought through this time, rehearsed with therapists, and I didn't even know if they were the right words, but I spoke them—taken there by anger and love that had refused to merge into any coherence. I spoke like a father and didn't weigh a word.

"It's pretty clear you want me to see that you're unhappy, and it's too bad that you are, but there's something you need to know. Whether you're happy or miserable is up to you, not me. I know you're mad at me, and I know you've been mad a long time, and I know why you're mad, but I'm telling you it's time for you to take responsibility for your own happiness. I'm done with it."

Adam listened. He didn't react except to stiffen his face. There was no movement in his expression—his mouth and the muscles of his face were frozen in anger. His eyes narrowed and burned. He said nothing back. He climbed into the raft and spooled his line onto the reel. Once he took his eyes off me, he refused to bring them back. He looked only at what he needed to look at: his rod, where he stepped on the ground, the raft. He cut me out of his line of sight. I didn't exist.

So now the trip was wrecked. The entire enterprise was a disaster. This was the moment I had wanted to avoid since coming to Alaska, but now it had happened, and since it had happened, well, so be it. I had tried my best, and I had failed, because everything I had done as a father on this trip had been wrong, so from now on I was going to enjoy what was left of it as best I could even if another word wasn't spoken between us for the next four days. I, who had never gotten to the Adirondacks, was in Alaska, and that was a fine thing in itself, goddammit. Here I was, fishing one of the world's great rivers, and that was a hell of a thing, wasn't it? Sure I had patched this trip together with not enough money, but I had made it happen. I had kept my promise, the promise to Adam and myself; we were catching fish, lots of fish, and I had cooked exactly twenty meals and gotten us this far down a river that I had never laid eyes on before, and I was doing it without a thousand-dollars-a-day guide, and for chrissake, what was I supposed to do anyway, stay in a marriage against all evidence that it was doing any good for either of the two people who were in it? I had taken that question on too many times already, fought it to a stalemate, and finished sick and exhausted, punched out, and I wasn't going to do it again now, not with a river spread before me. I was going fishing. I felt my heart pounding in my chest.

Silently, Adam and I slipped downstream. We spent the rest of the day not saying much more to each other than what was required to get down the river. And that, more or less, was how we spent the next two days.

VI. BACK IN PHILADELPHIA

Social critics who say divorce has become too easy haven't been through one. Every divorce is unique, I'm sure, but I also think for most people divorces have this in common: They're a last resort. I read the books on divorce as I struggled with my decision. They filled one entire shelf of one of my bookcases. Their longitudinal studies on the effects of divorce on children were useless. They treated divorce as if it were a choice of lifestyle. It is not: It is a struggle to keep one's self alive. There's only one good book on divorce that I know of, and it's called *Jude the Obscure,* by Thomas Hardy. It has more wisdom in a single page than all the books in the self-help section of a modern bookstore. It is less argument than illumination: It shows the cost of a marriage that fails to accommodate the natures of the people who inhabit it.

Of course divorce is bad for children. So is a death in the family. Death occurs; divorce occurs. We do not impute motive to death. Why should we set this burden on divorce?

Sara had come to visit me in Philadelphia during the first

summer I was in Philadelphia, and we were walking through a restaurant when I saw an old oil painting on the wall, from the nineteenth century. It showed a man in a frock coat with his wife and two children, a boy and girl, on a prosperous farm. It stopped me cold. I couldn't take my eyes from it. The father in the painting looked proud and confident. He stood tall, and his level gaze suggested rectitude. His wife and children, standing slightly in front of him, appeared happy, healthy, and secure. In the background, there was a big house and abundant fields. Birds flew in the sky. I knew that man: He had been my model. He and I were the same person. It was how I thought of myself and how I met the world. My family was my bulwark against the life I had left behind as a child. I had created myself as father and provider, and all that was missing was the frock coat. I was frozen there in front of the painting, staring at it. I wondered how I was going to step down from it.

"Are you okay?" Sara asked.

"Huh? Oh yes, I'm okay."

2

I wasn't okay.

My obsession with the details of the marriage went on. I wanted to know everything and put it in careful order so I could evaluate what had happened. Was I right or wrong in not wanting the marriage to continue? I called an old friend in Maine to check my memory of my marriage against his recollections of how it had appeared to him. Had I seemed like a good husband? I recalled some incidents when we all were together as couples. Had I treated my wife badly? He listened and tried to answer my questions. I felt my odd behavior reflected in his nervous laughter. I called my brother and cataloged my thoughts and feelings to him.

"Hey, Louie, you're beating yourself up."

And, every night, I called my mother. The calls were nearly all the same: I told her that I was feeling terribly stressed and that I was unable to decide what to do. She always responded with concern but made no attempt to move me toward a decision.

Then one night, after scores and scores of nights of the same words from me, she began to speak.

"Louis, I know it's hard to get divorced."

She went on to tell me, in greater detail than she had ever done before, the story of her own first marriage and divorce. I knew the basic outline of the story. It had seeped out through the years. Much of it was fuzzy and choppy; the film was broken. I say "film" because I had attempted to picture and splice together the disconnected incidents my mother had described to me over many years to make a story of her life that made sense to me. There had seemed to be no cause-and-effect logic between so much of what I had heard from her and what had happened to us. It wasn't coherent in a way that allowed me to grasp what had actually occured in her life and the beginning of mine. There were certain parts that she had told me—a freeze-frame here, a freeze-frame there—that I had memorized as episodes from some tale of the distant past.

There was the story of my birth, for example. Many times she had told me that she had been driven to the hospital in the back of a supermarket delivery truck. She had gone into labor during a snowstorm, and she had walked across the street, from our house in Monroe, to the Ideal Market, where she had shopped, to get help. She told the Italian man who owned the market that she was about to have her baby. He went around back, got his truck, and laid her down in the back with a blanket. He brought her through the wild storm and over the roads covered in snow to Middlesex General Hospital in New Brunswick, where I was born on December 28, 1950.

It was only after several tellings that it occurred to me what was strange about the story: not that she had been taken to the hospital in a grocery truck in a snowstorm, which was her point of emphasis, but that she was close to giving birth and my father was not living with her and available to drive her to the hospital. I deduced, they must already have been separated by her first pregnancy.

There was another episode, in particular, that she would mention to me from time to time. There had been a moment, at what I gathered was a divorce hearing, when a lawyer or maybe the judge had asked my mother a question or made an accusation that hurt and embarrassed her. The recollection of it would leave her angry and distracted for an hour or so after the telling of the story. In her telling, she lashed out at the men in the courtroom: "You cannot treat me like this!" That's what she had said, or something like it. "You cannot treat me like this!" The moral of the tale, from her perspective, was that I should not accept the judgment of others: "Don't let anyone hold you back, Louis." It was important to fight back. It was for that reason that she would tell me the story. "You cannot treat me like this!"

The incident was perfectly confusing to me as a child. Instead of absorbing it as a lesson in resisting injustice, my mind would be lost in trying to arrange the room in which all of this had taken place: My mother would have been on a witness stand, and a judge would have been seated above her, like in the courtroom scenes in *Perry Mason* on television, and a lawyer would be in front of her asking the question, and somewhere seated up front at a long table would be my father.

What was the accusation that had so stung her?

Now on the phone with me, as I struggled with the prospect of my own divorce, my mother was about to splice together some of those pieces of the film. To understand what she was about to say, it needs to be known that my mother had been raised by poor immigrant parents according to the strict customs of the Greek villages in which they had been born.

My mother worked in the family restaurant and later, during World War II, in a Western Electric factory in Kearny, New Jersey, where she wrapped wire onto spools that would become electric coils. She turned her sixteen dollars a week over to her parents. She had been emerging as a talented artist and designer when her parents forced her to give up entrance in the city's arts high school. I once asked one of my uncles, my mother's second brother, Constantine, what my grandfather's attitude was toward his daughter. I knew that my mother had loved her father, but he had died before my birth and I could never discern from what I had heard from her how he had felt toward her.

My uncle said, "Well, he never spoke about it, but if he had he might have said something like, 'It's just my luck to have a daughter.' "

On the phone with me, my mother began to speak: "My parents were terribly strict with me, Louis. I wasn't allowed to do anything. I met a guy at the first beauty shop I worked at in Newark. His name was Jack. He was a gentle guy, and very good-looking. He had wavy brown hair. He was a good dresser, too. He liked to wear double-breasted jackets. He looked great in them. He was crazy about me. He said I looked like Dorothy Lamour. You know, I was a pretty good-looking girl back in those days. Jack was Irish and liked to have a good time and he used to take me dancing. Of course I had to sneak out of the house, because my mother and father never let me do anything. I was like a prisoner in that house. All they wanted me to do was work. Work, and meet a Greek guy, and marry a Greek guy. That's all I was good for. My mother was the worst, and Pappou [a Greek word of endearment, meaning "grandfather"] just went along with her. He couldn't argue with her. She would just scream. I could only go out at night if one of my brothers came along. I wasn't allowed to date boys. So, my brother Johnny would lie for me, and he would tell my mother that we were going out together with friends, and then we would split up once we were out of the house. I would meet Jackie and we would go dancing. Sometimes we would go to a ballroom in Newark. Sometimes we would go to New York, to the Apollo. Jackie was a good dancer, and so was I. We were jitterbuggers.

"We had a lot of fun. We always got dressed up. People said we looked great together dancing. At the end of the night, Johnny and I would meet under the clock in front of Bamberger's on Broad Street in downtown Newark and we would go home together. My mother thought I was out with Johnny the whole time. I went out with Jackie for almost two years like that. Then one day he gave me an engagement ring. It was after work. He wanted to marry me. Oh, Louis, I was so happy. I loved Jackie. I went home and showed it to my mother. She was furious. She said to me, 'How long have you been seeing this guy? Have you been sneaking around? You're acting like a whore. You're going to disgrace this family.' That not all she said. Louis, my mother could be terribly mean to me. She said, 'If he works in the beauty shop, he's probably a queer. Take that ring back to him.' She said the most horrible things about me and him. She made me take the ring back."

She paused in her story. She was choking up on the other end of the line. I didn't say a word. Then she continued.

"Louis, I was heartbroken. I took the ring back, and I stopped seeing him. [There was another and longer pause.] Not long after that, one of the girls in the beauty shop, the first shop I had worked in, right in downtown Newark, said she was going to fix me up with a guy. My mother and father were out of town. They had gone to visit some relatives. This girl-friend in the shop had a boyfriend and he knew a guy, Gene Ureneck, and they were going to introduce me to him. Both of them worked on a farm out in Hackettstown. That was way out in the country back then. Hackettstown was all farms, big vegetable farms. Your father always liked working on a farm. He was a farmhand at heart. Both of these guys worked on the farm. So, my girlfriend and I took the train out to Hack-ettstown from Newark, and we met her boyfriend and Gene, and we spent the weekend together. Then, and it all began as a joke, after two days together Gene and I got married. We found a justice of the peace, and he married us.

"I knew immediately that I had made a big mistake. I went back to Newark by myself. I waited for my mother and father to get back. When they did, I told my mother what had happened. I said, 'Mom, I want to get out of this.' I was embarrassed. I told her that the marriage hadn't been con-summated. I thought there would be some way to get out of it. I don't think Gene really wanted to get married, either. It started as a joke. My mother screamed and called me the worst names—all in Greek, and they are so much worse when you know the words in Greek. '*Strickla,*' that's what she called

me. 'Witch.' She said to me, 'He's your husband now.' She
said to me, 'Go with your husband. You made this bed; now
sleep in it.' So I went to him. I had no choice. My mother
would not let me live at home.

"First Gene and I moved to South River, then to Spotswood.
Gene's brother said he could get him a construction job there,
but the work was never steady. I opened the beauty shop in
Spotswood, and Gene stopped working. I got sick of it. I was
killing myself working all the time. I wanted more to life than
just working. I told him, 'I'm not working anymore. I'm finished.' That's when he left me the first time. I was by myself.
I was terribly alone. While he was gone, I saw Jack again.
Gene came back, and he found out that I had seen Jack. He
went into a rage. When you were born, he was convinced that
you weren't his child."

I couldn't believe what she had just told me. My father
didn't think I was his child? How could that be? I had never
heard this before. Was this true? Everything I knew—all that I
had gleaned over the years—was thrown into a different light.
Things that I never had been able to understand before were
starting to fall into place. Gene Ureneck thought I was someone else's son. This would explain the scene in the courtroom.

This was too much, even coming from my mother. I had to
ask her.

"Mom, this is important. Was I Gene's son?"

"Yes," she said. "You were his son."

I was feeling sick to my stomach.

"I'm telling you all of this, Louis, because when I decided
to get divorced everyone was against me. Everyone. My
mother was against me the most. Nobody understood. Nobody was in my shoes. But I decided that staying married to
Gene was too big a sacrifice for me to make. I wasn't going to

give up my life to stay married to him. I held on to you kids, but I wasn't going to stay married to him. It was too much. I had my life to live."

3

Soon after the conversation with my mother, I sat down at the computer in my apartment and composed a letter. It began: "Dear Eugene Ureneck." I introduced myself as his son, described my job and career, and told him that I was married with two children. I acknowledged that the letter would come to him as a surprise and it might be difficult to receive after the passage of so much time. I said that I was not making any judgments about the past, nor did I intend to. I just wanted to know him better and have him know me. I said I would understand if he didn't respond. I asked if he would be willing to get together, even for a short time. Maybe we could talk on the phone. I thanked him and dropped the letter in a mailbox on Race Street on the way to work. I had signed the letter: "Your son, Louis."

4

In the fall, at the beginning of his sophomore year of high school, Adam and I staggered into our new life. He was fourteen.

We got up in the mornings, and Adam went to school and I went to work. I woke first, walked into his room and spoke his name to wake him up, and then went to get him breakfast from a lunch truck parked on the street. Philadelphia's streets are full of these trucks, serving a quick breakfast or lunch. The city smells like bacon at seven in the morning. I usually got Adam a bacon-egg-and-cheese sandwich on a bagel and a hot chocolate in a paper cup. I carried the meal in a paper bag back to our apartment while he got dressed. After he ate his breakfast, I walked him to the bus stop for the trip across the city to his school and then got myself ready for work.

At night, often late when I got home, as Adam played the music of Jimi Hendrix, Bob Dylan, and Kurt Cobain, I made some single man's sorry excuse for a dinner—pancakes, omelets, or spaghetti. Many times, too tired to cook, I brought home hoagies from the Fourth Street Deli or takeout from one of the Chinese places I passed on Race Street on the way home. His mother had been a great cook: meat, vegetables, and potatoes on the table every night, steaming in bowls and platters, water glasses, a pitcher full of water and ice, butter on a butter plate. Now Adam and I were eating in front of the television or over the chessboard we had set up in the living room, talking about our day or not at all.

Almost overnight, I had overthrown his old life. His assumptions of security and reliability were damaged. These were the unconscious and necessary assumptions of childhood that had been lived among family rituals and traditions: dinner at 7:00 P.M. with all of us, mother, father, daughter, and son, seated around the dining room table, late-afternoon Little League games where parents sat on lawn chairs and clapped in the warm summer light for their sons and occasionally their daughters, five-day family vacations to Florida that produced sunburns, shell collections, and enormous quantities of snapshots.

Adam had to find his place in a new high school in a big city. He had no friends in the beginning and no familiar places to hang out. He had entered a school in which most of the students had known one another since the first grade. They were city kids, street-smart and hip. Adam was a boy from a small town in Maine. He had to handle all of this as I started a new job.

The first apartment we lived in was in a section of the city that had been home to small manufacturers and wholesale supply houses. It was gradually gentrifying into loft spaces, but it was still a good place to buy, say, forty matching bar stools, a pizza oven, or rebuilt drill presses. Our apartment was in a building on a busy corner, on the fourth floor. The street level held a sushi restaurant that played cool jazz. To get to our apartment, you walked through an entrance of banged-up mailboxes and piles of free newspapers and restaurant flyers and took the elevator to a carpeted hallway with a hung ceiling and rows of doors with small gold knockers. Our apartment was No. 408. It had one bedroom with a door, which became Adam's room, and an open space intended for a studio or den, which was where I set my single bed. I put up curtains and bought a sofa and padded wing-style chair for the living room at a discount furniture store.

Our neighbor in the next apartment was a hot Colombian woman who brought boyfriends home on Friday and Saturday nights. Her bedroom abutted our living room. We heard her moans. Sometimes we turned up the television to drown her out. Other times we took the moans as a cue for our bedtime. One wall in the living room was big and white, like an art exhibit space, and I hung Adam's photographs on it. His photos were nostalgic and domestic: landmarks of the place we used to live, snowstorms lit by street lamps at night, a still life of fruit and bread in a bowl from the house in Maine, and many sunsets.

We had our dog, Rusty, with us, too. He was an aging Brittany, the last pup of a litter I had raised when we had lived in

the country. We walked him in the weeded lots in the neighborhood under the Benjamin Franklin Bridge and took him
with us when we went fishing. When he got angry at being
left alone, he raided the garbage in the kitchen or ate our
books. He preferred garbage to books. One day with no trash
available and Adam and me late in getting home from school
and work, Rusty consumed the better part of the alpha pages
in an expensive Greek lexicon that I had bought Adam soon
after he got to Philadelphia. Among the words on the pages
Rusty had torn from the book, but not eaten, was "antitos,"
the ancient word for revenge. At night, he slept with Adam on
the foot of his bed. They were inseparable.

There was one piece of our old life that persisted, though,
and it became a thread that kept us connected to better times.
We still had fishing. Some fathers and sons shared baseball.
Adam and I had flies and trout streams. The separation, and
what increasingly looked like a divorce, had shaken Adam's
view of me. I wasn't the hero he had thought I was. But the
fishing, I think, let him hold on to some better part of me. It
gave me some claim on being a capable man and father and
someone with a store of useful knowledge. I knew how to do
this part of life right and well. It was a remnant of me that
Adam could continue to believe in.

We could not find the words for the bigger problem between us, but we could always talk about fishing, the places
we had been, Nova Scotia, the Florida Keys, Montana, the
Bahamas, northern Maine, and we could always talk about
the places we wanted to go. Alaska was one of those places. In
fact, it was the most important place.

Adam had been in the seventh grade and reached only
halfway up my chest when we had started planning it. I had
been on a journalism fellowship at Harvard at the time, and

we had lived in Cambridge for the school year. I had gone down without my wife, and while I didn't know it then as I was stumbling through my distress and unhappiness, I saw later that it was a way for me to break out of the marriage or to at least step outside of it for a time. I had been married almost twenty years by then. Adam had come with me, a year with his dad, and he attended a middle school in Cambridge. We occupied a tiny apartment with one room, a kitchen, downstairs and two small bedrooms and a bathroom upstairs. The heat frequently didn't work, and I would turn on the oven of the gas stove and open the oven door to heat our rooms.

Right from the beginning, I had decided that he and I would do the year together, as a team. If there was a function that Adam couldn't attend, well, then I wouldn't attend it, either. I told him this. We were in it as a team. In the first week, I received an invitation from the White House for an evening reception with Bill and Hillary Clinton. I knew I was getting the invitation because I was a Harvard fellow, so I checked to see if I could bring Adam. I was told no. I declined the invitation. I was sticking to my promise. I wasn't going to have him come home from a new school to an empty apartment, and I wasn't going to begin our adventure together with an exception to my "we're-a-team" rule.

That same week, we received a printed invitation to dinner at the Harvard Faculty Club. This was a place I had never expected to find myself. For me, Harvard was mysterious and unattainable and the notion that I was there—actually there— seemed a dream. I had gone to a state college, admitted through the door of its agriculture school, which was where the forestry and wildlife biology programs had been lodged. The very name Harvard seemed a talisman and the university the magical idea of an elite education. The Harvard Faculty Club seemed its sanctum sanctorum. I could only imagine the conversations that had occurred there over codfish cakes or sherry.

On the day of the event, Adam and I went to a department store in Cambridge and I bought him a blue blazer and a new pair of shoes from the boys' department. The Harvard Faculty Club sits a small distance off the Harvard Yard. It's a redbrick Federalist building, and it looks like a house that could serve as a presidential mansion. Inside, the ceilings are high and the walls are hung with life-size portraits of university presidents and clergymen of the Massachusetts Bay Colony. Plush crimson carpets cover the floors. A stairway sweeps to the second floor, and that's where our dinner was to be held. We walked up the stairs and turned into a room with walls that were covered with maps and more paintings, mostly formal portraits and New England landscapes. The windows, gracefully curved at the top, reached from floor to ceiling, and outside, in the dark, I could see the black limbs of the big trees and the lights of Widener Library in the Yard. People had begun to gather in the room, and there was a bar set up against the wall. I examined some of the paintings. When I looked up, Adam was nowhere to be seen. I scanned the room. I saw about thirty people with drinks in their hands talking in small groups, but I didn't see Adam. At the far end of the room, a bigger group had gathered and the people seemed huddled around some center. I walked over, fitted myself into the packed shoulders and elbows, and saw that in the middle were two people, conversing back and forth. One of them was big and the other was small. The noted jurist A. Leon Higginbotham, our dinner speaker, and Adam were discussing that year's baseball strike. Ten Nieman fellows listened in admiringly, never interrupting.

And so it went for the year. I would come back to the Lippman House, the four-story colonial manse that was the fellow-ship's home on "Professors' Row," and there would be Adam's bicycle inside the front door and there would be Adam, in the office of curator Bill Kovach. Adam would be talking with Bill and the ambassador to China or some big newspaper's Washington bureau chief. Once a week, some important guest—a Nobel laureate, winner of the Pulitzer Prize, or fa-mous author—would speak to the fellows near the fireplace in the Lippman House living room and then take questions. Bill always gave the first question to Adam. The year bonded him and me even more tightly, and it brought back to me the good feelings that I remembered from the closeness that my mother, brother, and I had shared when I was growing up. It had always been us against the world.

Harvard welcomed us. Adam rode his mountain bike all over campus, up and down the steps of the law school, and through Harvard Yard, which was strictly forbidden. He would get a good start at one of the gates on Massachusetts Avenue and race over the pathways before the campus police, whistles blasting, could catch him. We ate our meals at Low-ell House among the overachieving undergraduates, and Adam swam in the Harvard pool. If we wanted fancier food, we crashed the receptions at the Kennedy School or the Clas-sics Department.

For me, Harvard was a dreamworld: I fitted in as many courses as I could and attended seminars at night by professors whose names were academic icons. My plan had been to study history and compare the methods of historians with the prac-tices of journalists. I attended an anthropology course, The Uses of History, taught by a scholar from Oxford University. To my astonishment, he invited me to lunch when I introduced myself to him after class. It was my first time eating sushi. We talked about journalism, anthropology, and Greece. (He had done his thesis on the island of Crete.)

I also spent two semesters studying ancient Greek. My fascination with ancient Greek went back to my college study of the English Romantic poets. Occasionally they had prefaced their poems with a Greek phrase, and I wanted desperately to unlock the code of those odd symbols that were Greek letters. Then, of course, there was that Greek pride that my mother had lodged in me, though the Greek she had grown up speaking was not the Greek I was learning at Harvard. Greek 101 was pure toil, like breaking stones in the hot sun. Ten of us, including the instructor, sat around a plain wood table in Boylston Hall and took turns reading six lines of Greek from Plato's *Apology* and then offered an English translation and an analysis of the grammar. The Greek verb has five hundred parts. The eight undergraduates in the class handled the work with speed and alacrity, crackling out the number, tense, and mood of the verbs and the identities of the innumerable participles. Then it would be my turn. Everything slowed down. I felt as if my mind was powered by an old-fashioned wood-burning boiler and soon smoke would come pouring out of my ears. I picked my way haltingly through the vocabulary and syntax and left the class exhausted. I sometimes had to nap after class. But I was learning Greek. This was no small thing to me: I was ready to put it on a par with having built a timber-frame house. At the end of the semester, I could conjugate a Greek verb and read the words Plato had used to convey the teaching of that most famous of teachers, Socrates.

Many of the Nieman fellows were from foreign countries. They were an astonishing group of journalists, some of whom were heroes in their nations. One, Kemal Kursparic from Sarajevo, had lost the use of one leg when Serbian gunmen attempted to assassinate him. Another had nearly died in a Chinese prison after the government jailed him for taking his Beijing radio program off the air to protest the Tiananmen massacre. I stayed up late into the night talking with them, mostly listening to their experiences. There was a woman from Poland, who had played a key role in the Solidarity labor movement, and another from Tanzania. She had brought her two young boys to Cambridge, and they and Adam often played together on the grass in front of the Lippman House. The international Niemans were curious about my experiences, too, and I told them about Maine and how we had remade the *Press Herald*.

One weekend, I brought the Chinese fellow, Wu Xiao Young, back to Maine and took him fishing. We caught some bass, which he steamed with scallions and then cooked again by drizzling the fish with hot peanut oil. It was delicious. On the way to the lake, he had gazed at the deep woods passing us by.

"Do you have tigers here in Maine?" he asked.

"No, no tigers, Xiao Young, but we do have moose."

A little later, we passed some small potato farms.

"Do the farmers grow bamboo here in Maine?" he asked.

"No, there's no bamboo," I said.

"It's a good crop," he said. "They should grow bamboo."

The year at Harvard was a gift for which I will be forever grateful, and it opened up my life at a time when I was desperately feeling the need for renewal and a bigger life. Sitting among my Nieman classmates during our discussions and moving among the classes at Harvard, I felt a tremendous sense of possibility. I felt connected to a larger world and a universe of ideas.

One winter night as the snow ticked at the window of our campus apartment, Adam and I were tying trout flies at the kitchen table and talking about fishing—our favorite places, the biggest fish, the best flies.

I said, "Adam, tell you what. When you graduate from high school, that summer, we'll go fishing in Alaska."

It was an extravagant promise even then. I was an editor at a small daily newspaper, and a trip to Alaska, arranged by an outdoor travel agency, with airfare, lodges, guides at five hundred dollars a day per person, and gear, could cost a semester's tuition at a private college. The money wouldn't be easy to come up with. I figured at the time that I had plenty of time to work it out. Adam's graduation seemed a long way off. I already had a record as a father for extravagant promises. When my daughter was ten, she had begged me for a horse. To the astonishment of us both, I bought her one. Actually, she had said she wanted a pair of riding boots, and over the course of the four months leading up to Christmas she had built up toward the horse. She worked her way, one small step at a time, from hunt cap, to riding lessons, to membership in the pony club, to the Big Request Itself. On Christmas morning, I led her out to the barn I had built that fall in anticipation of this gift and introduced her to Joker, a chestnut gelding with a split right ear and long brown eyelashes. These grand gestures were among the things I liked best about being a father. It gave me joy to be a little too generous, and they fitted the picture of what I imagined a father to be.

"Thanks, Dad."

The sweetest syllable in the language: "Dad."

When I had made the Alaska promise to Adam in the Cambridge apartment, he turned his eyes up from the trout fly in the vise that I had been teaching him to make. I think it was a Mickey Finn. He produced his trademark smile. For me, back then, it locked the trip in place as a promise.

. . .

In Philadelphia, we kept our rods in our apartment and some-times we got out of the city to fish. We drove to the Jersey shore for striped bass, which we caught in the surf at Island Beach State Park, and Central Pennsylvania for trout. One weekend, we drove to the upper Delaware River. We stayed at a cheap motel and explored the river as it snaked its way through the farm and hill country of the upper Poconos, and we watched in amazement as huge fish shot across the river's long, quiet pools. The fish refused our favorite New England streamer flies, Grey Ghosts, Black Ghosts, and other fresh-water smelt patterns, tied with bucktail, saddle hackle, and maribou on long-shanked hooks. These were the flies that al-ways had worked for us in Maine, on the Roach and Ken-nebago rivers. Only later did we learn that the Delaware fish were shad that had come up from the ocean and not trout. The way to catch them was with neon-green plastic-covered hooks. These shad darts, as they were called, were anglers' costume jewelry. They looked to us like the saltwater rigs used by the meat fishermen who sat on their ten-gallon spackle buckets on the State Pier back in Portland and jigged for mackerel. Adam and I had a good laugh about that.

5

At the newspaper, my job had shifted from the city desk to the news desk. The new job was "reading back" on stories headed to the front page and working with other editors to make sure the stories were complete and well written. The new job required a later start to my workday, because most sto-ries were handed in by reporters late in the afternoon. I came in at 1:00 P.M. The schedule meant that I would be at work when Adam came home from school, so I arranged for him to come to the newspaper office around 5:00 P.M. We had dinner together in the newspaper cafeteria. He then stayed at the paper and completed his homework at a desk in the newsroom. Either we went home together or, if there was a lot of news to handle, he went home first and I followed later in the evening when he and Rusty would be asleep.

One afternoon, the telephone on the news desk rang and I picked it up.

I gave my standard greeting: "News desk."

Usually the calls that came to me were from an editor in one of the newspaper's bureaus alerting me to a story that might be worth putting on the front page or the pressroom passing along information about a change in the deadlines. This time, though, the voice on the other end of the line was unfamiliar. It was a man's voice and not one that I recognized.

It said, "Is this Lou Ureneck?"

I said that it was. I was struck immediately by the fact that he had pronounced my name correctly. I have a difficult name for many people to say, and I was used to having it mangled. I sensed that something unusual or important was about to come to me from the other end of the line, and I felt balanced as on the pointed peak of the moment: Should I be alarmed, or could this be something good? I waited through a short silence. I could hear noise in the background, the hum of a crowd and a public-address system completing some announcement.

"I'm not really sure how to begin," the voice said, "and I'm in an airport, so I don't have a lot of time, but I wanted to call you. The letter you sent to Eugene Ureneck—well, I have it with me. There are some things I need to tell you."

There was a pause.

"I was Gene's nephew. I'm sorry to have to tell you this, but Gene passed away last year."

There was another long pause. I didn't know what to say.

The letter I mailed had been received by Gene's wife, the caller said.

"She's my aunt," he said. "My mother and Gene's wife are sisters. They're very close."

He told me that Eugene's wife had received the letter. It had shaken her and left her upset. She didn't know what to do with it, so she gave it to her sister, who in turn had given it to him.

"I'm sorry about all of this," he said.

"Can I ask you a few things?" I said.

"Yes. I will do my best," he said.

"Did Gene ever tell anyone that he had a son?"

"No, I don't think so. I didn't know it."

"Did his wife know?"

"I don't think so. No."

"Did you know him?"

"Yes," he said. "I was close to him. He was very good to me. He liked baseball and he used to take me to Mets games."

"What was he like?"

"Well, he was pretty easy to please, and simple in a lot of ways. He was great to me. He gave me my first car. That was really important to me. It was a used car, and he really liked giving it to me. He had fixed it up. I was in college, and I needed a car."

"What kind of work did he do?"

"He was retired. But he had worked for the city. He was a foreman for the Road Department."

"Did he have any children?"

"No, he didn't. He and my aunt didn't have any children. They were very close."

"And he didn't mention me, or my brother? He never said anything vaguely about it, sort of alluding to it? Nothing about another family?"

"No, I'm sorry. He never said anything. Like I said, I'm at the airport, and I'm going to have to go to catch a flight. So I'm going to have to run now."

"Okay. I appreciate it that you called."

"I thought I had to. I'm sorry about all of this."

"That's okay. Thanks."

I sat at my desk stunned. I remembered the small backyard of my grandparents' home in North Arlington, New Jersey. My father had taken me there when I was very small, maybe four or five years old. The recollection of it suddenly was strong and vivid: a narrow sloping rectangle of grass between adjacent yards separated by a low wood fence on both sides. I pictured him sitting there listening to the ball game. He was alone, with a radio on a table, in a lawn chair. Then a boy came into the yard, and they went off to the ball game.

I got up and went outside the building and walked around the block. My head was spinning. Had my father continued to think, as my mother had suggested, that I wasn't really his son? Had he ever thought back on me and Paul? Why hadn't he taken me to a baseball game? I took a second lap around the block and went back inside to finish my shift pulling together the day's news.

6

Adam talked to his mother on the phone from Philadelphia and went to stay with her on holidays. In the second year of our separation, she had returned to New Hampshire, near where she had grown up. At the end of his sophomore year,

Adam went back to Maine for the summer break. He lived with my brother, Paul, which was about an hour's drive from where Patti was living.

In Maine, Adam reclaimed a small skiff with an outboard motor that I had left behind. He patched it up and took it out on Casco Bay almost every day. He fished for mackerel and bluefish. In September, he returned to Philadelphia for the start of school. By then I had found a new apartment, which had a homier feel and was in a better part of the city. It had one bedroom, where Adam slept with Rusty, and an alcove next to the bathroom, where I set up my single bed. Together we tried to make it a home.

One day Adam said to me, "Let's buy some things for the apartment."

I agreed it was a good idea. I didn't have much money to spend on furnishings, but he was right. We needed to make the apartment our own. I was happy that he wanted to join in. We went downtown and picked out a big gilt mirror that he liked, and then we went to a gallery that was showing nature paintings and sporting art. It was full of ships and landscapes. There was one painting in particular, of an Alaskan landscape, that we both loved, but it cost twenty-five thousand dollars, far beyond anything I could even contemplate spending. We looked carefully through the gallery, flipping through prints, and we found a beautiful and delicate pen-and-ink drawing of the dunes and ocean at Cape Cod. I bought it and we took it home and hung it in our living room. For us it was an extravagance, but it added a touch of class to our little apartment.

At Christmas, we drove to South Philadelphia, a neighborhood of tightly packed row houses, and bought a tree from a stand that had been set up on the street. We decorated it with bulbs and lights I had bought at Kmart. The next morning, we awoke to find that all of the needles had fallen off. We were left with a spindly trunk and lots of bare branches. I covered its nakedness with more tinsel and left it up until New Year's Day.

The divorce became final in Adam's junior year of high school. Until then, I think he was hoping my wife and I would put things back together.

Adam was confused and angry about the breakup of our family and my long fall from perfection. As for me, I was torn by remorse and guilt. There was plenty of unspoken emotion between us. Confusion, disappointment, and anger, they were tightly packed together, and they resisted unbundling and explanation.

I had pushed him to talk about his feelings many times. I had pushed too hard, really, and my attempts only seemed to drive him deeper inside himself. I had always preached to my children the importance of sticking together as a family. It was an article of faith with me, and I had wanted it to be with them. I had felt a responsibility as a boy to take care of my mother, and more than once I had told Adam as he was growing up that sons should take care of their mothers. It was the code with which I had been raised by my mother: family first. And then, one day, I was telling both Adam and Elizabeth that I was breaking my commitment to their mother. I was splitting up our family. They took it as a broken commitment to them.

I had lost my footing as a father. I was on the phone at least once a week with a child psychiatrist who coached me on getting Adam to open up about his feelings. I had made a mess of things, and I needed every bit of advice I could get. I would go to his bedroom at night to rub his back and encourage him to talk. Those bedtime back rubs were moments of closeness that I looked forward to. He was still sleeping with his teddy bear on his bed and Rusty, too, and enjoyed the back rubs, but Adam would not open up. The result of pushing him was longer silences. Finally, I gave up on getting him to talk about his feelings. I rubbed his back and asked him about school.

He told me about each class and after-school activities, and to extend the backrubs he talked about the small group of friends he had made at school. There were three boys in particular who had befriended him: They were smart and hip urban kids who had grown up together in downtown Philadelphia, and the four of them, including Adam, the country boy, attended concerts and hung out at one another's houses.

By then, Sara had moved to Philadelphia and our relationship, which had begun as a friendship, had grown into something much deeper. I saw her frequently. This inflamed the situation between Adam and me. I was forging a new relationship with a woman at the same time that I was dissolving my marriage. On the one hand, the timing was all wrong. It was too fast, and his anger was justified. On the other hand, I knew in my own heart that my marriage was over, and I did not want to walk away from a person I had fallen in love with. In Adam's eyes, and Elizabeth's, too, I became small and unreliable. I was untrustworthy, repugnant, and unfaithful. There was no way that I could convey to them what I was going through without looking to them like a hypocrite. I was guilty as charged.

As Adam had approached the end of high school, we ran into more disagreements and even the fishing we had shared seemed in danger of becoming a casualty. One shouting match, over rules that I was laying down about how late he could be out on a school night, had brought us chest-to-chest in the kitchen of our apartment. The argument stopped just short of pushing and throwing fists. He was yelling at me, and I was yelling back at him.

He said, "Who are you to be making rules and to say what's right?"

It was a direct challenge to my authority as a father.

His words hurt me. My defense would have required more words and time than the heat of the moment would tolerate. I was struck dumb. I felt his surging need to throw a punch. His arm was back and low, his fist clenched, and his neck and shoulders bulging. His aggressiveness had lit my own anger, and I threw out my own chest and was ready to take back the respect, with force if necessary, that he had withdrawn from me. If he threw a fist, then I would throw one back. We were ready to brawl in the living room.

"I hate you," he shouted.

He stormed up to his bedroom and slammed the door.

It was one of the worst battles between us, but there were many others. One night, after an argument about Sara, he ran away. He said he was going back to his mother. He stormed from the house. Later that night, after hours of worry, the father of one of Adam's friends called me: Adam was at their house and was staying there overnight.

"I really appreciate your calling," I said.

"We care about both of you," the father said. "I wanted to let you know what's going on here."

For three days Adam didn't call and he went to school directly from his friend's house. Finally, Adam came home. He didn't say a word about his absence. I told him I was glad that he was back.

In the waning days of his senior year, his antagonism grew sharper. It was clear that he wanted to get away from me. I felt him moving farther and farther away. I worried that he had come to a judgment about us that might last a very long time, maybe a lifetime. For me, the Alaska trip began to take on even more importance.

Adam graduated from high school in June. I threw him a party in the small yard outside our apartment and invited his friends and their families. I stayed up most of the night making food: *satay* chicken on skewers, fresh-fruit salad, and *spanokopita.* His mother came down to Philadelphia, and Elizabeth was there from New York. There were awkward moments, but the party was a success. Then Adam went back up to Maine to work for the summer before entering college.

Before he left, I told him to plan on the trip to Alaska.

"Yeah, sure," he said.

There was no commitment in his voice.

Now that so much had changed, I couldn't say exactly what I wanted from the Alaska trip. It wasn't going to be the victory lap that I had originally planned during the snowstorm at Harvard. Neither did I figure that there would be a big talk between us that would clear things up. That was unrealistic. There wasn't much new to say, anyway. I thought it would be good for us to be together in the wilderness doing something we both enjoyed. I had made the promise to Adam that we would go to Alaska, and maybe I was keeping it for myself. I just couldn't bear being the source of another disappointment. For me, the trip began to take on the form of a final test of my reliability as a father. This reasoning wasn't clear in my mind at the time, but I felt the pull of it as kind of logic in my heart.

Over the summer, I called Adam once a week and we made small talk—weather, work, the news in Philadelphia, and the planning I was doing for Alaska.

"Are you sure we can do this?" he asked more than once. "You know, I'll understand if we can't."

It sounded to me as if he was suggesting that we forget the whole thing.

"Yeah, we can do it," I said. "We are going."

I knew that I was going to have to put together a trip on the cheap. I was over my head in bills: lawyers, therapists, alimony, private schools. I got books on Alaska and searched the Internet for information. I called outfitters, tackle shops, game wardens, and guides. Always I came back to the price. I bargained. Alaska is a huge state, and the number of possible fishing trips is almost endless. I made a list of regions and then listed the rivers within the regions. I studied the river reports put out by Alaska's fisheries biologists. I called several of them. Finally, I decided that we would take on one of the rivers in southwest Alaska, a river renowned for its fishing, but that we would do it without a river guide. It was a little risky, but it would save us thousands of dollars. With the right preparation, I thought, it would be doable.

I began running in the mornings before work, through the streets of South Philadelphia, past the vacant buildings, abandoned cars, and meat and fruit stands of the Italian Market, to get into shape. I went through a routine of push-ups and sit-ups at night before going to bed. I lost 10 pounds, which brought me to 185. I was getting some tone back to the muscles in my arms and shoulders. My stomach was losing some of the bulge that had appeared in the last few years.

We were going to need a lot of flies for the trip. So, I began tying some from the fly-tying chest that I had managed to hold on to through the divorce. I sent Adam a package of fly-tying materials and directions for Alaska patterns I had pulled from the L.L.Bean catalog. Each time I called him in Maine and asked him if he had begun tying, he said that he hadn't gotten to it yet. I don't think he believed we really would make the trip. I also think that to tie a fly for the trip would have committed him to going and he really didn't want to go. I felt the enlarging distance and the resistance in the phone calls.

At the end of July, I bought the airline tickets, through a discount travel agent, and secured a rock-bottom price from the outfitter who would fly us in to the river's headwaters. I called Adam with the dates of the trip.

"Really?" he said skeptically.

"Really," I said.

"Are you sure you want to do this?" he said.

"I've already bought the tickets."

"You already bought the tickets?"

"Yeah, I got a good deal. We're all set."

"Okay."

Adam said he would be back to Philadelphia the day before we were scheduled to leave. I met him at the airport. He came back taller and broader and fuller across the chest and shoulders. He had built up muscle lifting boxes and unloading fish at the waterfront market where he had been working. Despite my workout routine, I felt older and saggy in his presence.

He also had come back with more anger than he had left with, it seemed to me, and I assumed this was because he had stewed on his grievances while away. But I also was aware that I could be seeing hostility where there might be plain old adolescent separation at work. I was having trouble distinguishing between the two.

"Hey, Dad," he said at the airport.

"Hey, Adam," I said in response. "It's good to have you back."

I just tried to let things flow and not confront his irritability. I guessed that the trip must have felt to him like a reversal, or at least an interruption, of the direction toward independence that he had set for himself. He was chafing at this, I think, and it showed as sarcasm, annoyance, and distance.

In the days leading up to his return, I had worked my way down the checklist for the trip and set out all of the gear on the floor of our living room. There were rods, canvas duffels, a gun case, fly boxes, boots, new yellow rain jackets and rain pants, new polar-fleece shirts, wool socks, new flashlights, a fancy backpacker's water purifier, foil packets of freeze-dried food. All of this met him when he entered the apartment.

"This is amazing," he said on seeing it all. "This is really amazing."

I was elated that he was impressed. We began going through the gear together. He started checking for items that he wanted to bring (his waders and fishing vest) and he opened the boxes with the new reels I had bought and tried them out. He admired the two salmon rods I had ordered from L.L.Bean—they were my big splurges. He fitted the ferrules of one of the rods together and began whipping it in the apartment, making short false casts between the television and the sofa.

"Not bad, not bad," he said.

The next morning we left for the airport, the cab piled high with gear. After a long flight that took us through St. Louis, we landed in Anchorage, took a taxi to our Holiday Inn, and grabbed dinner at the motel's restaurant. The waitress who took our order and brought us our food, salmon and halibut, asked us where we were going, and when we told her she said that she used to work as a commercial fisherman with her brothers and father out of Kodiak Island. They had operated a dragger. She was a big woman, in her late thirties, and Adam and I talked and laughed with her through dinner. He knew about commercial fishing from his summer job in Portland and asked her about their catches, boat, and seasons. It was nearly midnight before we finished, and the restaurant was mostly empty. We asked her where we could buy fishing licenses and flies (Adam had never gotten around to tying them) and she said that the Wal-Mart was open all night. I asked if it was near enough so we could walk to it.

"If you want to wait until my shift is done and I cash out, I will drive you over."

I said we would appreciate the ride.

At the Wal-Mart, a clerk with long stringy hair, hollow cheeks, and black-circled eyes sold us several dozen flies that he said had worked for him on the Kenai River, south of Anchorage. He looked like the manager of a rock band who had barely survived the last tour. He set his long skinny hands on the glass countertop as if to keep from falling over. He recommended one pattern in particular, a purple maribou leech with a red head and weighted body. It was tied on a No. 2 wire hook.

"They call it an egg-sucking leech," he said.

I bought ten of them. Adam and I took a cab back to the motel. The cabdriver, in his late sixties, burly, bald in the back, and articulate, told us he had come up to Alaska from the Lower 48 decades earlier over a complicated family dispute that seemed to have a large sum of money and an important principle at its contentious core. It necessitated his remove to the frontier. As we drove by the city's fast-food joints and new strip malls with their lights ablaze under the northern sky, he chattered on, offering a wacko critique of the federal tax code, planetary travel, a secret army trained by the United Nations, and the Alaskan welfare system. At the Holiday Inn Adam and I collapsed in the musty room for a few hours' sleep, and then we caught a morning flight to Dillingham.

VII. ON THE RIVER, IN THE BRAIDS

On Tuesday morning, the rain had not diminished, the river was swollen and the maps had indicated more channels below. After a near fatal accident the day before, we decided to call BLM (Bureau of Land Management) to apprise them of our situation and try for a chopper to get us up past the braided section below, which would be choked with sweepers. . . . As a result of the field evaluation, we determined that the river is not suited to novice canoeists; that the topographic maps are "out of date" as they do not show the new channels; that the river can be run but it should not be attempted by one canoe as there are literally hundreds of sweepers ready to clutch a canoe and hold it fast; that the prospective traveler should be prepared to line and even portage often . . .

—U.S. INTERIOR DEPARTMENT LOG,

KANEKTOK RIVER JOURNEY, AUGUST 1973

I had become conscious of other fathers when I got serious about girls.

I had a girlfriend in college from Connecticut whose family owned a cottage (a mansion, by my measure) on Martha's

Vineyard. Her father, a small, alert, and quietly friendly man, was an engineer and an executive. He was skeptical of the skinny dark boy his daughter had brought home. I wasn't black or Jewish, but I must have struck him as exotic, and I guessed he situated me, ethnically, between Italian and Puerto Rican. He loved his daughter (as did I), and he was used to her rebellious ways. I sensed he was suspending judgment of me, in deference to her, until he could determine what I was made of. He had that strain of Yankee pragmatism that I've always admired: Go with what works. I gathered that some of the American boys she had brought home had been less than reliable. She invited me along for a weekend with her family at the Vineyard. To me, Martha's Vineyard was a foreign country. I marveled at their big old house with the wraparound porch and mansard roof and the small plastered bedroom I was to stay in with the lace bedspread and windows that looked out on Nantucket Sound. Her father took me out onto the porch, where we drank gin and tonic. I had never had a drink with an adult before. I could not remember even having had a mixed drink ("a cocktail"); in fact, I had never tasted gin. We talked. I saw the remnants of a tree stump on the big lawn that someone had tried unsuccessfully to remove by digging it up. I asked about it.

"I've been working at it a little each weekend I get out here," he said. "It's deep and stubborn."

I didn't know about Cape Cod or gin, but I sure as hell knew work. I got up early the next morning, took the shovel, a tool I had been intimate with for several summers working on a construction gang, and spent an hour clearing the roots so they could be cut with an ax. As I cleaned the hole around the roots, I looked up and saw him watching me from the porch. I finished the job and together we sat again on the porch overlooking the sound. He had brought out some lemonade. He was a delicate man, with small hands and thin arms, and courteous. He told me about sailing on the bay and about a favorite catboat he had owned as a boy and had sailed on these very waters. He waved out to the shimmering water. I felt like I was in a short story and watching myself as the scene unfolded. I was the boy on the porch, and I was the boy hidden behind a bush taking notes. As he talked, I could feel myself trying him out as a father. He was nice and straightforward, and he appreciated work and discipline and things done well. He knew his daughter through and through, so he must have known I had been having sex with her. Yet here he was talking with me quietly about things that mattered to him. This struck me as remarkable. I decided that he was a man I would want to impress if I were his son.

I had other experiences with the fathers of other girls, and maybe in the complexity of courtship even fathers are unconsciously drawn into the play as they evaluate young men as future sons-in-law. The father of another girl was a know-it-all and sure of everything and he dominated the life of his family. I wouldn't have lasted a night with him as a father. I don't know, but ultimately my imagination failed me. Try as I might, I could not conjure what it would be like to have a father. What was I supposed to feel? Respect? Awe? Love? I felt myself recoil at the idea of a person who would have authority over me. I never had had that in a parent and I didn't think I could accept it. It was an alien limitation. I wondered how others dealt with the idea of a father who could say no to them. I understood what it was like to be around your mother. It was acceptance and praise and a feeling of being known for what you are inside and for what made you who you are. A mother was a source of encouragement. What was a father? Did the feeling of being around a father ever become ordinary? What would it be like to be in the presence of your father? Maybe it was scary or reassuring. In some cases, like with the bullying father, it must be deadening.

What would *my* father be like if I were to imagine him into existence? Would he be big? Would he smell like aftershave or tobacco? Would his voice be deep, stern, slow? Would he wear a jacket and tie or a khaki work shirt? Would he look out for me and help me? If I were in a jam, would he get me out of it? How? Would he be willing to pay money? How much money? Where would he get the money? Would he have inherited money from his family, or did he make it in a business deal? Would he have a good job? Would he explain the situation to the police so that they would walk away agreeing that the matter was in good hands, in the hands of a father? Would he take responsibility for me and then tell me that I couldn't do again whatever it was I had done? Would he tell me about the time he had done the same thing as a boy? Would he say he understood? Would we sit and talk from time to time, say in his den or office? Would it be about his job? Hunting and fishing? About what I was doing these days, my studies, or the books I was reading?

As I worked to bring a picture of him into my mind, all I could imagine was fear, and that, I realized, was a suspect feeling, because the imagined picture contained a man I didn't know, a stranger, and he was laid over the memory of my own father. I was plucking men from a crowd and temporarily making them my father to assess the feeling they created. It didn't work.

Sometimes I would be around men who were older than I was, old enough to be my father, men whom I knew as bosses or teachers, and I would think, What if this man were my father? What would that be like? It might be in a business meeting, at lunch, or in a store. I would look at the man's face, his eyes, his hands, arms, the hair on the back of his neck, the slope of his shoulders, his shoes. You can tell a lot about a man by his shoes. Dress shoes, work shoes, casual shoes, sandals. Sometimes I felt repulsed by the fleshy faces or bodies of these men. Other times I felt like I was dying inside, with an up-welling of sadness, regret, loss, and emptiness, and I would have to fight back tears. I wondered if people who had fathers understood what it was that they had. Maybe it was like get-ting used to having a fortune in the bank.

Much later, I realized that I had already chosen my father and that I had done so quite unconsciously, and he turned out to be none other than God himself, the God I had found in the Episcopal Church as a boy. He was kind, generous, under-standing, and completely on my side. Actually, it was mostly his voice that I had taken from the Episcopal Church, that Elizabethan majesty speaking Hebrew wisdom, and he him-self was made up of many of the people I admired most—the priest in the Spotswood church who moved through town in his black cassock and white hair and who brought me into the choir; my uncle John, who was street-smart and generous and knew how to tell a story that made you laugh or cry; Jesus Christ, who stood among the poor people and told them not to worry about tomorrow; Socrates, who knew his way around the big questions; and my sixth-grade teacher in New Brunswick, Mr. Kachurack, a warmhearted man who had worn brown suits, parted his hair in the middle, told me to study, and given me As. He had captivated me with his stories to the class of growing up on a small farm in upstate New York. Oh, how I loved his classroom! This father that I had created, or intuited, and put in heaven was accepting, wise, merciful, and a good outdoorsman, too, and he was also fallible, which meant that I was drawing somewhat on my mother, which further meant that he was not completely a he but rather an accumulation of everything I had learned about goodness and living a full life that also meant its inevitable sadness and tragedy.

2

The name of the village that was our destination, Quinhagak, comes from a Yupik word that means "new river channel." Alaskan rivers are restless and frequently cut new channels on their way to the sea. Quinhagak was named for the restlessness of the river that passes by it.

Coming out of the hills, the Kanektok River ceases to be a single river. It becomes a skein of rivers, streams, back eddies, sloughs, ponds, and riverine cul-de-sacs. In this way, it walks over the landscape. Alaskan fishing guides call this varicose section of the river the Braids. Like a hank of sissel, the main stem unravels into many unruly strands. Some of these strands, or braids, stay close to the principal course of the river; others loop out into the tundra, usually connecting back to the main stem but not always directly and once in a while not at all. Sometimes a braid will reach into the endless pastures of spongy yellow tundra, flowing this way and that way, until it eventually peters out to marsh, miles from the river. For a rafter, the wrong choice can mean ending up lost in a labyrinth of waterways. The way back can be arduous, confusing, and, for some, because of panic, disorientation, or the failure of their equipment, fatal.

The river's braided section is shaped roughly like a delta except that the delta, at its widest spread, regathers most of its waterways and narrows back into a single river. In this way, the outline of the river resembles an aneurysm. Before the trip, I had seen an aerial photo of a braided section of the river, but it appeared to show not much more than the river breaking into four well-defined channels as it swept past three long and brushy islands. It hardly seemed a problem for Adam and me, who had other-rivers experience. The Braids turned out to be the compression of all the Kanektok's dangers into a single passage of about twenty perilous miles.

The first sign that something might be wrong appeared as we moved with the current, which was gaining speed from some large midriver tributaries, and we saw that the river split ahead into two channels, neither larger than the other and either one likely to be the main stem of the river. This struck me as odd since typically one channel is wider and deeper than the other and represents the true course of the river. Typically, the smaller channel buttonhooks around an island in a loose loop and soon regains the main river. In that case, the worst that can come from making a wrong choice about which channel to travel is that the raft strikes a long stretch of shallow water and the rafters have to disembark and haul the raft back to the place where the river split to regain the main stem. Some time is lost and the work is hard, but it's no big deal. So while the split ahead struck me as odd, I wasn't worried.

"Which way do you think we go?" I called out to Adam.

He looked up, right, and left.

"Left, I think," he said.

He waved his arm toward the left channel.

"Why left?" I asked. "What do you see left? Can you see anything?"

"More water to the left," he said. "I think there's more flow."

Possibly he saw something I didn't. I was moving my eyes back and forth as the split loomed closer. It was about three hundred yards off, and we were moving fast. There was an island between the two channels. From where I sat in the raft, I couldn't see downstream far enough to determine the island's length. It seemed to swell to a width of several hundred feet, and it was choked with thick, short willows that came down, and even into, the water. The basket weave of limbs, branches, and leaves looked impenetrable. I wouldn't want to have to walk across it, let alone drag a raft over it. By now it was evening, around nine o'clock, and the clouds had opened temporarily to admit some sunlight onto the river. It sparkled ahead of us. I examined the widths of the two river channels again as we drew closer, tried to discern their depths from the waves over submerged rocks, and peered down their lengths to see which reached farther. I wasn't seeing anything that gave me a clue as to how to make the choice. They were mirror images.

"You think left, huh?" I said to Adam, and then added, "Yeah, that looks like the way to go."

I had no basis for affirming the left fork over the right; I was speaking what I hoped would be true. It was an unconscious and hopeful incantation: Say it's so to make it so. The words amounted to throwing some salt over my left shoulder. In the rowing position, which put my back downstream, I pulled hard on the left oar, and the raft headed toward the downstream-left bank. We slid over a lip of gravel and into the left channel. As we did, I noticed a bluff, about a half mile back from the right side of the river. I guessed that it was an ancient glacial moraine, a massive pile of gravel washed from below a retreating glacier. Lichen and grasses now carpeted it. I held the sight of it as a landmark: It was something that would allow me to judge our direction and distance from the fork. Without it, if the clouds closed back on the sun I would be completely disoriented. It was my only reference point. I watched it move farther and farther away as the river carried us down and away, in a direction I judged to be south. I didn't want us to be going south. I wanted us to be going west to the sea, but a southward loop wouldn't be alarming as long we eventually regained a seaward direction principally to the west. My stomach sank when I saw that just one hundred feet down the braid the river split again. The second fork hadn't been visible from the first.

"Oh, shit," I said to Adam.

The wider channel, which was the logical choice for travel, turned farther to the south, to the left again. Should I take it? Or should I gamble on my sense of direction, my growing attachment to my friend the distant bluff, and choose the narrower right-hand channel and hope that it would put us on a more westerly course and back toward the channel we had departed from? I could still see the bluff hulking behind us and to the right. Its presence argued for choosing the narrower channel.

"What do you think, Dad?" Adam said.

He sensed some danger.

"I'm thinking this could turn into a major pain in the ass," I said. "Let's get closer and have a look."

The current was speeding up, by virtue of the narrower channels, I guessed. There wouldn't be much time to make a decision. Once the raft got close to the fork, the downward force of the river pushed the raft in one direction or another and it was nearly impossible to overcome the water's power with the oars.

"Let's go right," I said. "It's narrower, but it seems to flow in the right direction."

As we got closer, though, I could see that the narrower fork almost immediately tunneled into a wall of vegetation. It looked like a Florida mangrove. There would be no way we could float it. It was impassable.

"Okay, change that," I said. "We're going left again with the flow."

I worked the left oar, bounced off the willows, and spun to the left. We flew down the second braid. I could no longer see the bluff. A bank of mist and clouds had moved in and closed off the view of it. The sun was gone, too. The braid we were on was narrow, and the willows along the banks reared up above us. I couldn't see over them: There was no horizon line. So this was what it felt like to be a woodchuck walking between tall hedges. I could look down into the river and up to the sky, but my vision to either side was blocked by the jungle of willow and alders. They rocked in the swift water. The sky darkened, and it began to rain. We encountered one fork after another. They came on us fast. No sooner would we take one than it flowed back into the one we had departed; another braid would take us away from the general direction in which we had been moving and bring us to another fork. Everything began to look the same: the vegetation, the river, each fork and island.

Then, to the left I saw what seemed to be a brown stain in the water. It was only inches below the surface, a puddle of tawny color. It was waving a little, like a towel or rug that had snagged in the current. It wasn't moving downstream with the flow. It seemed to be fluttering at its edges. I got a bad feeling, and I glanced over at Adam. He was looking ahead. He didn't see what I was seeing. I decided not to say anything until I could identify the stain. I took a harder look as the raft brought me closer. Maybe it was a branch with brown leaves still attached to its tips—it was the exact brown of late-November oak leaves. But I was beginning to see that it was something else, something awful. It was a bear. The carcass was huge, slightly turned, and the head was upstream and facedown. I was sickened. It was an adult brown bear and about the size of the sow we had startled upriver. I wondered if it was the same bear. Had it been shot? It must have been shot. There was no other way for a bear on the river to be killed and end up like this in the water. The sense of a bad omen, a goose-on-the-grave feeling, came over me. I felt a shiver. This wasn't roadkill. It was like finding a corpse. Again I glanced over to Adam. He was still looking ahead. I stayed silent and kept working the oars quietly. We were passing right by the bear and I tried to gather the details of it through the swirling water. It was pushed against the bank. Yes, it was a big bear, and I picked out an ear, a shoulder, the wet shag carpet of a long back, and the dark sole of a hind foot. I hoped Adam wouldn't turn to see it. I didn't want him to see it. I stayed quiet as we slid by the dead animal. At last we were by it and the glare off the water blocked my sight of it. I was relieved that we had gone by and Adam had not seen it: It seemed to me that to have pointed it out to him would have brought something bad into the trip—something that would have cursed the better feelings that I hoped would prevail. A dead bear was a potent thing in the mind, and I didn't want the discord that had been in the air attaching itself to the depressing sight of the animal and I didn't want it staining the memory of this trip.

The bear had shaken me, but it was the Braids that I had to contend with. I had lost all sense of where we were: what was south or west, north or east. It was like being blindfolded and spun around. I had to admit to myself that we were lost. My heart was beating fast. I felt like I had a bird in my chest; it wanted to fly out. Here again was the old feeling of panic and a racing heart. It wasn't the first time that bird wanted to fly from my chest. Three years earlier, when I was deciding whether to separate from my wife, I had slipped into a cardiac condition called atrial fibrillation. I had spent seven days in a Philadelphia hospital as the doctors tried to return my heart to a regular and steady rhythm. A normal heart goes *thump-thump-thump*. Mine was going *thump-thump-thwip-thump-thwip-thwip-blip-thump*. It couldn't hold regular time. Instead of pumping when my brain sent the signal to pump, the muscle of my right atrium would just twitch and wiggle. *Thump-thwip-squish*.

The bird-in-the-chest feeling had come on me in the middle of the night. I didn't know what it was then, but I knew that it couldn't be good. I was lying in bed, but my heart felt as if I were pushing myself to finish a long race. It was a tight and tired fist under my ribs. Lying still, I was having trouble catching my breath. I began to sweat, and then I felt cold. It was 3:00 A.M. I got out of bed, dressed, and told Adam that I wasn't feeling well and needed to go the hospital.

"I don't think it's any big deal," I said, "but I want to get this checked out."

Of course I thought it could be a big deal, but I wanted to avoid alarming him with the phrase "heart attack."

"I hope to get back in a couple of hours," I said. "But you know how emergency rooms can be. So, if I get stuck waiting to see the doctor, I want you to get yourself ready for school without me."

His eyes were wide and looking into mine.

"Don't worry, Adam, everything will be all right, and I will let you know what's going on. Are you okay, with this? Can you get yourself off to school if I'm still at the hospital?"

"Yeah, sure. No problem, Dad."

I went down to the street and flagged down a cab. I was light-headed.

"Take me to the closest hospital," I told the driver.

He turned his head and looked at me dead-on. He saw that I was serious, and suddenly he didn't look bored. He checked the traffic and screeched through the red traffic light.

When I walked into the emergency room, I said to the sleepy receptionist, "I think I'm having a heart attack."

She picked up her phone. An orderly came from somewhere and put me in a wheelchair, pushed me through double doors and into the emergency room's inner chamber of curtained suites. There were doctors and nurses with clipboards and machines, and patients moaning on gurneys. A nurse took my blood pressure, and another told me I would feel a jab as she inserted an IV in my arm. A third nurse removed my shirt and pasted wires to my chest. I was breathing oxygen through a clear plastic tube inserted in my nose. I didn't know how it had gotten there. The nurses hid their looks of concern and moved competently around me. They seemed familiar with this drill. No one was reassuring me.

"Do you feel any pain in your chest?"

"Do you feel any pain in your left arm?"

"Are you short of breath?"

"When did this begin?"

"Mr. Ureneck, do you have any history of heart trouble?"

"Are you allergic to any drugs?"

I was getting my introduction to mortality, not from a car accident or fall or some youthful recklessness, which has no meaning, but by age, by my body running down, and by the agony I had inflicted upon myself.

"You will feel a pinch. I am going to take some blood."

"The doctor is on his way."

"Try to relax. Take deep breaths."

Here was the inescapable evidence of what lay ahead for me as a man past the middle of his years. On a gurney behind curtains with the monitor making the erratic pulse of my heart audible as liquid-sounding beeps, I saw my eventual death. Even if I escaped it this time, death would inevitably come to me as it comes to everyone. It was now real as it had not been before. How could I have not known this before? Life didn't last forever. Even *I* could die—would die. It was something I had to acknowledge that night in Thomas Jefferson Hospital and did acknowledge, just as the argument Adam and I had had the previous day on the river had forced me to acknowledge the end of something, and I had no choice but to accept the course my life had taken. We are born, we grow, we die, and there are things that we cannot alter. We accept them or we live in fear and anxiety of accepting them. My mother knew one line from Shakespeare, and she had repeated it to me often: "Cowards die a thousand deaths." She knew her son; he needed reassurance. I would try to take her advice. I was going to allow myself just one death.

I followed the nurse's directions. I breathed deeply and tried to calm myself. The pain in my chest turned out not to be a heart attack. I wasn't going to die, or so it seemed, but neither were the doctors through with me. Several hours later, after I had been wheeled, flat on my back, to the Intensive Care Unit of the hospital, a young doctor told me that the risk of atrial fibrillation ("that's what you have, atrial fibrillation") is that blood pools in the heart and sometimes thickens and clots. The clot gets pushed out by the ventricle and travels to the brain, where it causes a stroke. The result is paralysis or death. They had thinned my blood, he said, and administered a drug that was bringing my heart back from its hummingbird speed. But it was refusing to go back to its smooth rhythm. It was still syncopating and skipping, he said. They would watch me for several days, he said, and if the fibrillation continued they would take the next step up the ladder of medical intervention: cardioversion, a strong electric shock to the chest.

Six days later, I was sedated as the doctors put a high-voltage paddle over my sternum and administered a shock. The jolt stopped my heart momentarily, and then it resumed, back to its normal rhythm. When I awoke, my chest hair was singed and I felt the familiar and reassuring *thump-thump-thump*.

"Take it easy," the young doctor told me afterward. "Avoid stressful situations. That seems to be your trigger. You've had a warning. You're not twenty years old."

Funny, I thought as I listened to him, you look like you're twenty years old. When did I get older than my doctors?

There in the Braids my heart was speaking to me again in my chest and deep in the canals of my ears: The thumps were coming faster, but so far I hadn't heard any thwips or squishes. I calmed myself by breathing deeply. I ordered myself to stay cool. I had not only myself to worry about out here. I had my son, too. There was no cab to catch to the hospital. The nearest hospital was twenty miles of river and a bush plane flight away.

I concentrated on slowing my heartbeat. I pulled the air in slowly through my nose, filled my lungs, held the air in briefly, and slowly let it release. I did this five or six times in a row. I rested at the oars. But the current through the Braids was swift. When I stopped steering to rest and breathe, the raft immediately crashed into the banks and got fouled in the brush. Adam looked at me closely. My resting didn't make any sense to him. I saw his wonderment at my pausing to breathe. I smiled.

"Adam, take the oars for a while," I said. "You're a good rower, and you're a lot younger than your old man."

"Sure, no problem," he said.

I laughed, and we changed positions. I was doing my best to be calm and confident. I could see the worry in Adam's eyes. I felt him examining me. I kept smiling and concentrated on slowing my heart. I said nothing to him about it. It was beginning to work. I had pulled myself back from the racing heart. The thumps were coming more slowly. I knew I was going to be all right or at least I wasn't about to have a heart attack. We kept going. I concentrated on my breathing.

"What do you think, Dad?" Adam said. "Are we lost?"

"Lost? Hell, no," I said. "I know just where we are."

"Where?"

"In a raft, in Alaska, that's where the hell we are. And we're on our way to Quinhagak."

Now Adam was smiling, too.

In many places, the bushes along the riverbanks were broken and beaten down flat. I couldn't tell whether it was from bears or beavers. The braids were full of fish. Pods of sockeyes were packed into the channels, and in places there seemed to be more fish than water. I saw a few fish bodies in the grass that had been raked by claws and partially eaten, so I knew there was at least one bear working this area. This would be a very bad place to encounter one. The braid had narrowed to hardly more than the width of the raft, and it was twisting wildly. We would have no warning if a bear was ahead. We would be unable to avoid it. The braids were narrow, and they also were deep. We wouldn't be able to get out of the raft even if we wanted to. We were moving so fast, probably close to ten knots, and the braid turned right and left so often that we would undoubtedly collide with the animal if it was in the water.

There was an even more immediate problem. The numbers and size of the streamside trees had increased in the last ten or fifteen miles of river, and the river had pulled up and broken off many tree trunks and tree limbs along the way. These pikes, one inch to four inches around, had become lodged in the river bottom, usually pointing upstream. Often they were sharp where they had been snapped off. In some cases, the white flesh of the newly snapped wood flashed in the water like a knife blade. They swept back and forth in the current like serpents. They seemed to be searching for a victim. Given the velocity of the raft in the current, one of these sweepers could easily catch and puncture or tear the skin of the raft. We already had struck several of them, but the contact had been glancing, so they slid by without breaking through. Some of them poked through the surface of the water; others were sweeping deep and close to the bottom. The dangerous ones were just below the surface, hard to see but close enough to catch us as we went over them drawing our three inches of water. We encountered them with more frequency, and I tried to push them away with a long aluminum rod case. I thought of dragging our makeshift anchor to slow us down, but it would have been caught immediately in the welter of limbs on the bottom. I stood in front of the raft, and Adam was at the oars. I shouted directions.

"There's one to the right!" I called out. "Pull hard away from it!"

"Just keep telling me where they are," Adam said.

I leaned over the bow and pushed them away where I could and shouted to Adam when I had time to spot them. I called out their position by the clock: Ahead to the left was ten o'clock; to the right was two o'clock.

"There's an ugly one just ahead at noon, directly ahead."

He brought the raft toward the bank and I pushed the dagger end of the sweeper, a long black snake of a stick, out of our way. It slipped back, and I jammed it away again. Adam was doing a skillful job at the oars: It was physically demanding. I doubted that I would have been able to pull it off, even if I hadn't been concerned about my heart. He was young, and I was old. This was a job for two people—one to spot and guide and one to work the oars. We were working in harmony. There was no time or room for argument. The river required every bit of our concentration and cooperation. Everything else fell away. We were like two men, touching back-to-back, fighting off attackers. We had only time to shout warnings back and forth.

"Right, left, more left, at two o'clock, now hard right! More hard right, more!"

"There it goes. I see it."

"Good work!

"Thanks."

"Godammit, there's another."

We went on like this for hours.

It was still raining, and it was cold. I was tired. I had decided that the best thing for us to do was keep going through the Braids in the hope that we might pull back to the main river before the sky was completely dark. I didn't want to spend a night in this wet jungle of willow and alder and bears. Besides, there was nowhere to put a tent. If we stayed in the Braids, we would have to tie off the bushes and find some way to sleep in the raft. I couldn't see us doing that. Adam said he was okay with my plan to keep, going, though he looked dubious.

"Are you sure we shouldn't just sleep for the night?" he said.

"It may come to that," I said, "but let's push on for another hour or two."

"Okay, let's keep going. I can row this thing all night if you want me to."

We snaked our way through the Braids. I was getting more and more depressed about our inability to find the way out, but I wasn't going to let it show to Adam. I maintained my smile. At around 10:00 P.M., I smelled wood smoke. It lifted my spirits. For a moment, I felt I was back in New England in the fall. A thousand unformed memories burst from the smell: leaves, college, warm sweaters, a woodstove. I was momentarily happy and truly calm.

My first thought was that the smoke came from a campfire. A campfire meant people, and that in itself was reassuring. We weren't alone in this unknown and confusing place. But how could anyone be here? Who would stop to camp in a place this rough and wet? The odds of another party being lost in the Braids seemed beyond remote. So maybe it wasn't a campfire. Maybe it was wildfire. We had seen lightning the day before. Maybe the lightning had struck the ground and started a fire. That also seemed impossible given how much rain had fallen. Still, the smell was unmistakable, and it was getting stronger as we moved downstream. There was definitely a fire burning ahead of us.

The braid we were traveling had widened, and we were passing over fewer sweepers. The water seemed to be picking up speed, too. Something was changing. I was amazed at how fast we were moving past the muddy and overgrown banks. By now, there was very little light finding its way into our willow-and-alder-lined trench.

Then I heard voices. There was some laughter. Yes, somebody was talking. I couldn't make out the words. Suddenly, out of the dark and becoming visible as if a strobe light had been thrown on, two white-canvas wall tents appeared on the riverbank. There was a small yellow campfire. The voices had been coming from a guided party of fishermen that had set up for the night. The sight of them was like a single bright frame that been inserted into a fast-running movie that had been showing nothing but black for hours. It came and went that fast. One of the men wore a hat with the brim folded up in front, like an old-time prospector.

A voice called out, "Do you know where you're going?"

Of course I didn't, and the urgency and incredulity in his voice intensified my fears. Did he know something that I should know about what lay ahead? The water carried us furiously fast, at a sprinter's speed, past the tents and the hatted man who had called out, and then the strobe light went dark. We passed them before I could think what to do. The tents and the man were gone, swallowed up in the wilderness and the blackness of the willows and the night. Had I imagined them? No, Adam confirmed that he had seen them, too. At this speed, we both had been unable to react. We careened down the stream. We had passed them too quickly to even attempt a stop. The current pushed us on. Their voices disappeared. I no longer smelled the smoke.

Soon it was completely dark, which must have made it around 1:00 A.M., and despite my misgivings—and without any sense of where we were—I said to Adam, "I think we should put up for the night." He agreed, and soon we came to a gravel bar, our first in miles, where a smaller stream entered the one we were traveling. We beached our raft. The rain was pouring down, and the wind was blowing a gale. It was the worst weather of the trip.

We set about our nightly routine. Adam put up the tent, in the ferocious wind, using big rocks I pulled from the cold river to hold the corners in place while he fitted the poles together. I gathered more stones and set up them up to block the wind from the stove, then lit it and began preparing hot tea and dinner. We ate fish and noodles, prepared without any fuss, cleaned up thoroughly, and went to bed as the wind clawed the tent.

"That was pretty scary in there," Adam said.

"Yeah, it was," I said.

"How much more of this do you think we have?"

"I don't know, but I think we're going to be all right. I think we've done the worst of it."

"I think so, too. Good night."

"Good night."

In the morning, I was up first. I stepped out of the tent. The rain had stopped, but there was a deep wall of mist moving upstream. It smelled like brine. The river looked different. Instead of willow-choked banks, there were bars and banks of gravel and rubble covered with grasses and low bushes. Downstream, I saw a bird walking on the stones. It was a seabird. It looked like an eastern rail except it had yellow legs. It was scampering along the water's edge and dipping to feed. It was the first seabird I had seen along the river. I walked to get a better look. As I got closer, it lifted off and met another that looked just like it. The two flew over the water. I brought a false gun to my shoulder, followed them in flight, and just as if I were trudging the marshes of South Jersey I said, "Bang," as my gun pulled ahead of them. I walked down farther and came to a bend. Ahead, I saw that our braid flowed into a broad expanse of river. I looked back to our tent. Adam was standing there looking in my direction.

"What do you see?" he shouted to me.

"I see the river," I said.

"You do? You see the river?"

"I sure as hell do."

He came running toward me.

3

It is difficult to float a salmon river and miss the power of the story unfolding around you.

The salmon in this river had swum thousands of miles to return to the place of their own beginnings to deposit their eggs and sperm. Their odyssey had carried them through vast expanses of the North Pacific, among innumerable predators— seals, otters, orcas. In the great expanse of the Pacific, making the huge counterclockwise circumnavigations that took them from the Aleutian Islands to the seas off the Kamchatka Peninsula of Siberia, they had grazed on krill, shrimplike creatures that turned their flesh fatty and pink. It gave them the fuel for the massive exertion and body changes that lay ahead. Relying on the sun, the stars, ocean currents, electro- magnetic sensitivity, smell, and taste, the salmon found their natal rivers. They were doing this even as a speeding genetic clock ticked away their lives.

Riding the pulse of the rising tide, they entered the river as chrome-bright fish, darting like missiles into the fresh water. One imperative coursed through every cell of their bodies: As- cend the river; continue the species. In the river, their bodies began to change, turning fierce with hooked and elongated

jaws and humped backs, looking like frightful native spirits
or totems swimming out of the salt and foggy night. The
heads of the sockeyes turned green, and their bodies turned
red. Their skin thickened and grew rough as burlap. Their
blood chemistry changed; their internal organs adjusted to
the river. They lost their feeding teeth and grew caninelike
mating teeth. In the river, they faced new obstacles and
predators—bears, eagles, otters, man. (They included a father
and son in their raft.) The males flattened laterally, which
made them easier prey for bears than the females, whose eggs,
not coincidentally, were more precious than the innumerable
flagellant sperm of the males. A male wiggling through the
shallows with his back and dorsal fin exposed was more likely
to be caught by a raking bear than the more hydrodynamic female, who slipped upstream on her own appointment with
life and death.

So onerous was the journey back to the stream of their
birth that it had required that the fish, in these final weeks,
metabolize the organs of their own bodies. They drew down
their fat and protein for the energy to swim and grow their re-
productive organs, eggs and milt. Their guts are consumed by
their ravenous demand for caloric burn; with their bodies depleted and somatic tissue consumed, they absorb water to
hold their shape. They become spent watery ghosts.

The salmon's urge to reproduce runs on a time track over-
lapping and roughly ahead of the disintegration of its body.
The fish tries to outswim death. Close to the end of their journey, among the stones, sand, silt, and between riverbanks, the
salmon move more deliberately, like torpedoes. The males
fight among themselves to establish primacy; they nuzzle and
court the females. The female stirs the river bottom to create a

nest in the gravel. The male moves next to her. She drops her eggs, skeins of pink-orange balls the size of peas. He releases a cloud of milt. It's a ritual of instinct and ecstasy. The tails of the pair quiver in orgasm; their jaws gape in a dark show of pleasure. The female then looks for a place to make another nest. The male moves with her, or maybe he finds another female. Neither has much life force left. Already the flesh has begun to come off their bodies. They continue to fin in the current. The big rainbows and char eat the drifting flesh. Sometimes they don't wait for the flesh to separate from the dying salmon. They charge from behind rocks and tear it off.

Deep in the salmon's DNA, the order has been telegraphed and continues to be obeyed: Keep ascending, spawn, and propagate the species. Make another generation of salmon. Who cannot be impressed by this determination? Still, they keep swimming. It's hard to know when the life leaves them. They inhabit a place between life and death, and even as they die they fertilize the stream with their carcasses to create new life. The nutrients of the sea are dispersed into the river. It becomes food for the plankton that will feed the salmon's progeny. The new salmon will appear in the spring as alevins, fishlike embryos with egg sacs at their throats. The alevins will grow to smolts, and the smolts to young fish, and the young fish will drop down the river and eventually swim into the sea the following year as salmon.

The adult salmon is a biological Roman candle: It burns itself out in a burst of reproduction. With the act of sex complete, the fish dies. There is no overlap of generations. The link between one generation and the next, between the summer of death and the following spring of birth, is the tiny fertilized egg, sticky and vulnerable, holding to the bottom of the river.

4

Here on the river, I couldn't avoid the question: Had I been a good father?

Yes—and no.

Our children do best when we give them love and encouragement and the room to be themselves. I had given my children many things, love and aspiration among them, and stability at least for a while, but the divorce had taken away the world as they had known it. The sun had fallen out of the sky for them. I had broken the natural order of things: father, mother, daughter, and son. In the struggle to live my own life, I had removed some of the stability from theirs. It's a fearful experience, being the child of divorce. I knew it firsthand, and I once swore that it would never be part of my life as a parent. But it had been, and it was. And now I was beginning to learn to accept it. It was a death I needed to survive. I had a long way to go.

The river has its limits as a metaphor. People are not salmon, and we don't die after our children are born. We live on, and this makes our lives immeasurably more complicated. Our lives overlap their lives. Our lives may even overlap the lives of their children and, if we are fortunate, the children of their children. We are not Roman candles. Life is long. We try to understand our children, but we cannot expect them to understand us except possibly as they live their own lives and meet conflict and complexity and struggle to find their own ways.

As I floated downstream in those last miles, I remembered that among the Yupiks awareness in life counts for everything. The Yupiks must be aware of nature's dangers, alert to a shift in the wind or a crack in the ice. But they reach for something higher—self-awareness. It is the knowing of one's own story, and one's place in the world, that is necessary for survival. I saw that for some time I had been walking in my own wilderness, a wilderness of a different sort, and I, too, had to achieve my own awareness.

Adam and I never did speak of the divorce on our rafting trip, at least not directly, and that was okay with me. We had begun talking of it at home, a little, and Adam made it clear to me that he wanted to talk of it in his own time and in his own way. I would respect that and be ready to listen when he spoke. This trip hadn't been planned as family therapy. It was a father's promise and a boy's reward. It brought us together, and I was beginning to feel that we would continue to find ways to be together. There were many more rivers and streams for us to fish. Adam was commencing his own search for awareness. Maybe other rivers would help him along the way.

We could smell the ocean in the wind. The gravel bars held flocks of white-and-gray seagulls. The river was wide and flat, and we fished the backwaters and sloughs with the one beat-up egg-sucking leech we had left. The fishing was spectacular. We were taking fish from a fusillade of silvers that had just entered the river. They were as bright as chrome. We began to see other fishermen who were staying at a lodge nearby and occasional tar-paper shacks and wood drying racks belonging to the native Yupiks. For the first time in ten days, the rain held off for more than a few hours. We got a full afternoon of sunshine. Not far off, we saw a plane descend to a place that we guessed was the village airstrip. The end of our trip was around the next bend.

We reached the village at the end of the river and pulled our raft ashore as Eskimo children swarmed around us. "Gossack, Gossack," they called out, using the Eskimo slang for white men, a mangling of the word for "Cossack." We walked to the shed at the base of the runway and asked the radio operator to call for our pickup plane. When it arrived, we loaded the raft and gear on board and flew back to Dillingham. We caught another plane for Anchorage there, then another to Philadelphia, which flew through the night. At the airport in Philadelphia, I walked Adam to the gate for the plane that would carry him to college in Maine and a new chapter in his life. I gave him a long hug. I watched him move in line toward the door. He gave me a wave, and his smile. I picked up the gear—including our fishing rods—and caught a cab home.

EPILOGUE

O ur father and son adventures didn't end with Alaska.

In the five years since we took our trip to the Kanektok River, I left *The Philadelphia Inquirer* and Adam graduated from Bowdoin College, not in classics, as he had begun, but as a Latin American history major. He also decided to put himself on a path to explore a religious life as a Roman Catholic brother. Soon he will be entering a formation community in Peru that will lead, should he choose to complete the three-year regimen, to his status as a consecrated member of the church.

Last summer, Adam brought me to Peru to see the country and its people and to meet members of the Catholic brotherhood with whom he had grown close. He wanted me to understand what was drawing him to this life. The brotherhood lives simply in community, ministers to the poor, and serves the church in Latin America. We visited ancient cathedrals in Lima and Arequipa, slept on narrow beds in the spare plaster rooms of a religious community in the city of Chincha, toured clinics and schools, and walked among the poor of the shanty-towns that climb the hills around Peru's biggest cities.

Adam and I talked of his growing interest in the church. He told me of the many books he had been reading. He asked me, in particular, to read *The Seven Storey Mountain* by Thomas Merton. I asked Adam hard questions, challenged some of his assertions, and listened to his thoughtful and earnest answers. I never felt closer to him as he explained to me his search for a life of peace and usefulness.

Of course, we also found a day to go fishing. Brother Guillermo drove us into the lower Andes to fish the Rio Cañete. It is a glorious river that falls from the snowcapped peaks and waters a lush narrow valley of fruits and vege-tables, everything from coconuts to corn, on its way to the Pa-cific. I caught a Peruvian trout in a deep pool below a narrow bridge crossed by Andean shepherds and their herds of sheep and goats. I hooked it on a Maine muddler minnow. With Adam watching, I released the trout unharmed back to the cold mountain river (to the astonishment of a local shepherd).

I now teach journalism at Boston University. It's good to be back in New England. I'm close to my brother, Paul, and the brook trout fishing in Maine. This summer I plan to scout the striper fishing off Cape Cod. I like being a teacher. I have plenty of time to read, and each semester brings a new group of students eager to learn. The work satisfies the father in me.

January 2006

ACKNOWLEDGMENTS

Among those to whom I am grateful are my son, Adam, and daughter, Elizabeth. Both figure in this book, which is a true story, and both generously and courageously supported me in the writing of it. Adam was helpful in remembering details of the river trip, and Elizabeth, a creative actor and writer, was a careful and attentive reader of the text. A personal book leaves the writer exposed. Elizabeth's enthusiasm for the manuscript touched me as perhaps only a daughter's response could.

The spark that was the idea of this book was fanned by Sara Rimer, and she coaxed it into flame. A book is most precarious at its beginning when it is little more than a notion and an impulse. She saw its possibility from the start. Without her, there would have been no book.

It was my brother Paul's response to an early draft that kept me going and persuaded me that there was a story here worth telling.

Mark Bowden, Conrad Grove, Don Drake, and Hank

Klibanoff, colleagues at *The Philadelphia Inquirer,* were immensely helpful with advice. Was there ever a better hothouse for writers than the old Inky?

I benefited from the suggestions and reactions of many readers: Verlyn Klinkenborg, Steve Silber, Liz Rimer, Anne Bernays, Tom Ferriter, Sam Hammer, Mike Riley, Laura Angelone, Jose Pires, Doug Campbell, and Jack Hart.

I also want to thank Dr. Jason P. Briner for his primer on the geology of southwestern Alaska, and Rob McDonald of the U.S. Fish and Wildlife Service for information on the bird survey that he conducts of the Kanektok River. Also, Henry Mark of the village of Quinhagak helped me to confirm the accuracy of details in the book.

I will always appreciate the way my aunt Judith patiently read the entire manuscript aloud to my uncle John, over a string of sunny mornings in their loft in Greenwich Village, and the encouragement they gave me along the way.

I also want to thank Michael Flamini, my editor, for his skillful reading and suggestions, and Vicki Lame for her careful shepherding of the manuscript through the editing and publication process. She never seemed to tire of my questions.

These acknowledgments would be incomplete without a deep and appreciative "thank you" to my literary agent, Wendy Strothman. The late Jim Freedman led me to Wendy, and it was a marvelous gift that was given, sadly, in the final weeks of his life. I am indebted to Wendy for her skill, confidence, encouragement, and support.

ABOUT THE AUTHOR

Lou Ureneck is an outdoorsman, professor, and father. In his twenty years at Maine's *Portland Press Herald*, where he rose from reporter to editor, Lou crusaded to protect the state's environment against clear-cutting and commercial overfishing. He was an editor-in-residence at the Nieman Foundation at Harvard University and page-one editor of *The Philadelphia Inquirer*. He is now chairman of the Department of Journalism at Boston University. His work has been published in *The New York Times, The Boston Globe,* and *Field & Stream.* He lives in Brookline, Massachusetts.